The Discursive Construction
of Economic Inequality

Corpus and Discourse

Series Editors: Wolfgang Teubert, University of Birmingham, UK, and Michaela Mahlberg, University of Birmingham, UK

Editorial Board: Paul Baker (Lancaster), Frantisek Čermák (Prague), Susan Conrad (Portland), Dominique Maingueneau (Paris XII), Christian Mair (Freiburg), Alan Partington (Bologna), Elena Tognini-Bonelli (Siena and TWC), Ruth Wodak (Lancaster), Feng Zhiwei (Beijing).

Consisting of spoken, written or signed language, discourse always has historical, social, functional and regional dimensions. Corpus linguistics provides the methodology to identify meaning in discourse and make it available for interpretation. The goal is to expound the differences and commonalities in the attitudes and beliefs expressed by the members of a discourse community, both contemporary and historical.

The Corpus and Discourse series features innovative corpus linguistic research into a range of discourses; it publishes key texts bridging the gap between social studies and linguistics and it showcases a wide range of applications, from language technology via the teaching of a second language to the translation of discourses. It also explores how language frames the way we perceive reality.

Recent Titles in the Series

Corpus Approaches to the Language of Sports
Edited by Marcus Callies and Magnus Levin

Corpus Linguistics and 17th-Century Prostitution
Anthony McEnery and Helen Baker

Corpus Stylistics in Heart of Darkness and Its Italian Translations
Lorenzo Mastropierro

Investigating Adolescent Health Communication
Kevin Harvey

Keywords in the Press
Lesley Jeffries and Brian Walker

Learner Corpus Research
Vaclav Brezina and Lynne Flowerdew

The Prosody of Formulaic Sequences
Phoebe Lin

Representation of the British Suffrage Movement
Kat Gupta

Sadness Expressions in English and Chinese
Ruihua Zhang

The Discursive Construction of Economic Inequality

CADS Approaches to the British Media

Edited by
Eva M. Gómez-Jiménez and
Michael Toolan

BLOOMSBURY ACADEMIC
LONDON • NEW YORK • OXFORD • NEW DELHI • SYDNEY

BLOOMSBURY ACADEMIC
Bloomsbury Publishing Plc
50 Bedford Square, London, WC1B 3DP, UK
1385 Broadway, New York, NY 10018, USA
29 Earlsfort Terrace, Dublin 2, Ireland

BLOOMSBURY, BLOOMSBURY ACADEMIC and the Diana logo are trademarks of
Bloomsbury Publishing Plc

First published in Great Britain 2020
This paperback edition published 2022

Copyright © Eva M. Gómez-Jiménez, Michael Toolan and Contributors, 2020

Eva M. Gómez-Jiménez and Michael Toolan have asserted their rights under the Copyright,
Designs and Patents Act, 1988, to be identified as Editors of this work.

For legal purposes the Acknowledgements on p. xiv constitute an extension of this
copyright page.

Cover design: Ben Anslow
Cover image © Matthew Horwood / Getty Images

All rights reserved. No part of this publication may be reproduced or transmitted in any form or
by any means, electronic or mechanical, including photocopying, recording, or any information
storage or retrieval system, without prior permission in writing from the publishers.

Bloomsbury Publishing Plc does not have any control over, or responsibility for, any third-
party websites referred to or in this book. All internet addresses given in this book were
correct at the time of going to press. The author and publisher regret any inconvenience
caused if addresses have changed or sites have ceased to exist, but can accept no
responsibility for any such changes.

A catalogue record for this book is available from the British Library.

Library of Congress Cataloging-in-Publication Data
Names: Gómez-Jiménez, Eva M., editor. | Toolan, Michael J., editor.
Title: The discursive construction of economic inequality: CADS approaches to the British
media / edited by Eva M. Gómez-Jiménez and Michael Toolan.
Description: London, UK; New York, NY, USA: Bloomsbury Academic, 2020. |
Series: Corpus and discourse | Includes bibliographical references and index.
Identifiers: LCCN 2020009659 (print) | LCCN 2020009660 (ebook) | ISBN 9781350111288
(hardback) | ISBN 9781350111295 (ebook) | ISBN 9781350111301 (epub)
Subjects: LCSH: Income distribution–Great Britain–History–20th century. | Income
distribution–Great Britain–History–21st century. | Discourse analysis–Great Britain.
Classification: LCC HC260.I5 D57 2020 (print) | LCC HC260.I5 (ebook) |
DDC 339.2/20941–dc23

LC record available at https://lccn.loc.gov/2020009659
LC ebook record available at https://lccn.loc.gov/2020009660

ISBN: HB: 978-1-3501-1128-8
PB: 978-1-3501-9294-2
ePDF: 978-1-3501-1129-5
eBook: 978-1-3501-1130-1

Series: Corpus and Discourse

Typeset by Deanta Global Publishing Services, Chennai, India

To find out more about our authors and books visit www.bloomsbury.com and
sign up for our newsletters.

To Ledi, for being so gentle and generous ... and gorgeous!

Contents

List of illustrations	viii
List of contributors	x
Preface	xiii
Acknowledgements	xiv
List of abbreviations	xv

	Introduction: The Discursive Construction of Economic Inequality in the UK *Eva M. Gómez-Jiménez and Michael Toolan*	1
1	Poverty and social exclusion in Britain: A corpus-assisted discourse study of Labour and Conservative Party leaders' speeches, 1900–2014 *Nuria Lorenzo-Dus and Sadiq Almaged*	13
2	Inequality and 'the language of leadership' in the Second World War *Joe Spencer-Bennett*	33
3	Revisiting the welfare state through the decades: Investigating the discursive construction of the welfare state in the *Times* from 1940 to 2009 *Isabelle van der Bom and Laura L. Paterson*	49
4	What can be done about child poverty? What the *Times* said then and what it says now *Michael Toolan*	69
5	Inequality, accountability and responsibility in UK Press reporting on corporate fraud (2004–14) and modern slavery (2000–16) *Ilse A. Ras*	91
6	Health inequality and the representation of 'risky' working-class identities in obesity policy *Jane Mulderrig*	107
7	We are NOT all in this together: A corpus-assisted critical stylistics analysis of *Austerity* in Print News Media 2009–10 and 2016–17 *Lesley Jeffries and Brian Walker*	125
8	More inequality, but less coverage: How and why TV news avoided 'The Great Debate' either side of the financial crisis 2008–14 *Richard Thomas*	143
9	The democracy we live in: Can there be democracy without equality? *Wolfgang Teubert*	161
	Afterword *Danny Dorling*	183
	References	193
	Index	217

Illustrations

Figures

3.1	Sample of concordance lines for *welfare state* in the *Times* 1990s	52
6.1	Visual tropes used to achieve humour and evaluative health warnings in the C4L campaign	118
6.2	Visual modality in health warnings in C4L campaign	119
6.3	Cooking lesson from Asda: Representing mum as lacking parental control and domestic skills	120
8.1	Prominence of poverty, wealth, the squeezed middle and income inequality (PWSIE) issues in the news	150
8.2	ITV's report about Sienna Miller's trip on 23 June 2014	151
8.3	ITV's report that Manchester United have signed Falcao on 1 September 2014	152
8.4	Andrew Neil's comments about Conrad Black on ITV in 13 July 2007 and BBC on 10 December 2007	153
8.5	Various defending of free markets	154
8.6	The 'cost' of increasing the taxation system to Britain on the BBC on 20 June 2007	155
8.7	'Income inequality' in the *Telegraph* and the *Guardian*	157
A.1	'Here's to the brave new world!' By Illingworth, Leslie Gilbert, published in the *Daily Mail* 2 December 1942. Reproduced with permission from Solo Syndication	190

Tables

1.1	Poverty and Social Exclusion in Britain through the Labour and Conservative Party Leaders' Speeches, 1900–2014: Data Composition	18
1.2	Frequency of Use (n = Number of Concordances) of Each PSE Discourse in the BBPS Corpus	20
1.3	Percentage of Use of the TCFs of 'Debt' and 'Deficit' in the Conservative Finance Discourse across 1900–48, 1949–2000 and 2001–14	22
1.4	Percentage of Use of the TCFs of 'Debt', 'Deficit' and 'Low' in the Labour Finance Discourse across 1900–48, 1949–2000 and 2001–14	23
1.5	Percentage of Use of the TCFs of 'Need' and 'Poverty' in the Conservative Hardship Discourse across 1900–48, 1949–2000, 2001–14	24
1.6	Percentage of Use of the TCFs of 'Poverty', '(the) Poor' and 'Need' in the Labour Hardship Discourse across 1900–48, 1949–2000, 2001–14	25

2.1	Personal Pronouns against Popularity for Six Railway Posters (Adapted)	40
3.1	Hits of <*Welfare* State> in the *Times* 1940s–2000s	51
3.2	Collocates of <*Welfare* State> in the *Times* 1950s	55
3.3	Collocates of <*Welfare* State> in the *Times* 1980s	56
3.4	Collocates of <*Welfare* State> in the *Times* 1990s	57
4.1	Top Thirty Lexical Keywords in the *Times* 'Children + Poverty' 1970s Corpus	75
4.2	Top Thirty Lexical Keywords in the *Times* 'Children + Poverty' 2000s Corpus	79
4.3	Key Semantic Domains in the *Times* 'Children + Poverty' 1970s Corpus	82
4.4	Key Semantic Domains in the *Times* 'Children + Poverty' 2000s Corpus	83
5.1	Articles, Types and Tokens per Year in the Corporate Fraud Corpus (CFC)	95
5.2	Articles, Types and Tokens per Year in the Modern Slavery Corpus (MSC)	96
5.3	Relative Frequencies and Log-likelihood Values for 'Equality', 'Inequality', 'Responsibility' and 'Accountability'	97
5.4	C-collocates for 'Equality' in the Modern Slavery Corpus (MSC) and Corporate Fraud Corpus (CFC)	99
5.5	C-collocates for 'Inequality' in the Modern Slavery Corpus (MSC) and Corporate Fraud Corpus (CFC)	99
5.6	C-collocates for 'Responsibility' in the Modern Slavery Corpus (MSC) and Corporate Fraud Corpus (CFC)	100
5.7	C-collocates for 'Accountability' in the Modern Slavery Corpus (MSC) and Corporate Fraud Corpus (CFC)	101
6.1	Typology of Family Clusters in C4L Campaign	114
7.1	Focal Points for Data Collection for the Start of Austerity (SoA) Period	130
7.2	Focal Points for Data Collection for the End of Austerity (EoA) Period	130
7.3	Keyword Groupings for the Start of Austerity (SoA) Corpus	133
7.4	Keyword Groupings for the End of Austerity (EoA) Corpus	134
7.5	Broad Function Categories of 'Austerity' in SoA and EoA Datasets	136
7.6	'Austerity' in Head Noun Function in SoA and EoA Corpora	137
7.7	'Austerity' in Head Noun Function with Premodification in BoA and EoA Datasets	137
7.8	Head Nouns Premodified by 'Austerity' in SoA and EoA Datasets, where Figures in Brackets Denote Number of Tokens Greater Than 1	138
7.9	'Austerity' in Prepositional Postmodifier Following Time Nouns / Other Nouns in SoA and EoA Datasets	138
7.10	Unmodified 'Austerity' Acting as Participant in Transitivity Patterns in SoA Corpus	139
7.11	Unmodified 'Austerity' Acting as Participant in Transitivity Patterns in EoA Corpus	140
8.1	Summary of TV News (BBC and ITV) Wider Content Analysis	146
8.2	Types of News Story Associated with Poverty, Wealth, the Squeezed Middle and Income Inequality (PWSIE) Themes	148
8.3	Change in Number of Poverty, Wealth, the Squeezed Middle and Income Inequality (PWSIE) News Items 2007–14	149
A.1	The Most Equitable OECD Countries in the World as Reported in 2019	184

Contributors

Sadiq Almaged is Lecturer in English Linguistics at Thi-Qar University (Iraq). He researches in the areas of textual ideology, language of advertisement and political discourse, using corpus and discourse analysis methodologies.

Joe Spencer-Bennett (previously Bennett) is a Senior Lecturer in Applied Linguistics in the Department of English Language and Linguistics at the University of Birmingham (UK), where he is director of undergraduate programmes in English Language and Linguistics. His research concerns the political and ethical life of language, especially in recent British history. His book *Moral Talk* was published in 2018, and he has published in journals such as *Discourse & Society*, *Journal of Sociolinguistics* and *Language & Communication*.

Danny Dorling works at the University of Oxford (UK). His most recent book, published in 2019 with Sally Tomlinson, is *Rule Britannia: Brexit and the End of Empire* concerning what the 2016 EU referendum and 2019 'exit' reveal. In 2018, he published *Peak Inequality* on issues of housing, health, employment, education, wealth and poverty in the UK. In 2020, he is publishing a book, *Slowdown: The End of the Great Acceleration—and Why It's Good for the Planet, the Economy, and Our Lives*.

Eva M. Gómez-Jiménez is Lecturer in English Language and Literature at the University of Granada (Spain). Her research interests include Critical Discourse Analysis, Literary Stylistics and Graphology/Graphemics. She has recently published the paper '"An insufferable burden on businesses?" On changing attitudes to maternity leave and economic-related issues in the *Times* and *Daily Mail*' in *Discourse, Context and Media*. She is also the founder of the Poetics and Linguistics Association Special Interest Group on Graphology.

Lesley Jeffries is Professor of English Language and Linguistics at the University of Huddersfield (UK). Her work focuses on textual meaning in literature (mainly contemporary poetry) and non-literary communication (political language and reporting). She is interested in the development of rigorous and transparent methods of analysing how texts make meaning, both qualitatively and in conjunction with corpus methods. Her recent publications include *Keywords in the Press: The New Labour Years* (2018) and she has co-edited the *Routledge Handbook of Language in Conflict* (2019).

Nuria Lorenzo-Dus is Professor of Applied Linguistics at Swansea University (UK). Her research expertise lies in corpus and discourse analysis of institutional contexts, particularly politics and digital media.

Jane Mulderrig is Senior Lecturer in Applied Linguistics at the University of Sheffield (UK). Her research uses (corpus-based and multimodal) Critical Discourse Analysis to investigate the use of 'soft power', persuasion and 'nudge' tactics in contemporary policy and politics. She also researches the cultural political economy of education and ageing. Alongside a co-edited methodology volume *Critical Policy Discourse Analysis* (2019), recent publications include the paper 'Multimodal strategies of emotional governance: A critical analysis of 'nudge' tactics in health policy' (2018) and the book chapter '"Enabling" participatory governance in education: A corpus-based critical policy analysis' (2015).

Laura L. Paterson is a Lecturer in English Language and Applied Linguistics at the Open University (UK) and editor of the *Journal of Language and Discrimination*. She is a corpus-based sociolinguist and critical discourse analyst whose work is concerned with the discursive construction of UK poverty, audience response to UK poverty, media depictions of protest and discourse of marriage.

Ilse A. Ras works as a Teaching Fellow in Criminology at Leiden University (The Netherlands). She has completed degrees and has taught in both English Language and Criminology, and is a co-founder of the Poetics and Linguistics Association Special Interest Group on Crime Writing. Her work often crosses the boundaries between English Language and Criminology, focusing on the use of language to neg(oti)ate (capitalist) power structures and neutralize/condemn 'crimes of the powerful', using Corpus-Assisted Critical Discourse Analysis and Critical Stylistics to examine this language use.

Richard Thomas is a Senior Lecturer in Journalism at Swansea University (UK). Some of his main areas of interest are political communication and the coverage of elections. He has published many journal articles and book chapters on these topics and is the co-author of *Reporting Elections: Rethinking the Logic of Campaign Coverage* (2018).

Wolfgang Teubert held the chair in Corpus Linguistics from 2000 to 2013 at the University of Birmingham (UK). He had studied German and English Linguistics at Heidelberg University. Before he moved to Birmingham, he was Senior Fellow at the Institut für deutsche Sprache in Mannheim. His focus has always been on meaning: the meaning of lexical items, as well as the meaning assigned to the world by people talking about it. For him, a fruitful discourse is always dialogic and controversial, an exercise in interpretation, comparing and making sense of different perspectives, the only way to come up with new ideas.

Michael Toolan has been a Professor of English Language at the University of Birmingham (UK) since 1996, having previously taught at the National University of Singapore and the University of Washington, Seattle. He was educated at the Universities of Edinburgh and Oxford, and has main research interests in Literary Stylistics, Narrative and Critical Discourse Analysis. His most recent monograph publications are *Making Sense of Narrative Text: Situation, Repetition, and Mental Picturing* (2016) and *The Language of Inequality in the News: A Discourse Analytic Approach* (2018).

Isabelle van der Bom is the Practical Language Programme coordinator in the Department of English at Chemnitz University of Technology (Germany). She is a critical discourse analyst and stylistician, whose work focuses on the discursive representation of identity, reader responses to digital fiction, and media depictions of poverty and same-sex marriage. She also edits the *Journal of Language and Discrimination* and is the book review editor of the *Journal of Politeness Research*.

Brian Walker is a Visiting Researcher and part-time tutor at the University of Huddersfield (UK). His research focuses on the analysis of political texts and print news report using corpus and stylistic methods. His recent publications include *Keywords in the Press: The New Labour Years* (2018) and *Corpus Stylistics: Theory and Practice* (2019).

Preface

This book comes mostly as a result of a one-day symposium held at the University of Birmingham (UK) on 15 June 2018. It was sponsored by the European Commission, which had previously funded Professor Michael Toolan and Dr Eva M. Gómez-Jiménez with a Horizon 2020-Marie Skłodowska-Curie Actions-grant (reference no. 705247) to undertake DINEQ, a two-year research project on the changing discoursal representations of economic inequality in the British press, from September 2016 to August 2018.

Most of the chapters in this volume were presented at the symposium, where further discussion among presenters drove us to considering turning their contributions into a single volume. After the symposium, and having newly been aware of other academics' work on related topics, we also invited them to submit the additional chapters that gave form to the final version of this volume.

Acknowledgements

We are grateful for comments and suggestions from colleagues at the universities of Birmingham (UK) and Granada (Spain), which include Ruth Page, Joe Spencer-Bennett, Anna Čermáková, Leanne Bartley, Susan Hunston, Jeannette Littlemore, Michaela Mahlberg, Paul Thomson, Nick Groom and Viola Wiegand. We want to specially thank Wolfgang Teubert for his deep interest and big boost during these years, as well as Marta Falces-Sierra for her continuous support, which goes far beyond this project.

We also very much appreciate the useful advice and enthusiasm of the editorial team through the compilation of the volume, and the work and strong commitment given by all the contributors to this project.

Abbreviations

9/11	11 September 2001
BNC	British National Corpus
BoB	Box of Broadcasts
BPPS	British Political Party Speeches
C4L	Change4Life Campaign
CADS	Corpus-Assisted Discourse Studies
CDA	Critical Discourse Analysis
CEO	Chief Executive Officer
CFC	Corporate Fraud Corpus
CORPS	Corpus of Political Speeches
CSR	Corporate Social Responsibility
DOH	Department of Health
ECCE	Evaluation of Children's Centres in England
EoA	End of Austerity
H_0	Null Hypothesis
HWHL	'Healthy Weight, Healthy Lives' Strategy
KWIC	Keyword in Context
L1	Collocate immediate to the left
L2	Collocate preceding L1
LL	Log Likelihood
LR	Log Ratio
MI	Mutual Information
MI3	Mutual Information (cubic association)
M-O	Mass-Observation
MP	Member of Parliament
MSC	Modern Slavery Corpus
n	Number of Concordances
NAA	National Assistance Act
NESS	National Evaluation of Sure Start

NHS	National Health Service
NP	Noun Phrase
OCR	Optical Character Recognition
OECD	Organisation for Economic Co-operation and Development
Ofsted	Office for Standards in Education, Children's Services and Skills
Op-Ed	Opposite the Editorial Page
PMW	Per Million Words
PPI	Payment Protection Insurance
PSE	Poverty and Social Exclusion
PWSIE	Poverty, Wealth, the Squeezed Middle and Income Inequality
R1	Collocate immediate to the right
R2	Collocate following R1
RQ	Research Question
RQTR	Relative Query Term Relevance
SFO	Serious Fraud Office
SoA	Start of austerity
TCF	Textual Conceptual Functions (Jeffries 2010)

Introduction

The Discursive Construction of Economic Inequality in the UK

Eva M. Gómez-Jiménez and Michael Toolan

The Discursive Construction of Economic Inequality explores the linguistic representation of different forms of economic inequality in some of the mass media public discourses of modern and contemporary Britain. We understand wealth inequality here as broadly mirroring the social variable of class, an important defining characteristic of individuals and groups just as gender, sexual orientation, religion, country of origin or age are. As The Equality Trust (2019a) points out, economic inequality has several overlapping sources: (1) *pay inequality* (what somebody gets from employment only, which may include bonuses), (2) *income inequality* (what somebody (or a household) gets through employment (wages, salaries, bonuses, etc.), investments (interests, dividends), state benefits, pensions and rent) and (3) *wealth inequality* (the total amount owned by somebody (or a household), which may include financial assets, property and private pension rights). In simplified terms, economic inequality's two basic sources are wages and assets, enjoyed in sharply different amounts. Money is not everything, of course; it cannot buy you love, for instance. But it can buy your children places in the better private schools and subsequently cover their university and professional training costs with ease; it will pay for a nanny or plentiful childcare and a good preschool, private healthcare, comfortable spacious living accommodation, holidays, clubs, sports and hobbies, good food, reliable transport and everything falling under the heading 'nice things'.

The book approaches economic inequality through the analysis of a range of real text samples taken from public discourse, namely mass media (TV, newspapers), policy (Hansard, government campaigns) and political discourse (propaganda, parties annual conferences), in modern and contemporary Britain. Our goal is to show how economic inequality and related matters have been portrayed at specific points in British public discourse since 1900, particularly in the context of some of the significant events in the nation's life course, such as the Second World War, the introduction of the welfare state, the arrival of Margaret Thatcher to power, the financial crisis of 2008, and the most recent general elections (2010, 2015 and 2017).

The following sections explain why economic inequality deserves scholarly attention, both from a social and a linguistic-discoursal perspective (Section 1), overview the main research undertaken in this direction, particularly within the field of critical discourse analysis (CDA) (Section 2), briefly discuss on the methodological implications of this volume (Section 3) and outline the chapters to come (Section 4).

1 Why economic inequality (in Britain)?

1.1 The social side of the argument

Many reasons justify the importance of discussing economic inequality. From a societal perspective, high levels of income inequality correlate with health issues such as lower life expectancy (De Vogli et al. 2005; Wilkinson and Picket 2010; Kawachi et al. 1997; Kondo et al. 2009), higher rates of obesity, especially in adults (Wilkinson and Pickett 2010; Offer, Pechey and Ulijaszek 2012), higher rates of infant mortality (Wilkinson and Pickett 2010) and greater tendency to mental illnesses such as depression and schizophrenia (Burns, Tomita and Kapadia 2014) (see especially Rowlingson 2011). Inequality contributes to less stable economies, these becoming more prone to financial crises (Berg and Ostry 2011; Kumhof and Rancière 2010; van Treeck 2014), debt (Iacoviello 2008) and inflation (Beetsma and Van Der Ploeg 1996). It also leads towards more deregulated economies, ultimately with greater economic instability (Stiglitz 2009), lower labour productivity (Cohn et al. 2011, 2015; Stiglitz 2009) and more social competitiveness between citizens (Wilkinson and Picket 2009), which ultimately affects debt too (Frank, Levine and Dijk 2014; Kasser and Ryan 1993; van Treeck 2014). Studies have also demonstrated that inequality increases property-related crime, corruption and certain violent crimes such as homicide (Elgar and Aitken 2010; Elgar et al. 2013; Daly, Wilson and Vasdev 2001; Krahn, Hartnagel and Gartrell 1986), rape and robbery (Hsieh and Pugh 1993) (Whitworth 2012; Lederman, Fajnzylber and Loayza 2002). A drop in children's educational performance (Wilkinson and Picket 2009; Morrisson and Murtin 2013), lower levels of social mobility (Corak 2016; Blanden 2009) and higher social insecurity (Wilkinson and Pickett 2010) have also been linked to inequality.

From a more individual perspective, almost everyone would agree that life becomes harder for those on modest and low means. More concretely, many values and attitudes are influenced by income inequalities, namely those regarding political actions, religion and family (Pryor 2012), trust (Pryor 2012; de Vries, Gosling and Potter 2011; Elgar and Aitken 2010; Rothstein and Uslaner 2005), stereotyping (Durante et al. 2012) and friendliness (de Vries, Gosling and Potter 2011). Not just personality and attitudes, but economic inequality produces lower rates of social, civic (Lancee and Werfhorst 2012), political participation (Solt 2008, 2010) and cultural activity (Szlendak and Karwacki 2012) for low-income households. Overall, inequality leads to less happy and less healthy societies, with the population experiencing less general well-being than in more economically (and therefore socially, experientially and democratically) equal societies (Oswald 1997; Dorling 2016a).

Focusing on the UK, forms of economic inequality have systematically increased in this country since the 1970s.[1] As Toolan (2018) explains, since the 1970s, the share of the national income going to the poorer has deeply fallen, with only 8 per cent of the growth of real wages going to the bottom earners; the income of the richest 1 per cent has trebled; the UK has become one of the most economically unequal countries of the Organisation for Economic Co-operation and Development (OECD) (0.34 coefficient), with the richest 10 per cent holding the 45 per cent of wealth versus the poorest 50 per cent owning less than the 9 per cent; relative poverty has risen from 5 to 12 per cent since 1980s, with an estimate that, by 2020, there could be five million children living in relative poverty in this country; overall, top 10 per cent of UK society owns 100 times more than the bottom 10 per cent.

The current picture does not seem very positive for Britain. The £5,271,803 average pay for a FTSE 100 CEO is 165 times more than that of a nurse, and over 67 per cent of FTSE 100 CEOs are paid more than 100 times the average UK salary (The Equality Trust 2017); the richest 1,000 people in the UK have more wealth than the bottom 40 per cent, that is, 27 million people (The Equality Trust 2019b); today, Britain 'is the fifth most unequal country in Europe in terms of income, while inequality of wealth is even greater: the top 10 per cent of households own more wealth than the bottom 80 per cent' (Office for National Statistics 2018, in Roberts et al. 2019: 8). 'Fewer than half of "millennials" (those born between 1981 and 2000) are expected to own their own home by the age of 45, based on current trends' (Roberts and Lawrence 2017). Projections suggest that inequality will keep rising between 2015–16 and 2021–22 if current tax and benefit policy plans are kept to, thus reversing the minor falls since the last recession (Joseph Rowntree Foundation 2019).

1.2 The linguistic side of the argument: Language, media and the public discourse

All these signs of newly entrenched inequality are best understood within the framework of neoliberalism. We live in an order where economics is not just economics anymore, as it has covered many other aspects in our lives, such as education, health, culture and social relationships. To put it differently, we have passed from *having* a market economy to *being* a market economy (Sandel 2012), with all the dangers this change entails. Under unregulated shrunken-state neoliberalism where market forces rule, people can feel compelled to live so as to trade (their goods and services) rather than trading in order to live.

Notwithstanding the economic, political or historical reasons that may have driven some Western societies to become more unequal today, we need to look at how language has been used in the public discourse in relation to this matter. In the context of new capitalism (Fairclough 2012) or hypercapitalism (Graham 2012), 'language is becoming more central and salient than before' (Fairclough 2012: 163).[2] The contemporary transformations in society have driven us to a position where the economic system (and, by extension, all the other fields it has colonized) is 'knowledge-' or 'information-based', very much depending on new communication technologies and giving more prominence to branding and the success of products, companies, nations and even individuals (Klein 2000, in Fairclough 2012: 163–4). As Graham points out, 'We have reached a historical point at which specific identities, or ways of being, including ways of knowing and representing, become the most valuable commodity forms' (2019: 232). Therefore, knowing how language works in this socio-economic context will help us in understanding how this context works indeed.

Following a socio-constructionist theory (Fowler 1991; van Dijk 1988; 1998; Fairclough 1992, 1995), we believe that language has played an important role in this situation. This is so not just because of the recent transformations in society but also because the language we use (and the particular choices we make when using it) influences how we understand the world and how we (inter)act in it in relation to societal issues such as race, sexuality, age and gender. Our public discourses both rehearse and reaffirm the prevailing or hegemonic public understanding of who we are, what we are doing and why, and what we value. As Fairclough (2012) claims, if this new order we live in is knowledge-led, then 'it is also discourse-led, for knowledges are produced, circulated and consumed as discourses (economic, organizational, managerial, political, educational and so forth)', and 'discourses are enacted as ways of acting and interacting in society' (Fairclough 2012: 164) (see also Fairclough 1992). In the words of Chouliaraki and Fairclough (1999), 'It is an important characteristic of the economic, social and cultural changes of late modernity that they exist as discourses as well as processes that are taking place outside discourse, and that the processes that are taking place outside discourse are substantively shaped by these discourses' (Chouliaraki and Fairclough 1999: 4). This theoretical tradition (which is broadly represented by CDA), Toolan (2018) claims, 'understands a society's language habits and practices as shaping and influencing (but not straitjacketing) that society's customary and ordinary assumptions about everything' (Toolan 2018: 7).

Following this argument, one may also assume that the language used in the public discourse influences changes in societal attitudes and expectations, either facilitating or obstructing them. Events in society cannot be represented in a truly objective and neutral way in public discourses, because discursive report is always an interpretation, from one distinct perspective or another (see Chapter 9). In the case of mass media discourse, the interpretation is largely aligned with the dominant cultural values of the community, which Hall et al. (1978) called the 'central value system' (Toolan 2018: 15). This is the power of the news media to influence people's perceptions, particularly shaping the discourse on economic inequality, but by the same token applicable to any societal issue.

Some scholars have claimed that this situation distorts the original function of the media, which is now 'failing in its watchdog role' and 'acting as an ideological enabler of growing inequality' (Silke, Quinn and Rieder 2019: 247). What we discuss in our everyday conversations, in a way, is still influenced by the power of the 'old' journalism, as new channels disseminate news coming from (digital versions of) newspapers, which are particularly powerful in the case of opinion articles. We have changed the way we communicate, that is true, but it is no less true we want still to be informed, whatever the means, from traditional newspapers and television news to online discussions on Twitter. Is it possible, for example, that how the main political parties' leaders have talked about the poor and economic inequalities during the most recent general elections (2010, 2015 and 2017) has framed our perception of the topic? Is it possible that, among the dozens of tweets younger generations read every day, those discussing differences between CEOs and manual workers (but also other presenting

Beyoncé, the Kardashians and other celebrities' lifestyles, to mention a few) may have shaped how we understand such inequalities? By means of the dominant public discourses and the values they articulate, we believe British society today is encouraged to see and understand inequality in terms broadly congruent with a neoliberal mindset that is drawing us closer to the value system that prevails also in the United States. We also believe it is important to understand better how this situation has arisen. This motivates our interest in the representation of economic inequality in British public discourse.

2 Economic inequality in the British public discourse

Studies of different forms of economic inequality are relatively new in CDA, which, to our knowledge, has traditionally paid more attention to other forms of inequality-generating discrimination specifically sourced in gender, race, religion, country of origin or sexual orientation. Since the late 2000s, however, there has been growing academic interest in how different forms of economic inequality are mediated to the public (Machin and Richardson 2008), which subsequently has led to growing discussion in CDA.[3]

Most of the existing economic-related research within CDA has looked at the uses and users of the benefits system, these normally being represented in a negative way in print newspapers (Baker forthcoming), TV campaigns (Roberts 2017), the poverty-porn genre on TV (Jensen 2014) and Twitter responses to these (Baker and McEnery 2015a; Paterson, Coffey-Glover and Peplow 2016; van der Bom et al. 2018).[4] Results in these studies overall show that benefit claimants are presented as cheating, not wanting to work (which, in turn, is encouraged by a 'perverse' welfare system), smoking and/or consuming drugs, getting pregnant, carelessly and having poor dental hygiene; they are also described as lazy, feckless, pyjama wearing, subject to anger, disbelief and disgust. Moreover, viewers of TV programmes like *Benefits Street* evaluate certain practices by benefits claimants negatively, in what seems to be a process of homogenization in the evaluation of benefits claimants.

Also noteworthy on their own are those studies that have looked at the discourse of poverty, particularly in the media (Kress 1994; Street 1994; Hewitt 1994; Meinhof 1994) and as perceived by the audience (Richardson 1994). Lorenzo-Dus and Marsh (2012) found discursive evidence to support the claim that poverty has undergone a process of 'securitization', where the poor and poverty are displayed as a security threat, thus being linked to negative categories such as terrorism, insecurity and tyranny. In recent months, Paterson and Gregory (2019) have released a book on the representations of poverty that incorporates geographical text analysis to uncover the construction of poverty in the *Daily Mail* and *Guardian*, particularly foregrounding matters such as employment, housing or benefits and providing a London-centric coverage of poverty.

Supplementing the existing literature on the hegemonic negative discourse surrounding benefits claimants and the poor, further studies demonstrate the public defence of those more affluent in UK society, particularly the British royal family (Billig 1992), celebrities (Mendick, Allen and Harvey 2015), big corporations

(Graham and O'Rouke 2019) and the rich (Rieder and Theine 2019), who are even represented as victims.

Critical discourse studies have also acknowledged a denial of class struggle in UK society and the idea that class has disappeared from the political agenda in recent decades. This denial has been signalled in the political context, in particular cases such as the response by Cameron and Miliband to the Occupy Movement and the August 2011 British riots (Bennett 2013a), where both shared a neoliberal political discourse conception of class in their speeches and considered class to be something people choose.[5] Similarly, Ortu (2008) found that the anti-union discourse of several British governments from 1978 to 2007 denied class struggle systematically in UK society. This denial of the concept of class and class struggle as a social issue has also been found in interviews to television viewers (Paterson, Peplow and Grainger 2017) and the press (Toolan 2016; Grisold and Silke 2019; Rieder and Theine 2019).

Finally, the 2008 economic crisis and the subsequent recession led to nearly a decade of government-imposed austerity, and this in turn attracted CDA analyses. In this sense, Fairclough (2016) has discussed the consequences of the discourse of austerity in the UK press for social inequality, claiming that austerity measures oriented towards the most vulnerable in UK society were presented as inevitable and morally right. Harkins and Lugo-Ocando (2016) have similarly argued that coverage of austerity policies by tabloid newspapers in Britain reproduced and reinforced a hegemonic discourse of the undeserving poor. More recently, Jeffries and Walker's (2019) chapter on the grammatical context of austerity in House of Commons debates between 1803 and 2015 demonstrates how discussion of austerity has changed over the past 200 years.

To sum up, approaches to class and economic inequality in CDA have generally drawn on neoliberalism and the inequities of contemporary capitalism, overall displaying a society that is divided into workers and workless, the ones who give and the ones who take. They show, if they talk about class, that there is a hegemonic discourse as observed in different contexts (TV, politics, press, social media, etc.) that, in general terms, attacks (or at least questions) the welfare system. As Toolan (2018) argues, though, discourses around economic inequality should be more central to CDA, as empirical evidence indicates that this form of inequality is discursively more accepted than others, but also (and mainly) because 'the wider divide … between the rich and poor in this country, … which is probably growing yet larger, is causing and will continue to cause great harm' (Toolan 2018: 4). In particular, we believe attention needs to be drawn to how we have come to the present situation, particularly looking at the way the public discourse has been framed, with possible (and probable) changes, in modern and contemporary Britain.

3 Corpus-assisted discourse studies: An overview of the method(s)

In analysing the relationship between language, ideology and society, CDA comprises a variety of approaches that encompass different methodologies accordingly. In this sense, Hart (2010: 14) identifies four main approaches within CDA: *critical linguistics* (Fowler et al. 1979; Fowler 1991, 1996; Kress 1985; Kress and Hodge 1979), the *socio-semiotic approach* (Fairclough 1992, 1995, 2015), the *discourse-historical approach* (Reisigl and Wodak 2001; Wodak 1996, 2001) and the *socio-cognitive approach* (van Dijk 1995c, 1998, 2002). The reader of this book will see that the different chapters offer diverse approaches to economic inequality; hence, the methods they use vary significantly from one to the other. There is common ground, thus, in that (1) all the contributions are transdisciplinary (Fairclough 2005), as they address economic inequality and related issues through a constant dialogue with other disciplines beyond linguistics, namely anthropology, journalism or philosophy, (2) all of them approach different forms of economic inequality from a critical perspective (Wodak and Meyer 2009) and (3) all of them share the 'corpus-assisted' label, in that they incorporate corpus tools to a bigger or lesser degree to their objects of study.

Corpus-assisted discourse studies (CADS) (Partington, Duguid and Taylor 2013) is defined as 'that set of studies into the form and/or function of language as *communicative discourse* which incorporate the uses of computerised corpora in their analyses' (Partington, Duguid and Taylor 2013: 10). The origin of CADS is normally traced back to Mautner (1995) and Stubbs (1996), though other antecedents include Caldas-Coulthard (1993), Louw (1993) and Stubbs and Gerbig (1993), among others (see Mautner 1995: 2). More recent but also significant work in this field includes Partington, Morley and Haarman (2004), Morley and Bayley (2009) and Bayley and Williams (2012), as well as Baker (2006) and Gabrielatos and Baker (2008). The main features of CADS are best summarized by Partington, Duguid and Taylor (2013: 11–14), who particularly highlight the following:

- the *combination of quantitative and qualitative approaches* to discourse, whereby statistical and computerized overviews of large amounts of a particular discourse are combined with the close analysis of particular samples of such discourse;
- its *aim to try to analyse and critique as much as possible the discourse type* in question, which means approaching the corpus in a wide variety of ways;
- its *use of*, normally, *specialized corpora* that is built specifically according to the research questions or hypotheses that researchers aim to address; and
- its *comparative nature*, based on the notion that you can only approach and evaluate a corpus (discourse) if you compare it to something else. Again, this drives towards many different and possible comparisons that will also depend on the research questions or hypotheses that researchers aim to address (our emphasis).

As with CDA, CADS' overarching aim is to uncover 'non-obvious' meanings, or meanings which are not perceived at first sight, in the discourse under scrutiny (Partington 2010: 88). These 'non-obvious' meanings in discourse occur because, in speaking or writing, we make semi-automatic choices regarding linguistic aspects such as transitivity, modality or vocabulary (among many others) that can be more easily identified through the combination of quantitative (statistical) and qualitative (in-depth) tools. In this sense, CADS joins together what can be learned from corpus analysis (statistical insight) with other sources of information on a particular topic, either linguistic or sociocultural (Partington 2010: 90). Software tools are incorporated here because they have a potential 'in helping to unravel how particular discourses, rooted in particular socio-cultural contexts, construct reality, social identities and social relations' (Fairclough 1992: 64).[6] It is important to highlight at this point that, notwithstanding that the use of corpus tools complements the methods normally used in CDA, these should not replace them, as 'qualitative and quantitative techniques need to be combined, not played one against each other' (Mautner 1995: 2).

What is needed mainly include the corpora itself and computer software to analyse such corpora (Partington, Duguid and Taylor 2013: 14–20). The corpora used in this book are generally purpose-built, according to researchers' previous experiences with the matter or specifically designed for the aim of this volume. Examples include a corpus of the Labour and Conservative parties' annual conferences since 1900 to 2014 or another one of opinion articles in the *Times* about child poverty in the 1970s and 2000s. It is also quite common that already existing (and larger) corpora such as the British National Corpus or the Bank of English are used to compare such purpose-built corpora, following the comparative nature of corpus linguistics. Finally, dozens of software packages are also available so that the analyst inspects the discourse(s) embodied in the corresponding corpus. As Partington, Duguid and Taylor (2013: 17) indicate, the most important tools include 'first of all, the *concordancer*, then calculators of *frequency, keyness, clusters* and *dispersion*'. One may find that some of the commonest software packages used in CDA, such as *AntConc* (Anthony 2019), *Wordsmith Tools* (Scott 2019) and *Sketch Engine* (Kilgarriff et al. 2014), include most, if not all, of these tools.[7]

Although there is not a single method in order to undertake a 'corpus-assisted' CDA, we could identify a few standard stages in the process (see also Mautner 1995) that can be summarized as building (or gathering), annotating and analysing the corpus. At this stage of the analysis, countless options exist for the analyst, which will combine the concordancer with the additional tools provided by software, in a process where such tools are constantly feeding one to the others. This means that further methodological decisions will vary according to the hypotheses and/or research questions that instigated the study, as well as to the theoretical implications of the research in question. The chapters to come are a clear example of this, as authors have followed different methods in approaching their text samples.

4 Structure of the book

All the chapters in this book share a common interest in the discursive representation of different forms of exclusion, inequality and discrimination in the British media and other forms of public discourse, and all of them are produced within the realm of CADS. They differ, though, in their specific methodology, theoretical background and object of study. Also, some of the chapters provide empirical evidence to give readers an impression of how wealth inequality has been portrayed in different periods of modern and contemporary Britain; some others are thought-provoking reflections on the matter that should lead to further discussion on economic inequality and class in modern and contemporary Britain.

The chapters are organized chronologically, therefore, according to the socio-historical issues they address. Chapter 1 examines the discursive representation of poverty and social exclusion by the leaders of the Labour and Conservative parties from 1900 to 2014 through the parties' annual conferences. By organizing the data into three historical periods (1900–48, 1949–2000 and 2001–14) and by conducting an ideo-textual analysis (Jeffries 2010, 2014) of the concordance lines of the most frequent poverty and social exclusion keywords in their corpus, Nuria Lorenzo-Dus and Sadiq Almaged identify two recurring discourses in the leaders' speeches: a finance one, favoured by the Conservative Party, and a hardship one, favoured by the Labour Party. Their analysis also reveals some commonalities across the political parties and time: they are prone to describe poverty and social exclusion in terms of scale, to represent them as passive entities that need to be acted upon and to use third-person deixis to detach themselves personally from the responsibility of carrying out such actions. The authors observe an increase of personal involvement in the actions intended for addressing poverty and social exclusion after 2001, which they explain as the result of a process of securitization after the terrorist attacks on the West in the last few decades.

Chapter 2 addresses the discursive negotiation of inequality during the Second World War, particularly by inspecting metalinguistic sources from the Ministry of Information and the Mass-Observation project. Parting from the M-O project's proposal of a social deictic strategy to communicate with the civilian population (i.e. adopting a more vernacular, simple and personal language), Joe Spencer-Bennett results suggest that the 'mass' language was depicted in stereotyped terms and as a means for controlling the population indeed. Bennett argues that the project's proposal was far from the idea of democratization or egalitarianism that the twentieth century seems to have encompassed, linguistically speaking.

Chapter 3 investigates the representation of the welfare state in the *Times* between 1940s and 2000s. Isabelle van der Bom and Laura Paterson create their own corpus through CQPweb (Hardie 2012), and arrange this into decades for comparative purposes. By inspecting collocates, co-text and context, and through the application of van Dijk's notion of macropropositions, van der Bom and Paterson find that the welfare state is associated with restructuring and building metaphors, increased (im) morality and the creation/increase of an economic and cultural social underclass. All these findings keep stable over time.

Chapter 4 explores possible shifts in how child poverty was talked about in the *Times* between the 1970s and the 2000s. Michael Toolan postulates two contrasting explanatory narratives about child poverty in the UK. One implies that the UK is a country where nearly everyone is free to live decently and flourish, given suitable effort, so the state mostly should not intervene. The other narrative is one in which the 'playing-field' is so unlevel that living well is next to impossible for some (single parents with children, those on minimum wage, those dependent on the old-age pension) unless the state intervenes vigorously. The comparison of keywords in both periods suggests that in the 1970s the *Times* assumed that combating child poverty required financial aid from the state and governmental activism; by contrast, in the 2000s, it was more connected to charities and reported more anecdotally. A broader comparison of the semantic domains prominent in editorials and letters touching on child poverty in the two periods indicates that unemployment was a recognized link with child poverty in the earlier period but not in the later period, when the reality of 'hard-working poverty' arose; in the later period, 'schools and education' are thematized, possibly in recognition that poor children in the recent period are less adequately catered for by the state education system than fifty years ago. Toolan concludes by arguing that the identified shifts in the *Times*'s representations of child poverty show a shift in the paper's ideology away from one of collective social responsibility in the earlier period to a contrasting one of individualism in the latter, where far more responsibility for child poverty is transferred to families.

Chapter 5 deals with how UK national newspapers reporting on corporate fraud and modern slavery discuss economic inequality, responsibility and accountability from 2004 to 2016. By analysing the c-collocates of terms relating to corporate fraud and modern slavery, results indicate that they were presented in a 'neutralizing' manner in the years examined through a denial and/or transfer of the responsibility and accountability for these crimes. Particularly, Ilse Ras observes that the reporting on these crimes generally ignored where such responsibility lies and, if discussed, the regulatory parties and the governments were the ones who should take this responsibility.

Chapter 6 focuses on the UK Change for Life anti-obesity campaign and its construction of 'at-risk' social groups. It particularly inspects a corpus of documents about UK obesity policy from 1999 to 2019, and a compilation of thirty-three adverts that were broadcasted on UK television as a response by government to previous policy research. By combining policy discourse analysis, multimodality and corpus-aided discourse analysis, Jane Mulderrig finds that the adverts display patterns of representation which are aligned with neoliberalism: the working class is presented as chief culprit with regard to the rise in child obesity, while the freedoms of the food and drink industry are preserved in the campaign, which in the end also puts industry as an advantaged social actor. Furthermore, there is nothing in the adverts to address the powerful position of the commercial sector, but the ultimate responsibility is placed on the individual.

Chapter 7 compares the discoursal context of austerity in 2009–10, when the government drastically reduced its spending as a response to the financial crisis of 2008, and in 2016–17, when commentators and politicians claimed the end of the austerity period. Lesley Jeffries and Brian Walker combine corpus tools (keyword analysis and concordances) and qualitative research based on Jeffries's (2010, 2014) framework of analysis in order to inspect the national press. The exploration of naming and transitivity patterns in both periods suggests that, in general, austerity was presented as a viable and electable policy, as something inevitable in the context of the country in those years. Some shifts are found by Jeffries and Walker, who observe that while austerity was central in 2009–10, it became peripheral in 2016–17. In the latter period, the qualitative analysis indicates a negative evaluation of the government policy, less epochal sounding and more like moving forward.

Chapter 8 discusses the evolving landscape of inequality and looks for possible shifts in BBC and ITV 10.00 p.m. bulletins coverage between 2007 and 2014. By combining content and CDA analyses, Richard Thomas identifies a change in how these channels have reported inequality through time. Thomas suggests that income inequality and poverty issues were more prominent in 2007, which is complemented with a detailed discussion on why there has been such a decrease, bearing in mind that poverty has increased in UK throughout the same period. Thomas also claims both the BBC and ITV have defended a neoliberal approach to these issues in 2014, in those few cases in which they have discussed the matter.

Chapter 9 deeply probes the links between forms of economic inequality and the democracies we live at present in Western societies. Wolfgang Teubert claims in this chapter that Western democracies are not actually empowering their citizens to decide public issues collectively, instead citizens are exposed to a public discourse that is built on behalf of the ruling class. By developing thought-provoking ideas on concepts such as democracy, rights, minorities, hegemony, ruling class or class inequality, Teubert offers the readers an insightful perspective on inequality in UK public discourse. Applying collocational analysis to Hansard, he focuses on how the British parliament has discussed the concept of 'democracy' itself and its connection to economic inequality in gradually changing ways over two centuries. Teubert observes how Parliament firstly feared inequality, while with the passing of time, it has come to self-righteously approve it, secure now in the knowledge that the electorate have been deluded into quietly accepting direction 'in the name of democracy' from the ruling class.

Prof. Danny Dorling closes the book with a sobering reflection on economic inequality. In a very thoughtful tone, Dorling makes substantiated claims, such as that it is possible to gain greater equality (despite the effort of the greedy to preserve such inequalities) or that there was a time when UK was a much more equal country. Adapting Sandel's idea that we have moved from having a market economy to being a market economy (Sandel 2012), Prof. Dorling argues that society does need to keep that market ruled and delimited, as it was usually done in the past. After engaging in discussion with every chapter in this volume, Dorling's main contribution comes through his final and optimistic conclusion that though *The Discursive Construction of Economic Inequality* shows how the media has depicted economic and related matters so as to make us perceive such inequality as something natural or unavoidable, we do not know yet what will happen in future. There is much food for thought and action, then, in Dorling's afterword.

The book closes with a consolidated list of references that includes all the works cited in this volume. We believe this gives a strong sense of uniformity and cohesion to the chapters and also allows the readers to find any reference in an easier, more accessible manner. A final index is also provided with the intention to facilitate readers finding any topic through the volume.

We certainly hope that the readers of *The Discursive Construction of Economic Inequality* find this book a valuable contribution to the existing literature in CADS and economic inequality. We also expect that, by combining the strengths of CDA and corpus linguistics, this book helps in a better understanding of how the public discourse has helped in making increased inequality look more normal in UK society today.

Notes

1. On the growing economic inequality in the UK, see especially Cribb et al. (2012), Forsey (2017), Hills and Stewart (2005), Lansley (2012), Marquand (2013), Mount (2012), Piketty (2014), Rowlingson (2012), Stiglitz (2012), Westergaard (2012) and Wilkinson and Pickett (2010).
2. 'New Capitalism', as understood by Fairclough (2000), refers to 'the new form of capitalism emerging from contemporary transformations' (163).
3. The increasing interest within CDA studies in the 2000s has been made manifest by three especial issues of *Discourse & Society* (Fairclough 2002) and *Critical Discourse Studies* (Machin and Richardson 2008; Silke, Quinn and Rieder 2019). It is also worth noting here those studies that, though not properly from a critical perspective, have approached representations of different forms of inequality in the UK. This comes, naturally, especially from the fields of sociology and media studies. See, for instance, the Glasgow Media Group (1976, 1980), who approached elitism (among other things) in UK television coverage during a period of strikes, industrial action and economic issues. See also Mooney and Sifaki's (2017) *The Language of Money and Debt*, as well as Atkinson, Roberts and Savage's (2012) *Class Inequality in Austerity Britain*.
4. The so-called 'poverty-porn' TV genre includes programmes like *We Pay Your Benefits* (BBC), *Benefits Britain 1949* (Channel 4), *On Benefits and Proud* (Channel 5) and *Benefits Street* (Channel 4), first broadcasted in early 2010s.
5. David Cameron was the prime minister of the UK from 2010 to 2016, for the Conservative Party. Ed Miliband was the leader of the opposition between 2010 and 2015, as leader of the Labour Party.
6. Not just CDA, but also in many other linguistic fields, software tools have significantly contributed in the last decades. As Mautner (1995) explains, the application of corpus tools was traditionally in two areas, lexicography and more general linguistic research, either for descriptive or teaching aims in mind (Mautner 1995: 2). On this topic, see especially Hunston (2002).
7. There is no space here to note all the possible options that the analyst would have to choose from to research further, but we encourage readers of this volume to read, if not done yet, very significant publications regarding the methodological implications of CADS. In this sense, a good starting point is reading Fairclough (1992, 2015), Baker (2006), Baker et al. (2008), Bednarek (2008), Jeffries (2010), Gabrielatos et al. (2012), Baker and Levon (2015), Baker and McEnery (2015b) or the more recent Taylor and Marchi (2018).

Poverty and social exclusion in Britain

A corpus-assisted discourse study of Labour and Conservative Party leaders' speeches, 1900–2014

Nuria Lorenzo-Dus and Sadiq Almaged

1.1 Introduction

The impact of poverty and social exclusion (PSE) reaches beyond insufficient financial income to meet individuals' basic needs such as nutrition and shelter. As the World Bank Organization (2006) reminds us, PSE also concerns women, men and children feeling uncertain about their future, not having access to education and employment and surviving from day to day. The rise of PSE levels across a number of countries is concerning, and the UK, on which this study is based, is no exception. According to a June 2019 report by the UK Office for National Statistics, approximately 4.7 million people in the UK (7.8 per cent of its population) lived in persistent poverty in 2017 – with persistent poverty being defined as that which affects individuals whose 'disposable income falls below 60 per cent of the national median' in the year being measured and 'at least two out of the three preceding years' (UK Office for National Statistics 2019). The same report states that the UK's poverty rate in 2017 affected approximately 2.4 million *working* people. This resonates with Toolan's (2018: 221) statement that '[t]wenty and more years ago, people in poverty were mostly unemployed, whereas today they are more often in work, but lowly paid'. Further evidence of rising levels of PSE in the UK comes from 2014 to 2017 figures from the Organisation for Economic Co-operation and Development (OECD), which situate the UK within the top ten countries in the world for wealth inequality – the top 20 per cent of the country's population earn six times as much as the bottom 20 per cent (OECD 2019). In addition, a 2018 report published by the British think tank E3G highlights that more than 3,000 people are 'needlessly' dying each year in the UK because of 'fuel poverty'; that is, they cannot afford to heat their homes properly (E3G 2018).

Given the above, it is perhaps unsurprising that PSE have become the focus of political attention over time. O'Connor (2001) describes this as a 'politicization' of PSE, whereby political party agendas have come to play a progressively more influential role in determining PSE causes, measures and effects. There has also been a considerable rise in academic interest in PSE, in particular within the fields of politics, economy and sociology (see, for example Heath et al. 2013; Lansley 2012; Townsend and Gordon 2002; Westergaard 2012). An important body of discourse analytic scholarship into PSE has emerged over time, too, which has primarily examined the semiotic practices that individuals and groups deploy to represent PSE (see Section 1.2). Within this scholarship, however, there are some comparatively under-researched areas, which this study aims to address, specifically the discursive construction of PSE by political elites across time. Using the UK as a case study, this chapter examines the discursive means by which the leaders of the country's two main political parties – Conservative and Labour – have represented PSE across the twentieth and twenty-first centuries in their party conference speeches.

The chapter is structured as follows. Sections 1.2 and 1.3, respectively, review the relevant literature into PSE from a discourse analysis perspective and provide a brief overview of the ideology of the Conservative and Labour Parties, focusing on the political events to be examined in this paper, namely their annual party conferences between 1900 and 2014. Section 1.4 introduces the data and methodological approach adopted in our study, namely corpus-assisted discourse studies (CADS). Section 1.5 reports our key results, identifying similarities and differences in the discursive construction of PSE by political party and across time. In Section 1.6, we pull together these results, noting the relevance of British political leaders' discursive representations of PSE.

1.2 Representing poverty and social exclusion in discourse

Research into PSE within the field of linguistics, and specifically discourse analysis, has focused on how these issues are semiotically represented across a range of institutional contexts, especially the mass media. This research broadly agrees that representations of individuals and groups living in PSE are primarily negative, often involving some form of stereotyping (see, for example, De Melo Resende (2016), Garcia da Silva (2008), Lacerda (2015) in the context of Brazil, Pardo (2013) in Argentina, Pardo-Abril (2008) in Colombia, Summers (2006) in New Zealand, Fairclough (2005) in Romania and Toft (2014) in the United States). Within the UK media,[1] the first – to our knowledge – book-length treatment of the discursive representation of poverty in the UK is the edited collection by Meinhof and Richardson (1994), titled *Text, Discourse and Context: Representations of Poverty in Britain*. Only one chapter in this book examines media representations of 'home' (as opposed to 'Third World') poverty by the British media (Street 1994). The analysis reveals that, while regularly using 'supposedly comparable empirical data from other countries in order to highlight features of the home society', the British media mainly downplay poverty as a sociopolitical issue in the UK (Street 1994: 50).

More recently, several studies have been published that integrate corpus linguistics and critical discourse analysis (CDA) in order to find recurring patterns in the language used to represent PSE across UK media. Baker and McEnery (2015a), for instance, analyse Twitter responses to the British television show *Benefits Street*. These cluster around three main discourses: the idle poor, the poor as victims and the rich get richer. Van der Bom et al.'s (2018) analysis of Twitter responses to the same television show also reveals that benefits claimants are regularly constructed as social parasites and as morally inadequate and members of a flawed underclass. Focusing on a particular type of state-backed benefit in the UK (i.e. maternity leave), Gómez-Jiménez (2018) shows how representations of maternity leave became monetarized by the British press (the *Times* and *Daily Mail*) in the last thirty years or so of the twentieth century (1971–2001). Two main discourses (or 'macrostructures') emerged during that time: one saw mothers-to-be as facing numerous problems; the other regarded changes in maternity leave policy (three during the period examined) as leading to negative consequences for British society.

Two further corpus and discourse studies of PSE in the UK media across time of direct relevance are Toolan (2016, 2018). In Toolan (2016) the focus is on representations of wealth inequality and social class within television programme reviews published by the *Daily Mail* in 1971 (reviews by Peter Black) and in 2013 (reviews by Christopher Steven). Highlight findings include a disappearance of discussions about class and wealth inequality in the 2013 reviews, when compared to the 1971 reviews. Toolan (2016) warns that the absence of such discussion may become naturalized. In Toolan (2018) a comprehensive analysis of the representation of inequality in the UK media (primarily the *Times* and *Daily Mail*) over a forty-five-year period (1971–2016) is offered. In addition to confirming stigmatizing portrayals of those who experience some form of PSE, this analysis confirms the naturalization of wealth inequality, which is constructed as inevitable. As a result, Toolan (2018: 224) further argues, 'The rejection of egalitarian policies and redistribution as unreasonable and unjustified became considerably more discursively entrenched' over the forty-five-year period examined. Toolan (2018) continues to call for CDAs of wealth inequality to gain centrality within an otherwise prolific research agenda focused on other forms of inequality and discrimination.

Analysis of the representation of PSE in British *political* (rather than media) *discourse* is comparatively scarce. This is somewhat surprising, considering that politics is the main social field in which decisions regarding policy, including PSE-related policy, are made and that those decisions are articulated in and through discourse (e.g. Chilton 2004). Within this literature, several studies are particularly relevant to the work covered in this chapter. Koller and Davidson (2008), for instance, examine the discursive mechanisms used in 2017 UK policy documents about social exclusion and also the 2005 speeches by the then Labour Party leader Ed Miliband. Their analysis shows recurring use of conceptual and grammatical metaphors that portray British society as a physical space offering warmth and shelter to those who are socially excluded. Watt (2008) examines images of benefit claimants in a council housing campaign in the UK. The findings, which show them to be visually rendered as ordinary people, contrast with those from stigmatizing media portrayals of benefits claimants. For their part, Lorenzo-Dus and Marsh (2012) analyse representations of poverty in UK (as well as US and EU) National Security Strategies over a nine-year period (1997–2006). Their analysis finds discursive evidence to support the

International Relations thesis that poverty has undergone a process of 'securitization' (Balzacq 2005; Wæver 1995), whereby poverty/the poor are constructed as a security threat in high-level policy documents. This discursive evidence includes, among other, recurrent use of semantic-discursive categories, particularly post 2001, that link poverty to tyranny, terrorism, insecurity, security threat and security challenges.

For their part, McEnery and Baker (2017) use CADS to examine representations of PSE across time – in their case, throughout the seventeenth century – in England. Drawing upon a one billion word corpus of literary texts and examining the at-the-time commonly used terms 'beggars and vagrants', the study reveals the individuals thus labelled being systematically evaluated in hostile terms, including as being idle and fools. The study also shows a lack of compassion towards these individuals, whose social circumstances are not taken into consideration. Instead, a strong sense of personal responsibility and, therefore, personal blame, specifically of blaming beggars and vagrants for their own condition, characterizes their literary representation at that point in time.

Last, but not least, one must note the double-edged sword around the grammar of the noun 'poverty' in the English language. As Kress (1994: 29) puts it, in English 'poverty is something that you can be in, or get yourself into'. Poverty happens to individuals – it is grammatically a state of being beyond their control. The corollary of this non-agentive grammar is that individuals may fall into poverty accidentally, rather than intentionally. Yet, 'poverty itself can act agentively – poverty can drive us into despair, poverty causes the breakup of families, and so on' (1994: 29). This may conveniently support the causal connections often drawn in elite discourses of PSE whereby the poor are represented as both passive (idle) and agentive (blameworthy) – something that may enable the 'seeds for demonising poverty and the poor [to be] sown' while supposedly freeing political institutions from any agentive responsibility (Lorenzo-Dus and Marsh 2012: 278).

1.3 The British political party system: A focus on the Conservative and the Labour Parties

Although the birth of British political parties dates to the seventeenth century, given space constraints, this section outlines the ideologies of the two main parties – Conservative and Labour – across the period covered by our study (1900–2014). In the early twentieth century, the Conservative Party adopted a right-wing authoritarian ideology, which supported inequality and the survival of the fittest. Under the leadership of Margaret Thatcher in the 1970s to 1980s, the Conservatives most explicitly linked a social market economy to authoritarian populism (Pope, Pratt and Hoyle 1986). This increasingly shifted towards the adoption of a neoconservative ideology, which combined Liberalism with Conservatism, and currently embraces global interventionism (Fuchs 2016).

While being considered the most ideologically inclined of all British political parties, the Labour Party has been plagued by ideological struggle since its foundation

(Clark 2012). Through most of the twentieth century, the party advocated socialist policies, such as public ownership of industries, government intervention in the economy, redistribution of wealth and improved protections, healthcare and education for workers. In the late 1990s, the Labour leadership under Tony Blair and Gordon Brown re-modelled the Party's doctrine to create 'New Labour', also referred to as a 'Third Way' (Fairclough 2000: 21), which focused on issues such as minimum wages, health and education spending.

Like other British political parties, the Conservative and Labour Parties hold high-profile conferences annually. These conferences are their sovereign policy and decision-making body, as well as formal sources of party policy (Clark 2012). They also 'highlight their [the Parties'] extra-parliamentary existence and allow these organizations to address voters' (Faucher-King 2005: 11). The speeches delivered at these annual conferences therefore inevitably shape British politics.

From a sociopolitical perspective, and given the elite position that party leaders hold within their internal party structures, their speeches are the most important event of these annual conferences (Williams 2011). From a discourse perspective, party leaders' speeches illustrate the typical persuasive function of political rhetoric (Fairclough and Fairclough 2012). For instance, Thatcher used her conference party speeches to enthuse and inspire the mass membership and existing Conservative voters by assuring them that she shared many of their ambitions and their anxieties (Finlayson, Martin and Philips 2016). Party leaders' conference speeches are therefore not 'just' pieces of discourse where policy is verbally announced. They are also the discursive spaces where leaders (re)construct their parties' future in accordance with their agreed content, which is why they have been selected as the dataset for our study, to which we next turn.

1.4 Methodology

1.4.1 Data

Our data comprise all the speeches (203; overall word count = 1,019,328) delivered by 51 different Conservative and Labour Party leaders at their annual party conferences between 1900 and 2014. As shown in Table 1.1, we divide these speeches into three periods for the purposes of the present study. Each period covers significant historical events in relation to PSE.

Period 1 comprises all the speeches (76, number of words = 317,002) delivered by 32 different political leaders (7 Conservative, 25 Labour). The lower number of speeches by Conservative Party leaders during this period owes to war time preventing some conferences from being held and/or leader health issues. Between 1900 and 1948 the UK was involved in two world wars and affected by massive economic depression (Glennerster 2002; Lambert 2013). In 1911, the British government introduced the National Insurance Act to support health benefit and free medical treatment to workers. However, it was not until 1920 that health benefit policy was extended to those who were unemployed (Dorling et al. 2007). In the 1930s, Britain's trade fell

Table 1.1 Poverty and Social Exclusion in Britain through the Labour and Conservative Party Leaders' Speeches, 1900–2014: Data Composition

	Periods								
	Period 1: 1900–48			Period 2: 1949–2000			Period 3: 2001–14		
Parties	no.=W*	no.=L*	no.=S*	no.=W	no.=L	no.=S	no.=W	no.=L	no.=S
Conservative	163,276	7	30	244,847	8	48	79,926	3	14
Labour	153,726	25	46	328,163	8	54	85,390	3	11
Total	317,002	32	76	537,010	16	102	165,316	6	25

W*=words, L*=Leaders, S*=Speeches.

by half and depression spread over all sectors of industry, leading to unprecedented levels of unemployment and PSE more generally (Dimsdale and Hotson 2014). The economy gradually recovered in the 1940s, which also saw PSE reforms, notably the Beveridge Report that led to the foundation of the welfare state in 1942. In 1948, the Labour Government passed the National Assistance Act (NAA) to help citizens whose resources were insufficient to meet their needs (Gazeley 2003).

Period 2 includes all the speeches (102; total number of words = 537,010) delivered between 1949 and 2000 by sixteen different party leaders (eight Conservative and eight Labour). During period 2, economic improvements maintained the prosperity of most Britons under the Conservative Government led by Winston Churchill (1951–5), Anthony Eden (1955–7) and Harold Macmillan (1957–63). Under Conservative and Labour Governments in, respectively, the 1960s and 1970s PSE resurfaced, albeit that with less impact on the public than in period 1. This relative economic stability ended in the late 1970s under the Conservative Government of Margaret Thatcher. Thatcher's Britain was marked by a severe inflation crisis and an alarming rise in unemployment. Thatcher aimed at reducing public spending by raising the national tax levels on incomes (Glennerster et al. 2004). The policy caused economic deterioration that continued to the mid-1980s. In 1989, Thatcher introduced the very unpopular poll tax bill, which required every adult to pay a single flat-rate per capita tax, at a rate set by their local authority. This bill brought Thatcher's power to an end. In 1997, Labour won the general elections and Tony Blair became prime minister. In 1999, Blair announced the End of Child Poverty Programme, which aimed at increasing financial support to families to end child poverty in 2020 – an objective that has, sadly, not been met.

Period 3 includes all the speeches (25; total number of words = 165,316) delivered between 2001 and 2014 by six different party leaders (three Conservative and three Labour). This period was marked by a financial crisis in the UK and globally. Also, the deadly terrorist attacks in 2001 arguably changed the world's – and the UK's – views on multiple sociopolitical issues. After the 9/11 attack, PSE received renewed global interest from the world leading countries. In the UK, this led to a number of government initiatives to alleviate PSE. For instance, in 2010 the Labour Government enshrined the End Child Poverty Programme in legislation under the Child Poverty Act. In 2013, under the Conservative Government led by David Cameron, over 200

UK organizations teamed up to announce the Enough Food for Everyone campaign, along with the UK's presidency of the 2013 G8 forum.

1.4.2 Framework and procedure

This study uses a CADS methodology that enables synergistic integration of quantitative and qualitative analysis of language use. CADS typically follows a 'serendipitous' journey of discovery (Partington 2006: 12), whereby corpus linguistics software-enabled searches of datasets are treated as an initial '"map" … pinpointing areas of interest for a subsequent close analysis' (Baker et al. 2008: 284). Moreover, CADS encourages conceptual integration across relevant disciplines outside linguistics.

Our study comprises the following analytic steps:[2]

1. Extracting all the relevant party leader conference speeches from the publicly available repository *British Political Speech Archive* (British Political Speech 2019). In the small number of cases in which the repository did not hold a copy of a given speech, we located it in British public library and national archives. All the speeches were saved as txt files and uploaded – as two distinct corpora (Conservative Party and Labour Party) – to the corpus linguistics software Sketch Engine (Kilgarriff et al. 2014). We henceforth refer to this data set as our British Political Party Speeches (BPPS) corpus.
2. Using three thesauri (*Oxford Thesaurus* 2019, *Merriam Webster Thesaurus* 2019 and *Thesaurus.com* 2019) in order to identify synonyms of 'poverty' and 'social exclusion'. This resulted in 649 synonyms – our 'seed words'.
3. Identifying which seed words featured in the BPPS (Conservative and Labour Party) corpus, and selecting those that exhibited frequency levels ≥ 10. This yielded a list of sixty 'PSE words' in our corpus.
4. Conducting keyword analyses between the BPPS (Conservative and Labour) corpus and the British National Corpus (BNC)[3] and the Corpus of Political Speeches (CORPS).[4] From the resulting lists, forty-four keywords also featured in the list of sixty PSE words identified in step 3. Manual examination of all the concordance lines containing these forty-four words led to a number of them and/or concordance lines being discarded, as their meaning in context was not tied to PSE, such as the concordance 'We owe him great debt. We owe much to Heathcoat Amory, whose wisdom, charm and modesty made him both loved and trusted' (Harold Macmillan 1960, the Conservative Party) for the word debt. A final list of 28 words – to which we henceforth refer as the PSE keywords – and 956 concordances were derived. The PSE keywords were *poor, debt, deficit, bankruptcy, poverty, bankrupt, famine, low, misery, depressed, shortage, unfortunate, disastrous, terrible, reduction, modest, lowest, inadequate, waste, appalling, difficulty, short, bad, suffering, deprived, need, necessary* and *want*.
5. Manually categorizing contextualized use of the PSE keywords identified in step 4 into PSE discourses within the Conservative and Labour BPPS corpora.
6. Conducting an ideo-textual analysis (Jeffries 2010, 2014) of all the extended concordance lines containing the most frequent PSE keywords (see section

1.5.1) within these discourses. Jeffries' (2010, 2014) framework consists of ten 'Textual Conceptual Functions' (TCFs) that text procedures may use in order to generate ideologically laden conceptual meaning in different ways. They are *Naming and Describing, Representing Actions and States, Equating and Contrasting, Exemplifying and Enumerating, Prioritizing, Implying and Assuming, Negating, Hypothesizing, Presenting Other's Speech* and *Representing Time, Space and Society*.

1.5 Results

1.5.1 PSE discourses in the BBPS corpus

Two main PSE discourses were identified in our BPPS corpus, which we labelled 'finance' and 'hardship'. Within the finance discourse, PSE was explicitly represented in terms of economic and business needs, often through the PSE keywords *debt* and *deficit* (see below). For example, 'There is another thing – there is a War *debt* settlement' (Ramsay MacDonald 1930, The Labour Party), and 'I said the paper *deficit* might be over 320,000,000' (Winston Churchill 1949, The Conservative Party). Representation of PSE within the hardship discourse referenced various forms and/or sources of struggle – other than explicitly financial – to live in dignity. Most examples concerned general references to PSE through the keywords *poverty* and *need* (see below), such as 'You must not forget the *poverty* left by war' (Stanley Baldwin 1927, the Conservative Party, emphasis added), 'The worn-out veterans of industry are not only in *need*, but are deserving' (Walter Hudson, 1908, the Labour Party, emphasis added). There was also a third discourse, which we labelled 'other'. This encompassed a mixed bag of representations concerning living standards. The percentage frequency of presence of each of these discourses is shown in Table 1.2.

As can be seen in Table 1.2, the finance discourse covered 48.58 per cent of the PSE Conservative corpus and 29.10 per cent of the Labour corpus. For its part, the hardship discourse covered 41.95 per cent of the PSE Conservative corpus and 62.3 per cent

Table 1.2 Frequency of Use (n = Number of Concordances) of Each PSE Discourse in the BBPS Corpus

Discourse	Conservative corpus				Labour corpus			
	Period 1	Period 2	Period 3	Total/ % of corpus	Period 1	Period 2	Period 3	Total/ % of corpus
Finance	n=11 (7.14%)	n=52 (33.76%)	n=91 (59.09%)	n=154 (48.58%)	n=25 (13.44%)	n=94 (50.53%)	n=67 (36.02%)	n=186 (29.10%)
Hardship	n=27 (20.30%)	n=19 (14.28%)	n=87 (65.41%)	n=133 (41.95%)	n=96 (24.12%)	n=194 (48.74%)	n=108 (27.13%)	n=398 (62.30%)
Other	n=6 (20%)	n=13 (43.33%)	n=11 (33%)	n=30 (9.47%)	n=21 (38.18%)	n=18 (32.72%)	n=16 (29.09)	n=55 (8.60%)
Total	n=44	n=84	n=189	n=317	n=142	n=306	n=191	n=639

the PSE Labour corpus. Overall, therefore, the Conservative Party leaders, in their party conference speeches, talked about PSE in financial terms more frequently than in hardship terms. The Labour Party leaders, in contrast, favoured discussing PSE in hardship terms over doing so in financial terms.

There were cross-party similarities and differences regarding the PSE keywords through which the finance and hardship PSE discourses were realized, as well as their relative frequencies of use in the corpora. In the Conservative corpus, the finance PSE discourse comprised the words 'debt' (number of occurrences = 79), 'deficit' (n=42), 'bad' (n=10), 'bankruptcy' (n=9), 'lowest' (n=8), 'bankrupt' (n=4) and 'disastrous' (n=2). In the Labour corpus, the same discourse comprised the words 'debt' (n=57), 'deficit' (n=59), 'low' (n=50), 'lowest' (n=9), 'short' (n=6) and 'modest' (n=4). The words that comprised the hardship discourse in the Conservative Party were 'need' (n=67), 'poverty' (n=43), 'suffering' (n=11), 'want' (n=5), 'deprived' (n=4) and 'unfortunate' (n=3). Within the Labour corpus, they were 'poverty' (n=184), 'poor' (n=85), 'need' (n=81), 'suffering' (n=18), 'misery' (n=16), 'waste' (n=9) and 'want' (n=6).

In the Conservative Party corpus, therefore, 'debt' and 'deficit' accounted for 78.57 per cent of the total number of PSE keywords for the financial PSE discourse (n=154), and 'need' and 'poverty' covered 82.76 per cent total use of hardship discourse (n=133). In the Labour Party corpus, 'debt', 'deficit' and 'low' accounted for 89.24 per cent of all the keywords in the finance discourse (n=186) and 'need', 'poverty' and 'poor' for 87.93 per cent of the total use of the hardship discourse (n=398). The analysis of ideo-textual functions in these two PSE discourses presented in Section 5.2 encompasses all the extended concordances (n=747) of these particularly frequent words ('debt', 'deficit', 'low', 'need', 'poverty', 'poor').

1.5.2 Ideology within the PSE discourses of finance and hardship

The TCF analysis showed that six of the ten functions in Jeffries's (2010, 2014) framework were used in ≤10 per cent of the concordances selected for analysis, across the three periods by both parties: *Equating and Contrasting, Exemplifying and Enumerating, Implying and Assuming, Negating, Hypothesizing* and *Presenting Others' Speech*. Owing to space constraints, they are excluded from the analysis that follows, which focuses on the remaining TCFs, namely *Naming/Describing, Representing Actions/States, Prioritizing* and *Representing Person/Place/Time*. Tables 1.3 and 1.4 (PSE finance discourse) and Tables 1.5 and 1.6 (PSE hardship discourse) provide an overview of their frequency of use in, respectively, the Labour and Conservative BPPS corpora.

1.5.2.1 *Naming/describing PSE*[5]

The Conservative and Labour Party described the PSE keywords ('debt', 'deficit', 'low', 'need', 'poverty' and 'poor') in terms of three broad semantic properties: scale, locus and source. Scale refers to representations that concerned the quantity or size of specific PSE issues (e.g. '*huge* debt', '*massive* need' and '*big* deficit'). This category also

Table 1.3 Percentage of Use of the TCFs of 'Debt' and 'Deficit' in the Conservative Finance Discourse across 1900–48, 1949–2000 and 2001–14

	TCFs	Period 1: 1900–48 6 occurrences							Period 2: 1949–2000 38 occurrences							Period 3: 2001–14 77 occurrences						
1	Naming and Describing	6 (100%)							26 (68.42%)							30 (38.96%)						
		Locus 3 (50%)	Scale 2 (33.33%)	Misc. 1 (16.66%)					Locus 5 (19.23%)	Scale 19 (73.07%)	Misc. 6 (15.78%)					Scale 27 (90%)	Misc. 3 (10%)					
2	Representing Actions and States	Material 3 (50%)	Relational 3 (50%)						Material 21 (55.26%)	Relational 15 (39.47%)						Material 55 (71.42%)	Relational 16 (20.77%)					
3	Prioritizing	Active 6 (100%)	Passive 0						Active 32 (84.21%)	Passive 6 (15.78%)						Active 73 (93.50%)	Passive 4 (6.49%)					
5	Representing Person/ Place/ Time	Person	Place 1 (16.66%)	Time Present 6 (100%)					Person	Place 3 (7.89%)	Time Present 23 (60.52%)					Person	Place 7 (9.09%)	Time Present 44 (57.14%)				
		More distal Agent 4 (66.66%)							More distal Agent 33 (91.66%)							More distal Agent 34 (56.57%)						
		Patient 5 (100%)							Patient 5 (96%)							Patient 61 (66%)						

Table 1.4 Percentage of Use of the TCFs of 'Debt', 'Deficit' and 'Low' in the Labour Finance Discourse across 1900–48, 1949–2000 and 2001–14

	TCFs	Period 1: 1900–48 20 occurrences				Period 2: 1949–2000 89 occurrences				Period 3: 2001–14 57 occurrences			
1	Naming and Describing	16 (80%)				67 (75.28%)				39 (68.42%)			
		Scale 7 (43.75%)	Source 6 (37.5%)	Misc. 3 (18.75%)		Scale 40 (59.70%)	Source 20 (29.85%)	Misc. 7 (10.44%)		Scale 30 (76.92%)		Misc. 9 (23.07%)	
2	Representing Actions and States	Material 12 (60%)	Relational 8 (40%)			Material 61 (68.53%)	Relational 28 (31.46%)			Material 45 (78.94%)	Relational 12 (21.05)		
3	Prioritizing	Active 18 (90%)	Passive 2 (10%)			Active 84 (94.38%)	Passive 5 (5.61%)			Active 54 (94.73%)	Passive 3 (5.26%)		
5	Representing Person/Place/Time	Person	Place 3 (15%)	Time Present 12 (60%)		Person	Place 25 (28.08%)	Time Present 43 (48.31%)		Person	Place 11 (19.29%)	Time Present 29 (50.87%)	
		More Distal				More Distal				More Distal			
		Agent 17 (89.47%)				Agent 58 (65.16%)				Agent 34 (60.71%)			
		Patient 18 (100%)				Patient 66 (98.50%)				Patient 51 (100%)			

Table 1.5 Percentage of Use of the TCFs of 'Need' and 'Poverty' in the Conservative Hardship Discourse across 1900–48, 1949–2000, 2001–14

	TCFs	Period 1: 1900–48 16 occurrences						Period 2: 1949–2000 57 occurrences						Period 3: 2001–14 37 occurrences					
1	Naming and Describing	8 (50%)						31 (54.38%)						16 (43.24%)					
		Scale 6 (75%)			Misc. 2 (25%)			Scale 31 (100%)						Scale 13 (81.25%)			Locus 2 (18.75%)		
2	Representing Actions and States	Material 8 (50%)		Relational 7 (43.75%)		Misc. 1 (6.25%)		Material 38 (66.66%)		Relational 16 (28.07%)		Misc. 3 (5.26%)		Material 25 (67.56%)		Relational 11 (29.72%)		Misc. 1 (2.70%)	
	Prioritizing	Active 13 (81.25)			Passive 3 (18.75%)			Active 52 (91.22%)			Passive 5 (8.77%)			Active 35 (94.59)			Passive 2 (5.40%)		
5	Representing Person/ Place/Time	Person		Place 2 (12.25%)	Time Present 12 (75%)			Person		Place 5 (8.77%)	Time Present 40 (70.17%)			Person		Place 4 (10.5%)	Time Present 30 (81.08%)		
		More distal						More Distal						More distal					
		Agent 15 (93.75)						Agent 32 (56.14%)						Agent 30 (81.08%)					
		Patient 11 (100%)						Patient 44 (100%)						Patient 31 (100%)					

Table 1.6 Percentage of Use of the TCFs of 'Poverty', '(the) Poor' and 'Need' in the Labour Hardship Discourse across 1900–48, 1949–2000, 2001–14

	TCFs	Period 1: 1900–48 71 occurrences								Period 2: 1949–14 198 occurrences								Period 3: 2001–14 81 occurrences							
1	Naming and Describing	29 (40.84%)								73 (36.86%)								36 (44.44%)							
		Scale 24 (82.75%)		Misc 9 (17.24%)						Scale 64 (87.67%)		Locus 9 (12.32%)						Scale 24 (66.66%)		Locus 8 (22.22%)		Misc. 4 (11.11%)			
5	Prioritizing	active 65 (91.54%)		passive 4 (6.34%)						active 169 (85.35%)		passive 29 (14.64%)						active 77 (95.06%)				passive 4 (4.93%)			
10	Representing person/time/place	Person		Place 9 (12.67%)		Time Present 46 (64.78%)				Person		Place 28 (14.14%)		Time Present 151 (76.26%)				Person		Place 16 (12.67%)		Time Present 59 (72.83%)			
		More distal								More distal								More distal							
		Agent 60 (93.75%)								Agent 138 (75.82%)								Agent 47 (59.49%)							
		Patient 50 (98.03%)								Patient 141 (97.24%)								Patient 50 (100%)							

qualitatively compared PSE with other social challenges (e.g. 'debt and *unemployment*', 'need and *hunger*' and 'poverty and *crime*'). Locus refers to the geographical location of PSE issues, usually by drawing a distinction between the UK (e.g. '*national* debt') and overseas (e.g. '*overseas* poverty' and '*international* poverty'). Source refers to the origin of the PSE (e.g. '*war* debt' and '*trade* deficit') and those affected by them, that is, those to whom the PSE is a source of suffering (e.g. '*child* poverty' and '*needs* of the poor').

As Tables 1.3–1.6 show, with the exception of the Conservative finance PSE discourse in Period 1 (where the overall numbers are very small), all the political leaders favoured scale-based descriptions of PSE keywords over those linked to their locus or source. Scale-based descriptions often consisted of superlative adjectives, primarily 'large' and 'high'. The locus of PSE was sporadically referenced by both parties, albeit in different periods and in relation to different discourses. The locus of hardship-related PSE was referenced in Period 2 (Labour Party) and Period 3 (Labour and Conservative Party). Only the Conservative leaders referred to the locus of PSE in Period 1, in relation to financial issues. As for source-based descriptions of PSE, Labour Party leaders used them in their finance discourse only in Period 1, whereas Conservative Party leaders did so throughout the three periods. In the case of the Labour Party, this corresponded to the use of the keyword 'low' (not present in the Conservative corpus as a keyword), which premodified different forms of income (e.g. 'low wages', 'low rate' and 'low earning').

Regardless of the broad property being selected to describe PSE, nominalizations containing packaged-up information were used by the leaders of both parties across the three periods and the two discourse types. Packaged-up information hides linguistic values necessary to process the given texts (Fowler 1991; Halliday 1985; Simpson 1993). Linguistically, entities (e.g. 'debt') cannot be directly examined for time, place and agent, in contrast to processes, which extend over time, involve change and require a subject and a verb (Goatly 2007; Halliday 1985; see also Edwards and Potter 1992 for the discursive psychology of entities and processes). Halliday and Martin (1993: 39) argue that what justifies the existence of entities is difficult to contest because 'you can argue with a clause but you can't argue with a nominal group'.

In our corpus, packaged-up structures used to describe PSE typically comprised nominal groups that made use of attribute adjectives, as example (1) illustrates.

(1) What is their defence for all these broken promises, for the blunders, for the incompetence and for the very high debts? (Edward Heath 1965). [Period 2, Conservative Party, finance discourse]

In (1) 'high debts' functions as a nominal complement of the final prepositional phrase 'for the very high debts'. The adjective 'high' attributively modifies 'debts', which is also intensified via the adverb 'very'. Heath's description of debt in 'high debts' in example (1) is syntactically a block in that it is presented as an indubitable entity. This is supported by Heath's use of the definite deictic ('the' in 'the very high debts'), which presupposes the existence of the nominal complement ('very high debts'). The utterance leaves the audience without the possibility to question whether or not debt is actually high, as opposed to stating for example:

- Debt must (not) be high (deontic modality);
- Debt will (not) be high (epistemic modality); or
- Debt was (not) high (categorical assertion).

1.5.2.2 *Representing states and actions linked to PSE*

Overall, PSE issues were represented via material action – rather than relational – verbs across parties, periods and discourse types. Relational processes describe a state or being, pointing out the relationship between participants, such as intensive (e.g. someone is), possessive (e.g. someone has) and circumstantial (e.g. something deals). Use of relational processes linked to PSE therefore merely signals that PSE issues exist, rather than indicate the need to take any actions to address them. Nor does the use of relational verbs specify whose responsibility these PSE issues are. Material action verbs, for their part, denote physical doings, such as 'hit', 'fell' and 'rode'. They have two 'inherent participants' associated with them, namely the actor/agent and the goal/patient of the action (Simpson 1993: 82).[6] In our study, PSE issues were primarily represented as the goal of material actions. Consider example (2):

(2) I believe strongly that we need to reduce the deficit. There will be cuts and there would have been if we had been in government (Ed Miliband 2010). [Period 3, Labour Party, finance discourse]

In this example, 'deficit' functions as a direct object of the material action verb 'reduce'. The actor is first-person plural pronoun 'we' – an animate being who is explicitly identified as the one to perform the action of reducing the deficit. Since engaging in material actions is a 'direct enactment of social or institutional power' (van Dijk 1995a: 21), party leaders' frequent use of material action verbs in which they – or their parties – appear as subjects/agents may contribute to assert their party's political hegemony.

It is worth noting that material actions were more frequently used than relational actions by the leaders of the two parties in Period 3 for both PSE discourse types. This may be related to the security crisis after the 9/11 attack, which resulted in tougher security policies, including around financial issues of 'debt' and 'deficit'. Within the hardship discourse, the Conservative and Labour Party leaders resorted to 'challenging' verbal actions, such as 'fighting' and 'combating', which entailed combat metaphorical constructions (see, for example Charteris-Black 2013). This contributed to representing PSE as threats that required immediate aggressive (combat) action, as they overwhelmingly penetrated many social areas. Consider example (3):

(3) Labour still have the arrogance to think that they are the ones who will fight poverty and deprivation. On Monday, when we announced our plan to Get Britain Working you know what Labour called it? 'Callous' (David Cameron 2009). [Period 3, Conservative Party, hardship discourse]

In the subordinate clause of the first sentence '... that they are the ones who will fight poverty', Cameron also describes Labour Party members as arrogant individuals, expressing his disbelief in their ability to fight poverty and referring to them via the substitute pronoun' 'the ones' (Quirk et al. 1985: 387), which marks interpersonal (or, here, inter-group) distance.

Our analysis of processes for representing states and actions linked to PSE also identified some cross-party differences. These concerned the type of material actions verbs most frequently used across the three periods. Simpson (1993) distinguishes between three types of material action verbs according to the animacy and intention of the participants, namely:

- a Material Action Intention, intentionally performed by a conscious being – for example, '*We have to cut* the deficit' (John Major 1993 Speech);
- a Material Action Supervention, unintentionally performed by a conscious being – for example, 'I am certain, unless we can hold our own with the other great nations [...] *we shall fall* behind in the industrial race' (Anthony Eden 1955 Speech);
- a Material Action Event, performed by an inanimate actor, for example, 'Cut taxes or increase spending – these things won't work because *they lead to* more debt' (David Cameron 2011 Speech).

In the Conservative Party corpus, the most frequent verbs for representing PSE issues were Material Action Intention verbs, followed by Material Action Event verbs. Material Action Supervention verbs were not used. The semantic categories of these material actions comprised activities linked to reducing PSE issues, the most frequent ones being 'repay', 'wipe', 'run up' and 'tackle'. In these cases, PSE issues functioned as patients of reduction-aimed actions performed by third-person participants. Consider the illustrative example in (4):

(4) It is necessary to make a beginning in the reduction of our national debt (Bonar Law 1920). [Period 1, Conservative Party, finance discourse]

In (4), 'debt' functions as a post modifying noun in an adverbial prepositional phrase of a to-infinitive clause 'to make a beginning in the reduction of our national debt'. The example contains a Material Action Intention verb ('make'); the implied subject of the to-infinitive clause can be expressed by 'us', as in 'it is necessary for us to make ...' or 'we' as in 'it is necessary that we make ...' (see Hampe and Grady 2005). In (4), Law suggests addressing the financial issue of debt by 'making a beginning in [its] reduction'. The suggested actions are nominalized, that is, '*beginning*' from begin and '*reduction*' from reduce. Nominalizing verbs is a 'process of syntactic reduction' (Fowler et al. 1979: 41) that offers opportunities for deleting information regarding subject, time and modality of the action. In this case, it is not obvious who is going 'to make the beginning in the reduction of debt', because of the absence of the subject of these nominalized verbs. Law thus distances himself and his party from performing the PSE reduction-aimed actions by nominalizing them. This was a recurrent feature of the Conservative Party corpus within the representing states and actions TCF across the three periods and discourse types.

In contrast to the Conservative Party, Material Action Events were the most frequent type of the material action verbs used by Labour Party leaders in Period 1 and 2, albeit that it changed to Material Action Intention in Period 3. Semantically, most of the material actions in Period 2 were expressed via verbs that denoted general actions (e.g. 'make' and 'use'), and those were performed by third-person actors. By contrast – but like in the Conservative Party corpus – in Periods 1 and 3 the material actions represented in the Labour Party corpus tended to highlight reduction activities (e.g. 'relieve', 'cut' and 'eradicate') whose goals were finance and hardship-related issues. Example (5) is typical of this:

(5) That power could be multiplied beyond measure if the structures of security which are now amongst the ambitions of world leaders were established to promote aid, to protect the environment, to relieve debt burdens, to establish fair trade, to spread education, health care and housing in place of ignorance, disease and squalor (Neil Kinnock 1988). [Period 2, Labour Party, finance discourse]

In (5), the conditional clause contains a number of embedded to-infinitive clauses, in which 'debt burden' functions as a direct object of the Material Action Event verb 'relieve' ('to relieve debt burdens'). The subject of those embedded to-infinitive clauses is the inanimate third-person actor 'structures of security', which is the same as that of the main clause. Neil Kinnock argues that that relieving debt burdens would be met by structures of security, were these to be established. However, he does not make it clear who will establish them. He relates the activity to an unknown actor. Thus, he distances himself, as well as his political party, from the responsibilities that would fall upon the 'structures of security'. This in turn serves to distance himself and his party also from the task of relieving the 'debt burden'.

It is worth noting that most of the activities in Period 1 and 2 were performed by this type of inanimate third-person actor. It is also worthy of note that the majority of the occurrences of 'debt' and 'deficit' (as well as 'low' in Labour corpus) across the three periods functioned as 'recipient' of the material actions being considered. Thus the PSE keywords were acted-upon entities that played a subordinate role in the texts. Additionally, 'need' and 'poverty' frequently functioned as goals of those material actions across the three periods.

1.5.2.3 Prioritizing

When speaking about PSE in finance and hardship terms and across the three periods, the Conservative and Labour Party leaders mostly placed PSE keywords in the final part of the active voice sentences in which they were used. In other words, PSE terms were the focus of the information structures or sentence 'rhemes'. Rheme is the likely place to introduce new information in human utterances (Halliday and Matthiessen 2014). According to Hart (2014: 128), the use of the active voice represents a discourse order in which the audience is 'ego-aligned [rather than] ego-opposed' with the agent's viewpoint. These active voice alternates affect the order of participants relative to the audience, redirecting the audience's orientation such that it may be aligned with the agent. The audience is, therefore, less likely to question whether or not the agent (here, the Conservative and Labour Party leaders) are responsible for the PSE issues being mentioned – their attention being focused instead on the issues themselves. This pattern of the use of the prioritizing TCF is illustrated in (6):

(6) It is us, the modern compassionate Conservative Party, who are the real champions of fighting poverty in Britain today (David Cameron 2012). [Period 3, Conservative Party, hardship discourse]

In this example, 'poverty' functions as an object of the material action 'fight' – another typical example of the use of combat metaphors in the corpus, especially in Period 3, post 9/11 attacks. The noun 'poverty' is presented in the final position of the relative clause. Placing 'poverty' at the bottom node of the information structure tree reconstructs the term as new information, which in this context answers the question of 'what issue do we face?', rather than for example answering the question of 'who is responsible for the issue?'.

1.5.2.4 *Representing person/place/time (deixis) in PSE*

Use of place deixis was comparatively infrequent across the three periods, parties and discourses of PSE in the BPPS corpus. As for time deixis, the present tense dominated representations of PSE by both parties and PSE discourses across the three periods. This may serve to emphasize the relevance of PSE to the here and now of the leaders' speeches – the annual party conferences – and, in turn, to the policies to be ultimately derived from these political events. Rhetorically, the use of the present tense may also serve to create a sense of urgency about one's message – here regarding a range of PSE issues. Although less frequently, present-tense deictic references were also linked in the corpus to both past events and future consequences, hence presenting PSE as an ever-present challenge to the UK.

Overall, person deixis was most frequently of the more distal third-person type across periods, parties and discourses. This type of person deixis creates a separation between writers/speakers and text/speeches (Jeffries 2010), hence distancing party leaders from their responsibility for the PSE issues being thus referenced. It is important to note, nevertheless, that the use of proximal (first-person) deictic references by Labour and Conservative Party leaders across both the finance and the hardship discourse increased across the three periods examined. This means that the leaders became more personally involved in their own discussion of PSE, as illustrated in example (7):

(7) There are some low-paid workers here paying the price of defeat. Not the rest of us. I am heartily sick of seeing the victims who pay the price of our defeat (Neil Kinnock 1988). [Period 2, Labour Party, finance discourse]

In this example, Kinnock highlights a current finance-related PSE issue (low wages), linking it to his Party's (election) defeat. In doing so, he uses present-tense narration, in which the actor is a proximal (first person) 'I' and the patient is third-person 'victims' (workers). Kinnock, as an agent, explicitly states his feelings ('I am heartily sick of seeing') and uses emotive language, including labelling low-paid workers as 'victims who pay the price'. Rather than necessarily a sign of genuine commitment to PSE as individuals, or even figure-heads of political parties, this finding may simply reflect a broader shift towards personalization in political discourse in the UK (Corner 2003; Langer 2007) and beyond.

1.6 Conclusion

In this chapter we have examined the discursive mechanisms for representing PSE across time (1900–2014), and the ideologies that underpin such representations, within the context of British political leaders' (Conservative and Labour) speeches at their annual party conferences. Our findings reveal two main PSE discourses: finance and hardship. Although both parties made frequent use of these discourses across time, the Conservative Party made more use of the finance than of the hardship discourse, whereas the opposite trend characterized the Labour Party.

In terms of the ideo-textual mechanisms via which these discourses were articulated, and focusing on the most frequent TCFs in our corpus, the analysis has identified more similarities than differences, both cross-party and cross-period. The analysis of the describing TCF shows that the Conservative and Labour Party leaders characterized PSE in ways that sought to raise their audience's awareness of the crippling effect these issues have on British society. Most frequently when doing so, leaders resorted to packaged-up information structures that enabled them to present their propositions as entities to be taken for granted. Party leaders' 'unquestionable' propositions regarding PSE were reinforced by their frequent qualification of the issues as 'huge', 'excessive' and other superlative adjectives. This may have sought to focus people's attention on the sheer size of PSE challenges encountered and, in turn, away from their cause.

Regarding the representing actions/states TCF, the analysis has revealed that the Conservative and Labour Party leaders primarily relied on material actions, which may have helped them to reinforce their Party's political hegemony. Party leaders are known to draw upon challenging and reducing actions as means to exercise social power and control (van Dijk 1995a). This is what both political parties in our corpus also did, with the effect of representing PSE as posing a series of threats to the country. Most material actions used by the Conservative and Labour Party leaders were Material Action Intentional, performed by animate beings who were mainly distal third-person participants. In other words, when authoring their speech, party leaders did not overall present themselves as prominent in dealing with PSE. Material Action Events were relatively frequent in the Labour corpus during Period 1. This impersonalization of the actions being represented in their discourse helped distance Labour leaders from their direct responsibility to deal with PSE issues in early twentieth century. Furthermore, and regarding the prioritizing TCF, PSE terms were frequently presented in active voice sentences and placed as sentential rhemes. Through this use of the prioritizing TCF, the Conservative and Labour Party leaders sought to focus the audience's attention on the issues being discussed, rather than on whose responsibility it was to resolve them.

Finally, and regarding the use of personal deixis, the Conservative and Labour Party leaders frequently used third-person agents and patients. The ideological effect was to distance themselves from the suggested actions when discussing PSE. In Period 3, Conservative Party leaders showed increased use of first-person proximal agents, as an indication of their active involvement in their PSE discourse. The Labour Party leaders, too, appeared as discursively concerned about the financial issues as individuals, via increase in the use of proximal first-person forms in about one-third of occurrences in Periods 2 and 3. Our study did not entail a comparative analysis regarding party leaders' use of person deixis when talking about other issues. However, given the attested personalization of political discourse from approximately the 1950s in the UK, we do not see this finding as indicative of a political leaders' personal commitment to PSE per se.

All in all, the Conservative and Labour Party leaders represented PSE as issues to be acted upon rather than as issues that those suffering from PSE could actively change. In doing this, the stereotype of 'the poor' as idle/passive was perpetuated across time. Political responsibility for combating PSE was often delegated to third parties, including unspecific ones (such as 'the structures of security', in example 5). In the third period (2001–14) in particular, party leaders moved towards a more aggressive stance towards PSE, increasing their use of combat metaphors. This lends support to the thesis that PSE has become securitized by political elites. We see in this finding a reason for concern, given that the targets of such combative discourse are the many individuals in PSE who are also passivized and, hence, unable to escape their condition.

Notes

1 Scholarship in Media Studies that, using content analysis and ethnographic methods, has also examined British media constructions of PSE is noteworthy, too. Pioneer and since then influential works therein are the two volumes by the Glasgow Media Group (Beharrell and Glasgow University Media Group 1976, 1980), which showed elitism in British television coverage at the time of economic problems including recession, unemployment and inflation.
2 For further details of the procedure, see Almaged (forthcoming).
3 BNC is a 100 million word corpus of general English language use, available online: http://www.natcorp.ox.ac.ukl
4 CORPS is a corpus of political speeches comprising more than 3,600 of UK and US presidential speeches (7.9 million words) (Guerini et al. 2013).
5 As 'naming' concerns the actual PSE keywords, the analysis offered here concerns the 'describing' part of this TCF.
6 For a detailed review of the main transitivity models see Bartley (2018).

2

Inequality and 'the language of leadership' in the Second World War

Joe Spencer-Bennett

2.1 Introduction

In stratified societies, language is often interpreted as what Foley (1997: 313) calls a 'social deictic' phenomenon; it indicates the 'high' or 'low' position of its users relative to others in social space (e.g. Bernstein 1971; Labov 1972; Bourdieu 1991; Rampton 2006). This chapter is about the social deictic concerns of a particular British political institution: the Ministry of Information during the Second World War (1939–45). The Ministry of Information was the main propaganda wing of the British government during the war, and its leaders – drawn largely from upper-class British society and tasked with maintaining the morale of the civilian population at large – felt themselves faced with a social deictic problem. They were worried about the morale of those who one Minister of Information, John Reith, called 'the less informed classes' (quoted in McLaine 1979: 35). It was the job of the Ministry to do something about this morale (Dibley and Kelly 2015). But many of the propagandists felt unsure of how to best talk to this socially distant audience.

One of the ways in which the Ministry dealt with this apparent problem was by employing social researchers, prominently Mass-Observation (M-O henceforth), to provide feedback and advice on their attempts at communication, and on the civilians with whom the Ministry was trying to communicate.[1] M-O, a quasi-anthropological research organization, proposed to solve the problem by encouraging the Ministry in more vernacular and personalized linguistic directions. They encouraged greater and more careful use of personal pronouns – a shift away from abstract, 'educated' vocabulary – and a general avoidance of the Ministry's 'upper-lipped' official English. M-O proposed a new 'language of leadership' which was, as they saw things, best suited to getting the masses on side.

In this chapter, I consider whether M-O's work – and the social deictic strategies it encouraged – can be understood as a moment of increased egalitarianism in twentieth-century British English. Many linguists have argued, using a range of related terms, that English became more informal, colloquial, conversational or egalitarian during the century, perhaps especially in political discourse (e.g. Pearce 2005; Mair

2006; Farrelly and Seoane 2012). I will suggest that, in some ways, M-O clearly did seek to be agents of a kind of linguistic egalitarianism. They encouraged the Ministry to aspire to what George Orwell would call a more 'demotic' linguistic style, and this was motivated by a sense that the views and behaviour of ordinary citizens mattered. However, there were also significant limits to their egalitarianism. M-O and the Ministry's interest in personalized and vernacular forms of English was an exercise in 'synthetic personalization' and perhaps 'synthetic vernacularization' to adapt a term used by Fairclough (2015). Further, though M-O did conduct some empirical research into the vernacular English of working-class British citizens, the vision of vernacular English that they presented to the Ministry was in significant part an imagined one, refracted by a stereotyped view of working-class language as simple, personal and concrete.

Before I discuss the details of the Ministry of Information, M-O, and their linguistic strategies, it may be worth making a methodological point about the study presented in this chapter. It is intended as a study in political discourse, indeed a *critical* study of the ways in which political discourse is implicated in the reproduction of social inequality (e.g. van Dijk 1993; Fairclough 2000, 2015). However, unlike most studies in this field, the properties of political texts themselves are not the central focus. Instead, I look at the metalinguistic practices that surround those texts, the ways in which language was conceived as a resource for managing the problems that the Ministry of Information saw in social inequality. Such metalanguage is revealing of aspects of political discourse that have been neglected in text-based discourse analysis: the significance accorded to that discourse by those who produce political discourse and, to a slightly lesser extent in this case, by those who receive it. In terms often used in linguistic anthropology, where 'folk' metalanguage is a prominent focus of study, they are revealing of the 'language ideologies' (Woolard and Schieffelin 1994; Keane 2003) that inform political communications, and which themselves have social and political content, making implicit claims about people and their relations with one another.[2]

2.2 The Ministry of Information and Mass-Observation

When Britain and France declared war on Germany on 3 September 1939, planning for a Ministry of Information had been underway for some time. On 4 September, the Ministry was established in Senate House, London, with Lord Macmillan, a Conservative Peer, in charge. The Ministry's key concerns, on the 'Home Front' at least, were with the monitoring of civilian morale and the production and distribution of propaganda.

The existence of the Ministry of Information was a consequence of the fact that the Second World War was the first (and only) 'total war' in British History. Because air power and radio transmissions could reach far into enemy territory and because the war required huge amounts of industrial production, it involved the entire civilian population, as contributors to the war effort and potentially as casualties too (Hobsbawm 1994; Gardiner 2004; Calder 1969). Communications between the government and civilians were therefore of utmost importance. The war was, among other things, 'a war of words' (Briggs and Burke 2009: 197), and the Ministry of Information was there to fight this verbal war, at home as well as abroad.

In the early years of the war, however, the Ministry was widely regarded as incompetent, often laughably so (McLaine 1979: 1). The BBC radio programme *It's That Man Again*, caricatured the organization as 'The Ministry of Aggravation and Mysteries' (Gardiner 2004: 135), and, to cite one Ministry mishap, in October 1939, with German bombing raids widely anticipated, the *Daily Express* reported that a postcard showing an aerial view of Senate House was on sale at the front desk (Harrisson 1939d). John Reith wrote that, when the prime minister asked him to take over as Minister of Information, things were 'most unsatisfactory. ... Not only was the ministry in thorough bad odour, it had no terms of reference and no authority' (Reith 1949: 353).

Social inequality was a particular concern in relation to the Ministry. For many within the organization, the concern was that working-class British people may not be on board with the war effort and that much work would be needed to bolster their morale. McLaine cites a pre-war planning meeting as indicative of the Ministry's propagandists' 'preoccupation with class', their 'assumption that the mass of their fellow citizens would need to be cajoled and wheedled into acceptance of their obligations' (1979: 21–2). The meeting centred on the idea of using an image of a bowman from the Hundred Years' War to stir patriotic feeling among the working class. 'The archers, who provided the mainstay of the English Army, were drawn from the lower classes,' the meeting's minutes state, 'The dress of the archer should make this point clear' (1979: 20).

For critics of the organization, the problem was with the class make-up of the Ministry itself (Calder 1969; McLaine 1979; Gardiner 2004). Richard Crossman, future Labour Member of Parliament and 'token' Labour representative in the Ministry (McLaine 1979: 6), took this line of criticism in conversations with his friend, and leader of the Mass-Observation project, Tom Harrisson. Crossman, according to Harrison's report, had been trying to encourage the Ministry's civil servants to 'make things popular'. But he had faced difficulties: 'a large number of Dons are getting into the ministry because they have taught the Civil Servants at the universities, and the civil servants do them a good turn in exchange in time of war.' The dons, Crossman thought, were 'the most unsuitable people for these jobs'. They 'lived retired from the world', they had 'the least popular contacts' and they treated their political communications like they treated their university lectures: 'So long as they have the exact facts ... the effect on those who attend the lecture is very subsidiary' (Harrisson 1939a).

Whether the problem was seen as being with the Ministry's 'privileged ignoramuses' (*New Statesman and Nation* 1940) or with the apathy of its audience, there was a sense of a gulf between the Ministry and many British people. This was clearly problematic for an institution which existed primarily to mediate between government and citizens. Therefore, a 'Home Intelligence' department was established in January 1940 in order to find out more about how ordinary people felt about the war and about the effects of the government's propaganda efforts. The Ministry's early attempts at collecting such intelligence, however, could be cited as further evidence of their distance from the majority of British people. In a September 1939 meeting, recorded by Harrisson, one of the civil servants reported that the Ministry was to use a group of '50 regional committees, of churchmen, aldermen, etc.' and that such a system 'represents every shade of opinion'. Harrisson took it upon himself to point out 'the utter diff[erence] between these leader types on such committees, and the led. That they do not at all tackle [the] problem of the DUMB masses at whom propaganda is really aimed' (Harrisson 1939b).

In April 1940, Harrison's Mass-Observation organization won a regular contract to help the Ministry in its attempts to gather home intelligence, having already submitted a number of ad hoc reports beginning in October 1939. M-O was itself established in early 1937 primarily by Tom Harrisson (an anthropologist and ornithologist, recently returned from Vanuatu) and Charles Madge (a poet). The project was based in a mixture of psychoanalysis, surrealism and anthropology (Highmore 2002). It had bases in London and in Bolton, a nationwide panel of observers, and was geared towards producing what Harrisson and Madge called an 'anthropology of ourselves' (1937: 10). Before the war, M-O had investigated such things as attitudes to the coronation of King George VI (1937), smoking habits and pub-going in Bolton (1938a), and, in unpublished work, the colour of men's ties at political meetings (1938b). The unorthodox methods of the project, and the non-academic background of its leaders (and most of the staff), meant that it received criticism from leading anthropologists such as Raymond Firth, though Bronislaw Malinowski was an early supporter (Malinowski 1938; Heimann 1998: 150–1). Within the Ministry of Information, there were also those who suspected M-O's methods, which, compared with those of Gallup pollsters and the British Institute of Public Opinion, were small scale and qualitative in orientation (McLaine 1979: 23). They were often, as M-O itself would put it, 'indirect', which is to say that observers made it a point of principle not to tell their subjects that they were being observed at all. This indirectness was a concern to some in the Ministry, and was controversial at various points during the war. In the summer of 1940, questions were asked in parliament about the Ministry's clandestine 'intelligence' gathering, and the Minister at the time, Duff Cooper, downplayed M-O's government role (Hansard 1940). However, this indirectness was also well-suited to providing the kind of information about 'the masses' that some in the Ministry felt they needed. Even if they had not seen this, Harrisson, a 'self-publicist of genius' (Calder 1985: 121), worked hard to demonstrate the utility of his project. In early 1940, M-O published what Hinton (2013) interprets as a direct pitch to the Ministry, the book *War Begins at Home*. 'We believe,' M-O write 'that one of the vital needs now in this war is that the government should be fully aware of all the trends in civilian morale. They need an accurate machine for measuring such trends; a war barometer' (1940, v). However, it is difficult for those in government to act as 'barometers' themselves: they 'are living at a different level of income and intelligence' than 'the mass of people who left school when they were fourteen' (1940: 7–8).

M-O provided the Ministry with regular reports on morale in various parts of the country, which the Home Intelligence department used to produce 'Home Intelligence Reports' (Addison and Crang 2011). M-O also produced a range of other documents, some of which were requested by the Ministry, others seemingly dependent on the whims of M-O. The reports that are most directly relevant to the concerns of this chapter have to do with propaganda. Some of these, such as *Government Posters in War-time* (1939, 2) and *Reaction to Eden's speech* (1940, 112), were reports on propaganda that had already been distributed (or broadcasted). In other cases, M-O were asked to 'pre-test' Ministry of Information ideas, often with a focus on particular words and phrases – *fifth column* (1940, 84) or *crusade* (1940, 363). M-O also produced a number of more general propaganda reports, such as *Propaganda Ideas* (1940, 197), *The Yardstick Memo* (1940, 250), *Unintelligible Words* (1940, 305) and *Personification Processes (YOU)* (1940, 448), and considerable attention was paid to propaganda in a number of their publications for wider audiences, such as *War Begins at Home* in 1940 and *Home Propaganda* in 1941.

Assessments of the *language* of propaganda certainly fell within the remit of M-O's work for the Ministry. In his earliest exchanges with the Ministry, Tom Harrisson seems to have been regarded as someone in a position to give linguistic advice. At the beginning of the September 1939 meeting, before all had arrived and before tea had been served, Harrisson notes that he was asked, 're BBC language—does grammar need simplifying?' (1939b). A month later, Harrisson describes a visit to see Crossman in Senate House. The two of them shared their dismay about a BBC broadcast which had 'an elaborate title including the words "attitude to"'. The broadcast was intended to get propaganda about Germany out in an accessible way, but 'had turned to the usual upper-class stuff' (Harrisson 1939c). In another case, in the first few months of the war, the Ministry wrote to M-O, requesting a list of 'unintelligible words' which some civil servants had heard as part of an M-O broadcast on the BBC (Charles 1939).

Part of the function of M-O, then, was to act as a source of what Cameron (1995) calls 'verbal hygiene', that is, evaluative commentary on language. Theirs was an interesting kind of verbal hygiene, since it was partly (but not entirely) based on empirical investigation of 'audience response'. Some of the methods used by M-O were:

1. 'Indirect interviewing without the person interviewed realising it'.
2. 'Direct interviewing'.
3. 'Direct interviewing facing the poster'.
4. 'Detailed documentation from the national panel of 2,000 part-time observers all over the country'.
5. 'Verbatim reportage of Overheard conversations'.
6. 'Objective studies of poster behaviour'.
7. 'Study of other posters, and examination of previous poster investigations, including previous investigation of our own'.

Mass-Observation 1939, 2

'Indirect interviewing' meant engaging shopkeepers or people on the street in conversation without letting them know that the conversation was an interview at all. 'Overheards' were, literally, snippets of conversation overheard while on a bus, in the pub or queuing at a shop till. 'Objective studies of poster behaviour' meant such things as standing next to posters and keeping a tally of how many passers-by had looked at the poster. The results of some of these investigations will be discussed below. They constituted the 'observation' that gave M-O its credentials as a social research unit, and allowed them to claim insight into the lives of the civilian population.

The relationship between M-O and the Ministry of Information hinged on questions of communication and often on very specific linguistic concerns. M-O was there to help an elite institution – a government Ministry – to communicate effectively with their mass audience. M-O's ideas about how this should be done seem to have been formed early in the war, and much of what they had to say to the Ministry consisted of variations on a basic theme. This theme placed great emphasis on (1) the use of personal pronouns to personalize communications (or 'personify' them, as M-O would sometimes write); (2) the avoidance of words and phrases that would be 'unintelligible' to a mass audience; and (3) the general importance of a 'language of leadership' which was in tune with the masses to which it was addressed. I now address each of these points in turn.

2.3 'An absolute battery of YOUs': Personal pronouns

At the very beginning of the war, in September 1939, the Ministry distributed posters which read, in white letters against a red background:

<u>Your</u> Courage
<u>Your</u> Cheerfulness
<u>Your</u> Resolution
WILL BRING US VICTORY

Hundreds of thousands of these posters were printed, some as large as 240 × 120 inches (roughly 6 × 3 metres). Their planning had been underway for some months, and they were up within weeks of the declaration of war (Lewis 2017: 47–49).

In the literature on British life during the Second World War, this poster is presented as a particularly *bad* piece of propaganda, which served only to draw attention to inequalities of power between 'you' – the citizen – and 'us' – the government (e.g. Calder 1969; Longmate 1973; Gardiner 2004; Welch 2016). Anthony Burgess saw the poster as 'ham-handed': 'You and us, you see. No wonder we all became bloody purple' (1980: 38, quoted in Hatherley 2016: 131). M-O's first job for the Ministry was to report on the effectiveness of the poster and of its less-widely distributed companion, 'Freedom is in peril – defend it with all your might'.[3] Their findings were very much in tune with the general feeling of Anthony Burgess above: 'On every possible criterion and by every possible research technique', they wrote, 'we got a large amount of unfavourable criticism' (1939, 2: 102). However, for M-O, the problem with the poster was not that *you* and *us* are inherently divisive. Presumably, the Ministry's intention was to be inclusive: *you* were intended to be one of *us*. But it was read as exclusive, M-O found, akin to a sign in a pub saying 'Your purchase of beer will bring us profits' (1939, 2: 98).

Why did this exclusive reading of *you* and *us* come about? M-O addressed this question in some detail in a twenty-five-page report on personal pronouns, written under pressure of 'a direct hit next door' (1940, 448). They claimed that the answer had to do with the ways in which ordinary British people had come to think, and to talk, about their relationship with government. M-O based their claims on evidence from the 'analysis of many thousands of comments on current affairs, etc'. In such comments, they found that citizens use *we* to refer to themselves and the government when the government is acting abroad, as in:

"We shall win."
"We're doing all right."
"We've got a long fight coming."

Mass-Observation 448: 14–15

However, the report goes on to say, 'comment about Home policy practically never refers to WE, but goes like this':

"They're going to ration soap."
"They haven't got anything else to tax."
"They've fired somebody for careless talk."
"They're enforcing the Factory regulations again."

Mass-Observation 448: 14–15

The suggestion is that, in ordinary talk about Home affairs, the government is never *we*. It is always *they*. It was therefore rather a lot for the Ministry to expect to be able to go against ordinary usage and use *us* in the inclusive way intended. They had what M-O called 'the THEY-gulf' (1940, 448: 15) to contend with, a linguistic reflex of 'a growing gulf between the leader and the led, between the high-ups and the lowdowns' (4). Use of *you* alone offers little hope of crossing that gulf. The second person is 'the sad cheer with which [the propagandist] decorates his upper class, upper understanding vocabulary' (4). Though the public may face 'an absolute battery of YOUs', they are unlikely to be moved (1939, 2: 91).

This was not to say that personal address was in itself a mistaken strategy, however. M-O argued that it was the right approach, if done properly, as evidenced by popular 1930 advertisements like 'Guinness is Good For You' (1940, 448: 12). In October 1939, M-O assessed the popularity of six posters produced to inform the public of sacrifices they would be forced to make when the railways prioritized troops and munitions (1939, 5). M-O found 'an almost perfect grading of popularity directly related to personal appeal' (35). The most popular poster read:

FOODS, SHELLS AND FUEL
MUST
HAVE PRIORITY

If your train is late or crowded –
DO YOU MIND?

Table 2.1 Personal Pronouns against Popularity for Six Railway Posters (Adapted)

Order of Popularity	Personal Pronoun
1	YOUR, YOU
2	YOUR safety
3	you (black type)
4	YOUR (prominently), you
5	OUR
6	(None)

Source: Mass-Observation (1939, 5: 35). Emphasis in original. It represents underlining and capitalization on the posters themselves.

The least popular poster did not use any form of second-person pronoun. Its main text read:

> GOODS TRAINS MUST STILL BE LOADED
> IN
> THE B L A C K - O U T

Other popular posters also used *you*, M-O found, while the unpopular ones did not (see Table 2.1).

M-O argued that the railway companies, like Guinness and other commercial organizations, were in a better position than the government to use direct address. They did not have such a significant 'THEY-gulf' to contend with; they were seen as less distant from ordinary citizens, and therefore as less hectoring in their direct address. The way forward for the Ministry of Information, M-O argued, was not to drop the personal address of the 'Your Courage' poster. It was to continue it, but to do so alongside other devices, linguistic and otherwise, which would help to demonstrate the government's affinity with the masses.

2.4 'Unsuitable for mass use': Unintelligible words and phrases

The failure of the 'Your Courage' poster was apparently exacerbated by two other features of its wording. First, *you*, M-O rather dubiously claim, is 'a word much less used by the working and artisan classes than by the upper and middle classes' (1939, 2: 92, cf. Bernstein 1971: 115–16). Second, it is used alongside abstract words that name 'hardly understood properties', *resolution*, in particular (1939, 2: 95–6).

These two points were important for M-O more generally. They placed a great deal of emphasis on what they saw as the classed distribution of particular words and phrases, and on the supposed unintelligibility of abstract vocabulary among the working class. In a number of reports, particular words and phrases were identified as being 'unsuitable for mass use', 'not a good mass phrase', 'out of line with mass grammar [and] understanding', 'obscure to the masses', a 'difficult mass-word', 'not operative on the masses' and similar. 'What I have called unintelligible words,' wrote Harrisson in a report of that name, 'are only unintelligible to that portion of the population which left school at 14'. They are 'Suitable, no doubt for Whitehall. Unsuitable, probably, for Whitechapel' (1940, 305: 2). M-O provided a list (alphabetized by first letter) of 161 words and phrases. To give an indication, below are those beginning with *i*:

> in default of present concrete satisfaction
> inherent
> integration
> in the aggregate
> integrity
> improvise
> Iron Guard
> imminent
> immobilise
> indiscriminate
> improvisation
> integral
> issued subject to revision
> involved in harship [*sic*]
> invoked
> indomitable resolution
> implement
> inculcate
> isolated land units
> inflicting
> intermittent
>
> Mass-Observation 1940, 305: 3

Unintelligible words and phrases were mentioned in many other M-O reports too, and occasionally those words were subject to tests of understanding. Of *resolution*, M-O reported that 'The commonest definition observers got when they asked what people thought [the word] meant was, from working class people, something you made at New Year' (1939, 2: 72). Comments from other reports include the following:

> in spite of words like debris and deteriorate, the style and language are an attempt to be popular.
>
> Mass-Observation 1939, 3: 24

> [The poster] contains certain difficulties for the mass of people ... such as the heavy emphasis on the difficult mass-word NEVERTHELESS.
>
> Mass-Observation 1939, 5: 55

> the plural of FOOD is never used in ordinary talk or writing, where it would be: FOOD, SHELLS, FUEL.
>
> Mass-Observation 1939, 5: 68

> avoid the words "economy", "sacrifice", and all that group ... that would pay you, and get you round a whole lot of confused class and stigma ideas and tentions [sic].
>
> Mass-Observation 1940, 197: 5

As these comments suggest, M-O's objection to particular words and phrases was based on a mixture of a sense that the forms in question were unnecessarily abstract, that they were infrequently used in working-class speech, and that they were not well understood by working-class people. These three, potentially very different things, were seldom teased apart, even when M-O did investigate words' understanding empirically. For instance, upon finding that 'upper-class' people were better at remembering the abstract words on the 'Your Courage' poster, M-O wrote, 'We have seen how the uncolloquial language of the posters, which is associated of course with their abstract phraseology, lends to the confusion and non-registering' among working-class poster readers. Upper-class people were more favourably disposed towards the posters 'largely because of greater ability to understand the language and abstractions' (1939, 2: 76–7).

2.5 'The language of leadership'

M-O's arguments about personal address and the importance of mass-appropriate words and phrases were put forward very early in the war; they can be found in relatively articulate form in M-O's first report for the Ministry (1939, 2). As the war went on, these arguments came to have the feel of general principles, presented in documents such as *A New Attitude to the Problems of Civilian Morale* (1940, 193) and, in 1947, in a pamphlet *The Language of Leadership*, in which M-O sought to recast their wartime propaganda advice for an audience of peacetime public relations professionals. Arguments established in reports on the early posters were repeated even in relation to later propaganda which M-O's research found to be highly effective. A May 1941 report about a new gas mask information leaflet, for instance, found that 'the leaflet is exceptionally successful and effective, unusually clear and to the point' (1941, 681: iii). Nonetheless, the report included three pages of line-by-line commentary on the leaflet's language, suggesting various improvements in wording where no misunderstanding was reported: '<u>Impeded</u> is unsuitable for mass use'; '<u>In case the day comes</u> is not a good mass phrase' and 'In four years fieldwork experience, we have never heard any inhabitant of the British Isles refer to any article of clothing as a <u>garment</u>' (1941, 681: i, iii, emphasis in original).

What M-O came to be presenting to the Ministry of Information, and to other later clients, was a general theory of propaganda language. Leaders must use 'a language which the people can understand and respond to'; they must 'work, sing, look, smell and speak a language of leadership which can either be understood or reacted to emotionally by the masses' (1940, 193: 9). As things stood:

> Statesmen making important speeches use words and phrases which their audiences cannot follow. They say "In jeopardy" and "capitulate" when they mean "in danger" and "surrender". Quotations from Meredith or Cromwell, obscure to the masses at any time, and with no immediate reference to the matter in hand, are used in place of clear simple instructions.
>
> Mass-Observation 1940, 193: 18–19

But, for M-O, this state of affairs was no good. Total war meant that 'everyone matters equally', that 'everyone is offering the same thing, their lives'. Therefore, 'the leaders and experts, the Ministry of Information, must ... be in sympathy with everyone' and their language must reflect this (1940, 19, emphasis in original).

M-O's *Yardstick Memo* provided a list of positive and negative 'technical elements' of propaganda. The first two positive elements are 'identification (sympathetic identification between leaders and led)' and 'personification'. These are contrasted with, respectively, 'Out of touch leadership. Upper class approach. Differential treatment' and 'Impersonality and removeness' (1940, 250: 13). A July 1940 report on a Ministry-orchestrated public rally begins as follows:

> The Rout-The-Rumour-Rally ... seems to have been a large-scale venture in the new propaganda technique that is being tried out on the British people; the technique of appealing to them in a friendly, man-to-man sort of spirit; a spirit in which authority lays aside its insignia and joins with the common man in his jokes, his interests, his slang.
>
> Mass-Observation 1940, 298

Similar comments were made about the appearance of a Ministry of Information speaker at Speakers' Corner in Hyde Park. Despite the perception that the speaker was 'too polite and slightly 'upper-lipped'' and that he 'suffered from the stigma of officialdom', the fact that he was speaking in a place of relatively informal, popular discourse and that he conspicuously gave over to the norms of this discourse apparently worked in the Ministry's favour (1940, 219: 2). A *Propaganda Ideas* memo for the Ministry of Food suggests that the Ministry should (1940, 197: 2–5):

1. emphasise the fact that the Minister of Food, Lord Woolton, had been involved in slum clearances, with Liverpool University Settlement. The words *university* and *settlement* should be avoided, of course, since they are 'not operative on the masses'. But 'the more [Woolton] can be made "one of us" the more we are likely to follow him'.
2. 'have gramophone records, e.g. of Gracie Fields singing about food'.
3. organise dances, comedy performances, music hall shows. Comedians, in particular, 'do continuous provincial tours which reach millions of people'.

4. make use of the Northern sea-side resort Blackpool in some way, since 'Somewhere near half the population of the North of England, and overwhelmingly the poorer half, pour through Blackpool during the summer'.

Finally, a 1941 report was dedicated to the role that songwriters might play in government propaganda. They could be employed 'to write quickly and well any ideas the government wish to put over ... using the emotional appeal at the moment needed, and disguised as entertainment' (1941, 795: 3–4). Songwriters were finding it hard to make a living, M-O claimed: they might be glad of the work.

2.6 Democratization, egalitarianism and vernacular English

As noted at the beginning of this chapter, the twentieth century has been seen as a time of linguistic democratization (Farrelly and Seoane 2012). Given the efforts made by M-O to shift the Ministry of Information's language towards that of their mass audience, perhaps the Second World War was a key moment in this democratization. M-O certainly worked to present their advice as fundamentally democratic; democracies and propaganda, they argued, went hand-in-hand (1940, 193). However, propaganda, as M-O well knew, was just as important for the non-democratic enemy, and, even in Britain, the Second World War was not really a time to speak of democratization in any political sense. No general election was held between 1935 and 1945, most by-elections were uncontested, and the very existence of the Ministry of Information marked a contrast with the previous system of party-based political communications (Calder 1969: 58; Welch 2016: 12). So, it may be better to think here in terms of 'egalitarianism' and to ask whether M-O's linguistic advice pointed in egalitarian directions or not.

The answer to this is mixed. On the one hand, M-O's attitude towards language clearly does not fall into the kind of snobbish prescriptivism so often identified in commentary on British English (e.g. Crowley 2003; Mugglestone 2003). M-O saw great value in how the masses spoke, arguing to those with RP accents and Oxbridge educations that they need to learn to use language *more* like their mass audience. There is a kind of egalitarianism in this, in accord with M-O's founding conviction that the ordinary, the everyday, the mass is important (Highmore 2002). The poet Kathleen Raine – very briefly a member of M-O before the war – writes that the project involved the 'search for the lost lineaments of the most high in the most low'. This was a search that she was not entirely on board with, however. While her then-husband Charles Madge 'saw the expression of the unconscious collective life of England ... literally in writings on the walls', she saw the crowd at a football match as 'scarcely human ... its only language a roar' (1991: 168, 173). Raine's attitude to 'the masses' speaks of the conservative ideologies that have been said to dominate English thought about working-class language. The M-O project more generally struck against such views.

M-O's linguistic ideas are akin to George Orwell's well-known arguments about the superiority of clear, vital working-class English to the stuffy, formulaic language of upper-class officialdom (Fowler 1995). It may even be that Orwell took some inspiration from M-O in developing his views. In a diary entry of 24 June 1940 –

the diary entry that Fowler (1995: 24) cites as Orwell's first use of the term 'demotic speech' – Orwell wrote that

> there is still nothing in really demotic speech, nothing that will move the poorer working class or even be quite certainly intelligible. Most educated people simply don't realise how little impression abstract words make on the average man.
>
> Orwell [1940] 1968: 355

He went on to mention M-O's work. The author of a war-time political pamphlet had 'had the first draft vetted by the Mass Observers, who tried it on working men, and found that the most fantastic misunderstandings arose' (1968: 355–6; see also Orwell [1944] 2010).

M-O shared Orwell's concern for the colloquial, the vernacular and the concrete, and his concern for the importance of 'demotic speech' in political communication. But there is none of Orwell's concern for the state of 'The Language' more broadly and none of his wider political ambition. In contrast to Orwell's section on 'The English Language' in his essay 'The English People' (2001, written towards the end of the war) or his 'Politics and the English Language' ([1946] 2004), M-O's writings on language have much narrower scope. They are about propaganda and how it can be done better. Orwell wrote that 'the first sign that things are really happening in England will be the disappearance of that horrible plummy voice from the radio' ([1940] 1968: 356), but M-O's writings on language show little concern with 'things happening' in any broader political sense. Indeed, Harrisson, who led M-O's work for most of the war, was not particularly radical in his politics. His biographer writes that 'he had no wish for an egalitarian society', that he 'liked hierarchy and was comfortable with inherited privilege'. His interest in mass life – and in mass language – arose from a sense that 'leaders needed to be in active dialogue with the common people' in order to lead them well (Heimann 1998: 125). Charles Madge, more radical than Harrisson, left M-O in 1940, citing the Ministry work as one of his reasons, and many of the more left-wing observers were uneasy about the government contract (Hinton 2013: 161–3).

It is probably useful to understand M-O's linguistic egalitarianism as 'synthetic', in Fairclough's terms (2015: 89). Fairclough's 'synthetic personalization' captures the ways in which large institutions use personalized language in order to compensate for the fact that they are communicating with thousands or even millions of people in fundamentally impersonal ways. This is part of what M-O encouraged. But they encouraged a 'synthetic vernacularization' too, foregrounding the classed nature of this mass communication. These people were not only a mass audience in the purely quantitative sense. They were also 'the masses' (Williams [1976] 1983: 192–7). For M-O, the language used to communicate with them must therefore be suitably simple and vernacular. Mass language was important, but as a technology of governance. Indeed, Calder (1969: 470–2) has argued that the Second World War was a point at which, through bodies like the Ministry of Information, the British government's use of social investigation as means of control was accelerated. M-O, for Moran (2008), was implicated in 'the birth of the focus group'. Here we see M-O's role in the development of a linguistic strategy that, though undoubtedly present before the war, would be a particularly salient aspect of post-war mass communications (Hoggart 1957; Williams [1969] 2005).

A further limit on the egalitarianism of M-O has to do with their somewhat stereotyped view of what actually constituted mass language. The project suffered from the obvious problems that attend any attempt to describe the linguistic competence of millions of people. It was selective, partial, and shaped by the perspectives of those doing the observing. As Crossman put it in his internal Ministry of Information memorandum on M-O's poster research, M-O's insights were, for better *and* for worse, 'partly the result of ... fertility of imagination', a 'subjectivity' which was 'the inevitable defect of Mass-Observation's virtue' (Crossman 1939). Some of the M-O work was, of course, based on close empirical investigation. But even that could only capture a very limited range of Britain's linguistic diversity, and much of what they had to say was only very loosely based on empirical observation in any case. For instance, their list of 'unintelligible words' is based on M-O's own impression of what *might* be unintelligible to others, and, as noted above, linguistic advice was offered to the Ministry even when M-O's research found propaganda to be effective.

Though M-O's view of mass language certainly did resist some traditional snobberies, it was nonetheless dependent on a familiar dichotomous picture of language, and of social life more generally, which, for Bourdieu, 'has its ultimate source in the opposition between the "élite" of the dominant and the "mass" of the dominated' (1984: 468). It is a view which sets up a series of oppositions, roughly as follows:

working-class	upper-class
masses	leaders
concrete	abstract
personal	impersonal

M-O's critical energies were ostensibly aimed at the 'upper-class' side of this dichotomy. But their critique seems to have come at the expense of a stereotyped view of the other side too. In this respect, M-O's linguistic advice might be seen as an emergent point in the development of the set of political ideas that Kennedy (2018) calls 'authentocracy'. Authentocracy, for Kennedy, involves a dual perspective on working-class life: on the one hand, positioning it as something to which elites should be especially sensitive and, on the other, characterizing that life in reified, stereotyped terms – as simple and concrete, lacking in creativity and often as politically regressive. Kennedy cites such examples as Enoch Powell's 1968 'Rivers of Blood' speech, in which Powell presented his racism as rooted in the talk of 'a decent, ordinary fellow Englishman' (Kennedy 2018: 33–4), and, more prosaically, Labour MP Owen Smith's 2016 claim that he would call a cappuccino a 'frothy coffee', and always drink it from a mug rather than 'a posh cup' (2018: 19–20). For Kennedy, M-O, in delving into the varied details of working-class life, was largely an exception to such authentocratic thought (80–108), and indeed a good deal of M-O's work can be considered much more radical than that discussed in this chapter (Jeffery 1978; Hinton 2013). However, when we see what they had to say to the Ministry of Information about the language of propaganda, Kennedy's 'authentocracy' seems to capture well the picture of mass life and language that they promoted.

2.7 Conclusion

It is difficult to tell how much influence M-O's linguistic advice had on the Ministry of Information's propaganda. Certainly, even before the start of the war, concerns to do with the masses and how they might best be talked to were present in the Ministry's discussions, as is clear from the case of the Longbowman poster. Beyond the first year of the war, criticisms of the 'upper-lipped' manner of the Ministry seem to be less prominent. This may, in part, be the result of M-O's work, but it may also be because changes in the Ministry's leadership and changes in the circumstances of the war meant that the Ministry felt it increasingly unnecessary to boost the morale of the masses (McLaine 1979; Gardiner 2004). Nonetheless, M-O's employment by the Ministry is indicative of the sense, during the Second World War, that inequality posed a problem for official discourse. This problem was not so much one of representation. That is, it was not about how the government talked or wrote *about* inequality, hierarchy or class. The problem had to do with how the social deixis of a class society was to be communicatively negotiated by those in power. M-O offered a particular solution to this problem. They encouraged the Ministry to shift towards a more personal, vernacular style of communication. In so doing, they stood in partial contrast to a tradition of linguistic elitism. But this was only partial contrast. The egalitarianism they offered was one which promoted a reductive view of mass language as a means by which those masses might be controlled.

Notes

1. Many of the references in this chapter refer to items which can be found in the Mass-Observation archives. Where this is the case, the number that follows the date refers to the item's unique report number in the M-O archives. Not all M-O items have report numbers. Some, such as *War Begins at Home* (1940), were published as books. Others, such as M-O's 1938 noted on a Labour Crusade Meeting, were not produced as formal reports. They exist as boxed notes in the M-O archives, and details of the box in which they can be found have been included in their reference here. In all cases, M-O materials can be accessed online by subscription through Adam Matthew Digital, or in hard copy at The Keep, University of Sussex. For more information, see the Mass-Observation website here: http://www.massobs.org.uk/.
2. A terminological note might also be useful: M-O and the Ministry of Information were concerned with communicating with a large group of British citizens who they variably conceived of as 'working class', 'mass', 'the less informed classes'. Because it is primarily this group as imagined by the Ministry and by M-O that is the subject of my discussion below, rather than with any more clearly defined sociological category, I will largely use terms borrowed from their discourse. This is, therefore, a 'folk' category, even if the 'folk' in question are those employed by a government ministry.
3. The third poster in this 'Red Poster' set was the 'Keep Calm and Carry On' poster. This now has gift-shop-ubiquity, but it was never officially displayed during the war, mostly because the bombing that the Ministry hoped civilians would keep calm about did not take place until nearly nine months after the posters were printed (Lewis 2017). By the time the bombing came, the Red Poster campaign was old news and the Keep Calm posters were not displayed.

3

Revisiting the welfare state through the decades

Investigating the discursive construction of the welfare state in the *Times* from 1940 to 2009

Isabelle van der Bom and Laura L. Paterson

3.1 Introduction

The concept of a 'welfare state' became established in the UK following the publication of the famous *Beveridge Report* in 1942. As a notion, the welfare state was established to tackle social inequality through a series of government policies that provided (among other things) a safety net for the unemployed, access to education and nationalized health care. Today, however, the term 'welfare state' is often discussed in terms of rising costs, austerity measures and a system under strain. This chapter traces whether and how policy and attitudinal changes to the welfare state are evident in newspaper discourse. To ascertain whether and when attitudes have fluctuated, we use seven-decade-long corpora of the *Times* held in CQPweb (Hardie 2012) to investigate how the newspaper reported on the welfare state from its initiation in the 1940s to the end of the 2000s. Acknowledging that we only have data from a single source which covers this seventy-year time span, we use the *Times* as a case study of how discourses surrounding the welfare state (as indexed through language) have developed over time. Our corpus-based discourse analysis of the *Times* begins with collocation analysis and expands to include an analysis of co-text and wider social contexts. We address the following:

1. (How) do reports about the welfare state change over time?
2. Is the welfare state associated with any core concepts which remain unchanged over time?
3. How does the language used to report on the welfare state index wider discourses about the UK welfare state from the 1940s to 2009?

3.2 The changing welfare state

Political arguments surrounding the unsustainability of the welfare state, the dismantling of welfare state policies and austerity have been ongoing in the UK for decades. Taylor and Powell (2017: 191) note that from the 1970s onwards, the modern British welfare state was called into question and subject to a number of invasive reforms that were very much led by a surge in neoliberalism (see also Toolan 2018). Since its formation, the British welfare state has undergone a number of changes, implemented by both Conservative and Labour Governments. In the 1960s and 1970s, reforms were made to allow the Treasury to plan and control public expenditure; in the 1980s and 1990s, the civil service and administration of welfare were restructured, which led to the creation of separate administrative agencies (e.g. NHS Trusts), the adoption of an economic market-like model and the introduction of a management layer in public service (Taylor and Powell 2017: 194). These reforms, meant to cut costs, maintain budget and planning control and improve administrative efficiency, have continued in this vein since the 1990s, with a perceived need for cost-cutting and marketization invigorated by the 2008 financial crash (Winckler 2012: 213, 218). The most recent, large-scale change is the Welfare Reform Act (2012). Our data, which runs to 2009, does not extend far enough past the financial crash to facilitate the analysis of newspaper reports on the impacts of 2008 or the implementation of Welfare Reform. However, the analysis we present stands as a foundation for future work comparing newspaper discourses before and after the financial crash.

To analyse attitudes towards the welfare state throughout its history, we take the stance that newspaper discourse, as a constituent of public mass media discourse, both reflects ongoing sociopolitical issues in society and has the capacity to shape and construct these issues and attitudes towards them (Fairclough and Wodak 1997; Fowler 1991; van Dijk 1988, 1998). Discourses represent ideologies, and the 'naturalizing tendencies' of newspapers (Gómez-Jiménez 2018: 101), where certain attitudes are represented as common sense and particular policy changes as inevitable, may lead readers to be more accepting of such changes (c.f. Toolan 2018). Our hypothesis is that a right-of-centre newspaper such as the *Times* will display a somewhat critical attitude to the welfare state. However, we do not expect the newspaper's position to hold constant. At the inception of the modern welfare state in the 1940s we expect more positive evaluation, given that it was initiated relatively soon after the economic hardship and rationing associated with the world wars. Following the structural changes to the welfare state starting in the 1970s (and the surge of neoliberalism in the 1980s) we expect more negative evaluation as significant welfare reforms were introduced (mainly by the *Times*-backed Conservatives).

3.3 Data and methodology

Our primary data consist of seven-decade-long corpora of the *Times* newspaper articles held in CQPweb (Hardie 2012). Each corpus contains a decade's worth of material from the *Times Digital Archive*, which runs from 1785 to 2013 (Gale n.d.). For this paper we focus on the seven corpora which include data from the 1940s through to the 2000s (1940–2009). While the later corpora can be interrogated rather unproblematically, given that they comprise texts which were 'born digital', the earlier corpora need to be treated with more caution as they contain texts which were originally printed and have been digitized using optical character recognition (OCR). Common errors in OCR are well documented, and the accuracy of OCR when scanning old newspaper texts has been questioned (see Gregory et al. 2016 on nineteenth-century newspapers). As such, it is possible that OCR errors meant our corpus query did not return all relevant hits.[1]

We adopt an integrated corpus linguistics and discourse analysis approach to our data. The combination of these two methodologies is now well established and has been used successfully to interrogate the discursive construction of issues closely related to the (modern) UK welfare state, such as poverty (Paterson and Gregory 2019, Gregory and Paterson 2020), welfare receipt (Baker and McEnery 2015a; van der Bom et al. 2018), housing (Toolan 2018) and state-backed maternity leave policies (Gómez-Jiménez 2018). For example, Gregory and Paterson (2020) investigated how the term 'poverty' is located in geographical space by the *Times* between the 1940s and 2000s (drawing on the same corpora we use here). Baker and McEnery, on the other hand, used a corpus of tweets about UK benefits debates to identify several overarching discourses about benefits recipients used repeatedly by members of the public. They found 'scrounger' and 'idle poor' discourses (with van der Bom et al. 2018 finding similar discourses expressed in their own Twitter corpus). This paper builds on these studies, and similar works, to take a historical slant on the discursive construction of the welfare state. As such, it has the potential to shine a light on how the discourses identified in contemporary work developed into their modern realizations. Corpus-based discourse analysis helped us to establish key themes in our corpus and contextualize our qualitative findings on the use of the *welfare state* over time.

We searched each of the seven corpora using the query <*welfare* state> and downloaded all the concordance lines within a span of +/− 50 words to facilitate close analysis. The corpus wildcard (*) was used to ensure we included any alternative forms of *welfare state* that occurred in the corpora. For example, there are occasions where *welfare* is encased in quotation marks, as in 'the so-called "welfare" state'. The queries returned a total of 7,553 hits (see Table 3.1).

Table 3.1 Hits of <*Welfare* State> in the *Times* 1940s–2000s

	Hits	Texts	Normalized frequency (pmw)	No. of collocates
1940s	114	64	0.39	5
1950s	1350	858	3.21	41
1960s	978	725	1.88	28
1970s	685	482	1.43	19
1980s	1,402	797	2.61	58
1990s	2,034	1,020	2.65	109
2000s	991	675	1.2	38
Total	7,554	4,621		298

Our analysis took two forms: (i) the computationally aided analysis of the collocational patterns of *welfare state* in each decade and (ii) the close reading and manual coding of 10 per cent samples of all concordance lines returned by the query (we took four 10 per cent samples in all, meaning that we manually analysed 40 per cent of the hits returned by the query). The analysis of collocates is useful for discourse analysis as collocates can shine a light on wider trends in a dataset. Furthermore, semantic groupings of collocates can suggest that particular topics/semantic fields are particularly relevant to the query node. In the present case, the semantic groupings were determined on an ad hoc basis rather than relying on semantic tagging software, which was due largely to the format of our data. To expand upon the collocate analysis, we took four 10 per cent samples of all 7,553 hits across our corpora. Each author was given a different 10 per cent sample (755 concordance lines each) for initial analysis. Concordance lines present all occurrences of the query node within their wider co-text left and right (see Figure 3.1). They allow for the systematic interrogation of all the hits of a given search term and facilitate the identification of language patterns (these can be grammatical, lexical, semantic and/or discoursal).

To analyse the concordances, the authors worked independently before reconvening to discuss their findings. There was considerable overlap and, as a result, the following analysis highlights the key macropropositions (see below) repeated in the concordance lines. To ensure that the conclusions made here are robust, each author took a second 10 per cent sample of concordance lines to ensure that no major patterns in the data had been missed. This method is similar to that used by Baker (2006) who suggests taking samples of fifty concordance lines for close analysis, identifying any patterns, repeating the analysis with an additional fifty concordance lines, testing the patterns and finding new ones, repeating this process until no further patterns can be found. As we are working across a relatively large time scale, it was important that we did not restrict our analysis to small numbers of concordance lines, as such, due to our use of 10 per cent samples, we closely analysed a total of 3,020 concordance lines (40 per cent of the hits across all corpora). This is a larger proportion than would be expected in most corpus-based discourse analyses, but gave us the advantage of being familiar with a large proportion of our data.

Our data was categorized using van Dijk's (1988, 1995b) discourse approach to media analysis. Van Dijk's approach is particularly suitable for our data because, together with our quantitative analysis, it allowed us to capture relevant themes within the data and examine the ideology/ies which underpin them. In his 1988 work, van Dijk proposed a way of analysing the thematic structure of the organization of news discourse. He suggests that a text can be analysed in terms of a hierarchy of propositions which represent linguistic meaning. Propositions capture, in other words, what utterances,

reality greater than myself) . And I have never regarded the **welfare state** as anything but a threat to this . Not only is Gray
of the " Virginia school " , which tell us that the **welfare state** will in time become a colony of " rent seeking " bureaucrats
den has , of course , risen since 1979 ; the **welfare state** has to be financed . The main difference is over the balance
affluent to make their traditional fair contribution to the costs of a **welfare state** . Until Nigel Lawson 's tax giveaway in 1988 , the top
Health Service was set out in three paragraphs , as was the **welfare state** . Churchill forbore to mention apple pie , but was unabashed in
Iron Curtain and the end of the Nordic model of the socialist **welfare state** has overtaken M Delors 's game plan ; however , and the

Figure 3.1 Sample of concordance lines for *welfare state* in the *Times* 1990s.

sentences or discourses 'are about'. A text is made up of individual propositions, which form the lowest hierarchical level of van Dijk's thematic analysis. Through the use of, for example, modality and the description of social actors, the linguistic structure of propositions may reveal underlying ideologies (van Dijk 1995b: 258). These individual propositions may then be grouped under several distinct macropropositions. Van Dijk typifies macropropositions as 'organized sets of propositions', which 'unlike the propositions expressed by clauses or sentences, ... are only expressed, indirectly, by larger stretches of talk or text' (1988: 32). Macropropositions capture the 'theme' or 'topic' of a text, and may also be hierarchically structured, with one macroproposition on top of the entire hierarchical structure, summarizing the whole text.

In our use of van Dijk's methodology, we approach our entire dataset as the 'text', rather than, for example, treating each query hit as a separate text. We thus grouped out concordance lines into macropropositions following van Dijk's (1988: 32) three steps: (i) delete irrelevant information, (ii) generalize a group of propositions into one macroproposition and (iii) replace sequences of propositions that denote part of an act or an event by a macroproposition that represents the act or event as a whole. While these steps area somewhat subjective (i.e. deciding what information is 'irrelevant') our decision to independently analyse samples of concordance lines before sharing our findings with each other minimized individual researcher bias, as we only include here the clear trends identified by both authors. Our analysis led us to identify three macropropositions: the welfare state is ripe for reconfiguration, the welfare state breeds immorality and the welfare state facilitates the creation of a social underclass. Each macroproposition is discussed in detail below, but first we present an overview of the collocate analysis.

3.4 Trends in the data

Table 3.1 shows the number of hits for the query in each corpus, as well as the number of texts which included the search term. As each corpus was of a different size, the penultimate column in the table shows the normalized frequencies for each corpus (the number of query hits per million words (pmw)). The normalized frequencies indicate that, overall, references to the welfare state increase throughout the decades from 0.39 hits per million words in the 1940s to 2.65 hits per million words in the 1990s.

The lower number of hits in the 1940s is somewhat expected given that the major policies which led to the welfare state – particularly the National Health Service Act (1946) and the National Assistance Act (1948) – were not made law until late in the decade. These Acts could potentially account for the fact that the 1950s corpus bucks the general trend, as it has the highest normalized frequency at 3.17 hits per million words. This decade is thus a potential case study for extensive discourse analysis. In a similar vein, in the 2000s references to the welfare state decrease to 1.2 occurrences per million words. By considering the co-text and the social context of the texts produced in the 2000s, it may be possible to determine why this decrease occurred. For example, it could be that another term has arisen to take the place of *welfare state*, discourse has shifted away from conceptualizing particular issues (education, benefits receipt, health care, etc.) as part of the welfare state or (in a somewhat unlikely scenario given the global financial crash in 2008) the newsworthiness of the welfare state has decreased.[2]

3.4.1 Thematic collocate analysis

To move beyond raw numbers and start to identify trends in the co-text surrounding the welfare state, we generated collocates of <*welfare* state> for each corpus. There are a total of 298 collocates (see Table 3.1) calculated using log ratio, 'a collocation measure very similar to Mutual Information', but results are filtered through log likelihood to measure statistical significance (Hardie 2014). We chose log ratio because it avoids the potential for overemphasis on high-frequency words (as with the cubed version of the MI statistic (MI3) or log likelihood) or low-frequency words (as with mutual information (MI)). Our calculations returned markedly frequent lexical collocates, facilitating our analysis of the discourses associated with the welfare state. (We were not, for example, interested in the function words which collocated with *welfare state*.) Collocates were calculated using a span of +/−5, minimum frequency = 5, minimum collocation = 5. All collocates in the analysis have log-likelihood values above 16.04 ($p<0.0001$) – we chose a high level of statistical significance to make the number of collocates manageable – and we used a threshold value of 3.0 (c.f. Baker 2006: 101 for a discussion of cut-off points). Thus, while our scope for collocates, in a statistical sense, is quite narrow, these parameters ensure that our analysis focuses on those words most strongly associated with the welfare state in each decade.

Using the established cut-off points, in the 1940s, there are only five collocates of *welfare state* (*employment, social, full, could* and *what*). However, despite being so few in number, the collocates can still tell us something about the discourse surrounding the welfare state; there is clearly a relationship between the welfare state and employment, and the occurrence of *could* supports the idea that, as the 1940s was the decade where the welfare state was initiated. The co-text for the search term relates to how the concept of a welfare state *could* or *could not* be realized in the future, as shown in example (1).

> (1) All these extravagances and follies were coming home to roost and at the end of the argument when the taly [sic] was struck the welfare state could guarantee its citizens everything except the two things that really mattered. The only things with which they could not provide them were food or work. (1949)

There are forty-one collocates meeting the thresholds set out above for the 1950s. To identify patterns in the collocates they have been grouped semantically as shown in Table 3.2. The collocates were grouped on an ad hoc basis, with semantic categories being data driven. As such, some semantic categories differ between decades while others are relatively stable (see Table 3.2).

To determine the appropriate categorizations for each collocate, concordance lines were manually analysed. The grouped collocates suggest some initial trends in how the *Times* characterizes the welfare state. There is conflict between the welfare state's potential social good – providing security and benefits to all – and its perceived social ills. For example, the collocation of *welfare state* and *dangers* clusters in one text in particular (2), where Conservative MP David Gammans claimed there would be negative moral/spiritual ramifications of the welfare state.

Table 3.2 Collocates of <*Welfare* State> in the *Times* 1950s

Benefits: welfare state	benefits, welfare, provisions, pensions, employment	5
Destruction/Opposition	attack	1
Economic	economy, economic, maintain	3
Idea/notion/concept	concept, so-called, idea, principles, true, whole	6
Initialization/building	advent, foundations, fabric, creating, structure, depends, existence, become	8
Letter sign off	faithfully, yours	2
People	citizen, nation	2
Politics	Socialism, democratic, Socialist	3
Social good	survival, social, voluntary, luxury, security	5
Social ill	dangers, demands, needs, danger	4
Other	Sweden, itself	—

(2) Possible dangers in the welfare state were suggested by Mr. L. D. Gammans, M.P., when he spoke in London yesterday at the founder's day meeting of the Church Army [...] not merely the danger of malingering or abuse of the national health service, but the danger of attending to people's physical wants and forgetting they had souls. (1950)

Given the proximity of the 1950s to the creation of the welfare state, there is debate about its intentions at its origin, as well as references to the ideas that underpin it (3). These ideas are also associated with building metaphors, linking the *foundations* of the welfare state to the *structure* of society.

(3) The fact that the whole economic programme of the Labour Party is pivoted upon Keynesian economics is not, perhaps, generally appreciated. It is, however, the foundation of the whole Socialist concept of the welfare State. (1952)

Moving into the 1960s, there are twenty-eight collocates, many of which are shared with the 1950s (*benefits, depends, welfare, voluntary, social, structure, employment, needs*). Of those collocates that are different, many relate to the same semantic groups used in Table 3.1: *creation, create* and *developed* fit into the initialization/building category, and *Conservatives* and *unions* fit in the political category. However, it is interesting that the Conservative Party is not strongly associated with (opposition to) the welfare state in the late 1960s, given that they lost power to a Labour Government in 1964. One additional semantic group which occurs in the 1960s collocates includes references to *casualties* and *health*, which initially may appear to suggest links between the welfare state and the NHS. While in the latter case this is a fair representation, *casualties* is used in a more metaphorical sense, as shown in the headline in (4).

(4) CASUALTIES OF THE WELFARE STATE 'WHERE POVERTY STILL PINCHES' (1960)

In (4) reference is also made to *poverty* (another collocate) and this is one of the earlier indications of claims that the welfare state does not work for all, but rather it is *overworked* and *cannot keep pace with the growing need* (a phrase which is associated with the welfare state eight times in the 1960s corpus).

The 1970s only have nineteen collocates meeting our criteria and, again, many are shared with previous decades: *fabric, poverty, welfare, burden, benefits, created, social, employment, economy, health, towards*. This repetition of collocates across decades suggests that by the 1970s the core components of and issues associated with the welfare state (as presented in the *Times*) have become established. Indeed *benefits* is a collocate for every decade bar the 1940s, although the meaning of this collocate shifts between *benefits* in its generic sense and the use of the term more specifically to refer to welfare payments given to benefits recipients (5):

(5) Jack Cooper, the Chesterfield man who discovered that he could draw more money in welfare state benefits than he could by working, was sentenced to seven months' imprisonment by Chesterfield county magistrates on Saturday. (1960)

Although there is no indication that Jack Cooper committed benefits fraud – a topic which is prominent in twenty-first-century press coverage of welfare receipt (see Lundström 2013) – an implicit association is made between claiming benefits and the deviant criminal behaviour for which Cooper was sentenced (stealing copper and non-payment of fines).

Moving on to the 1980s, there were fifty-eight collocates, which may suggest that the welfare state had come to be associated with multiple different issues. However, when grouping the collocates semantically, it became clear that most collocates fit neatly into a smaller number of semantic fields (Table 3.3).

Table 3.3 shows how, in comparison to Table 3.2, there are some semantic fields which now seem relatively stable in terms of their association with the welfare state, particularly the use of a building metaphor. The most salient change between the 1950s and the 1980s collocates, however, is the marked increase in collocates relating to the destruction and/or opposition to the welfare state. Changes are framed using

Table 3.3 Collocates of <*Welfare* State> in the *Times* 1980s

Benefits: welfare state	*beneficiaries, welfare, benefits*	3
Destruction/opposition	*dismantle, dismantling, overhaul, destroy, reform, attack*	6
Economic	*financing, funding, privatization, economy, socialist, Conservatives, spending, expenditure, employment*	9
Idea/notion/concept	*mentality, consensus, attitudes, radical, concept, principles, thinking, principle*	8
Initialization/building	*rebuild, founding, foundations, creation, created, existence, shape, structure, basis*	9
People	*Beveridge, Fowler*	2
Politics	*Tories*	1
Social good	*compassion, social, provision*	3
Social ill	*undermining, burden, crisis*	3
Temporal	*post-war, future, modern, towards*	4
Other	*hidden, mixed, NHS, scope, debate, review, aspects, effects, health*	—

negatively loaded terms such as *dismantle, attack* and *destroy* (6), which are associated with government policies:

(6) Mr Leon Brittan's audacious admission that the Cabinet is indeed contemplating a wholesale dismantling of the welfare state. (1982)

The 1990s has the highest number of collocates (109) but they are mostly all associated with the same semantic fields as were found in the 1980s (compare Table 3.4 and Table 3.3). The number of collocates shows an increase in the semantic field of destruction/opposition and the role of economics in debates about the welfare state, but still the building metaphor remains. Only one additional semantic field was needed to categorize all the collocates – that of scope – and, thus, it seems that there was a trend in the 1990s data to refer to the welfare state in terms of its size (7):

(7) The British tax burden is greater than in America and Japan, but less than the European average because of variations in the scope of the welfare state. (1992)

Overall, however, it seems that by the 1990s the language the *Times* uses to talk about the welfare state has become relatively fixed in terms of the semantic fields drawn upon. The destruction/opposition category is more heterogeneous than in other decades and not all words in this category carry the negative semantic prosody associated with 'destruction' – *reform*, for example could be interpreted positively – but nevertheless, the notion of reconfiguration holds constant for many of these collocates.

Table 3.4 Collocates of <*Welfare* State> in the *Times* 1990s

Benefits: welfare state	*welfare, benefits*	2
Destruction/opposition	*dismantling, reforming, dismantle, redesign, overhaul, reform, shake-up, reforms, axe, reformed, transform, shake, restructuring, assault, replace, review, changes*	17
Economic	*privatizing, nationalization, privatize, affordable, financing, poverty, taxes, privatization, reducing, taxation, pensions, spending, cuts, afford, economy, budget, costs*	17
Idea/notion/concept	*rethinking, mentality, radical, consensus, fundamental, principles, argues, principle, proposals, existence, commitment, promised, culture*	13
Initialization/building	*foundations, blueprint, creation, preserve, establishing, architects, founded, creating, created, structure, foundation, parts, built, create, basis*	15
People	*Beveridge, Lilley, Portillo, Blair*	4
Politics	*right-wing, Tories, voters, Labour, Tory, government*	6
Scope	*far-reaching, wide-ranging, broadly, sweeping, universal, wholesale, scope, comprehensive*	8
Social good	*generous, social, encourage, safety, security*	5
Social ill	*dependency, burden, crisis*	3
Temporal	*cradle-to-grave,[3] modernize, modernization, cradle, post-war, post-war, modern, 1945, 21st, future*	10
Other	*Swedes, middle-class, unemployment, defend, functions, NHS, Sweden, speech*	–

The number of collocates for the 2000s drops to just thirty-eight, and the same semantic fields can account for most collocates. As a final point, the collocates and indeed the close analysis of the concordance lines (discussed in section 3.4.2) also included numerous references to welfare states in other countries, such as Sweden. We have not examined these references in any detail; although it would be interesting to examine the depiction of the welfare states of other countries in the *Times* and compare these to representations of the British welfare state, this goes beyond the scope of this paper. What the collocate analysis has shown is that, while individual collocates vary across decades, the semantic fields these collocates are drawn from begin to stabilize in the 1970s and are continued in differing proportions into the 2000s. This warrants further qualitative analysis, but suggests that the core elements of the *Times*' reporting of the welfare state are relatively static. We thus interrogated our data further to determine how these core components were realized as macropropositions.

3.4.2 Macropropositions

3.4.2.1 Macroproposition I: The welfare state is ripe for reconfiguration

Despite the relatively small number of hits in the 1940s corpus, there are some minor trends evident in this decade that continue throughout the data. First, the welfare state is used to advance political arguments in the run up to the 1951 UK general election (a trend which continues for subsequent elections). Secondly, even at its beginnings, the welfare state is categorized as underfunded and ripe for reconfiguration:

(8) It is not a question of dismantling the welfare state but of building it upon rock instead of sand. (1949)

The examples clearly depict the welfare state metaphorically, with (8) drawing upon the building metaphor found in the collocate analysis. It is useful to examine these with the help of conceptual metaphor theory (Lakoff and Johnson 1980), which is based on the premise that metaphor is not just a feature of language, but that thought itself is inherently metaphorical. Unpicking the metaphors in our dataset allows us to examine how one thing (X) is conceptualized in terms of another (Y). In (8) the welfare state is conceptualized as a structure that has been built on unsteady ground, revealing the underlying conceptual metaphor COMPLEX SYSTEMS ARE BUILDINGS (Gibbs 2017: 26). Example (8) suggests the welfare state should not be taken apart, but rather built on different grounds. However, it is very difficult to move a building onto different foundations without dismantling it, despite the author's claim that 'it is not a question of dismantling the welfare state'.

In addition to the use of metaphor, examples (9–10) show how policies of different political parties are either made explicit (10) or are criticized (9). Perhaps unsurprisingly, the welfare state continues to be at the centre of political argument and policy debate throughout the decades (11–14):

(9) Continuance of the present course can only mean that the Labour Government's experiment in the welfare state will come down with a crash. (1949)

(10) The Conservative Party accepts the welfare State with all its implications. It will try to keep wages at their present level and to maintain – or even to increase – the social services. (1949)

(11) Conservatives believe the time has come to make the individual worker see the truth that [t]his welfare state cannot be maintained merely by Acts of Parliament. (1950)

(12) We make jokes about Government guidance from womb-to-tomb, but nobody sane would dismantle the Welfare State. (1967)

(13) The party conferences have drawn the battle lines for the coming general election. The future of the welfare state will be at the centre of the argument. (1977)

(14) Blair, who has been almost silent since last weekend, will argue the need to reshape the welfare state. (1994)

In the 1950s, the Conservatives and Labour favoured different models of the welfare state, with different conceptions of the extent and purpose of government welfare expenses. Example (11) provides one example of how political parties – in this case the Conservatives – used the welfare state in their political messages. Here, the 'individual worker' is addressed to see the 'truth' that the welfare state 'cannot be maintained merely by Acts of Parliament'. The emphasis on the 'individual' worker can be seen as the Conservative's attempt to emphasize individual liberty (as opposed to state responsibility) or address the non-unionized worker.[4] The negation 'cannot be maintained merely by Acts of Parliament' further suggests that the welfare state *is* currently solely maintained by Acts of Parliament and that this is unsustainable (cf. Gómez-Jiménez 2018: 105).

The discussion about restructuring the welfare state seems to be less active in the 1960s and 1970s. This could suggest that in (relatively) more prosperous times, there was greater acceptance of the welfare state, although there are examples from each decade which mention the need for reform (see 13). In the 1980s however, the debate around reforms seems to pick up again, with more concordance lines referring to change. This is not surprising given the 1980s was associated with Conservative prime minister Margaret Thatcher and the rise of neoliberalism (Thatcher favoured reduced state intervention, free markets and entrepreneurship (Apple 1983)). It is also clear, however, that the welfare state was established enough by the 1980s that people did not want to get rid of it. This is evident in the increased reporting of opposition to government plans (15), despite the Conservative Government positioning itself as 'not intending' to 'dismantle the welfare state' (16). Yet, the welfare state is deemed 'incompatible' with government-endorsed ideologies (17).

(15) Mrs Anne Spencer, National Union of Tailors and Garment Workers, said during a debate on the welfare state. She proposed a motion, carried unanimously, condemning repeated and damaging attacks by the Government. (1987)

(16) Foot's question, said the Government was not intending, as he knew full well, to dismantle the welfare state. It was determined to give individuals and families more choice and freedom to exercise it. (1983)

(17) So if there is one central truth in this campaign it is that the survival of the welfare state is incompatible with Mrs Thatcher's grand design. (1983)

Discussion of welfare reform continues in the 1990s and 2000s, where – in line with New Labour's discourse (Fairclough 2000: 38) – the role of the individual is foregrounded and the welfare state is reframed as an enterprise (18):

(18) Malcolm Wicks, the Pensions Minister, said that the project would enable the welfare state to adopt a more 'customer-focused approach'. (2004)
(19) He [Tony Blair] will lay out a 'new Labour vision' of the welfare state. This is one in which people do not wait to be helped but become 'active citizens'. (2005)

In (19), Blair is said to announce a new vision of the welfare state, in which people 'do not wait to be helped', but become 'active citizens'. The implication here is that responsibility for one's welfare is shifted from the state to individual citizens; in this reformulation of the welfare state, people 'do not wait to be helped' because they help themselves. Furthermore, the marketization of the welfare state – where public services are increasingly made to function more as businesses – is evident in the nomenclature in (18) where people accessing the benefits of the welfare state are labelled as 'customers'.

Although the examples given above have different linguistic realizations, they all point towards a wider overarching idea that links the welfare state with restructuring, reformulation and change. Thus we identified our first macroproposition – that the welfare state is ripe for reconfiguration – which is found throughout the seventy-year time span of our corpora. This was somewhat surprising given that there appears to have been no 'bedding in' time for the welfare state's inaugural policies. This early push for reformulation may be accounted for by the fact that the welfare state was primarily a Labour Party initiative, but the Conservatives held power from 1951 to 1964. Similarly, the neoliberal stance of the 1979–97 Conservative Governments is also incompatible with a welfare state founded on ultimately socialist principles. But it is important to note that the Labour Government of 1997 also proposed changes to the welfare state (see 19) in line with a neoliberal ideology. In the examples given so far (including the collocates), there is little indication of the justification for why the welfare state is so closely linked with reconfiguration. While some objections to the welfare state were based on economic grounds, by far the more prominent argument relates to our second macroproposition.

3.4.2.2 Macroproposition II: The welfare state breeds immorality

In addition to references to the affordability of the welfare state, we found moral talk featured very prominently in our data. Moral talk, or language which is 'oriented towards making moral judgements' (Bennett 2014: 73), is repeatedly used to negatively evaluate the welfare state and the effects it (allegedly) has on wider society (20–1, also 22–3):

(20) The comprehensive social planning of the modern welfare state may have produced in some people the feeling that responsibility towards their fellow-

men has been in large measure removed, and no doubt in some particulars this is true. (1949)
(21) The political economic philosophy of the welfare State is not only bad economically but it is also morally bad. (1953)

Throughout the decades, the welfare state tends to be characterized as an agent or social actor which has the potential to alter people's behaviour. In the first instance (20), this takes the form of laments about declining rates of charity and people's unwillingness to look after or take responsibility towards others. The naming of the value 'responsibility' points to morality here (Bennett 2018). The argument is that the welfare state breeds a form of individualism where no one cares about anyone but themselves and, furthermore, they expect the state to take care of other people. This argument is particularly prominent in earlier decades.

A related position occurs in (predominantly later) examples where the welfare state is positioned as stifling individuality and independence, creating 'idle', morally weak people that show little initiative or personal responsibility (22–3). Beyond expecting the state to care for others, the 'idlers' now expect the state to take care of them:

(22) The Welfare State has gone too far. It is breeding a nation of idlers. Families and individuals should stand upon their own feet. (1962)
(23) She [Thatcher] told Mr Major to tackle the 'dependency culture' which was becoming an increasing burden on the State. The welfare state was initially set up to help the genuinely poor and ill, she said. Some people were now abusing the welfare state by claiming benefit when they should be working. (1995)

To return to the wider co-text of (21) the welfare state is both 'economically' and 'morally' bad, because it is based on 'spite', 'envy' and 'sentimental altruism' and because the 'foundation of dependence on the State' it creates is unsustainable. The author of (21) argues that 'a man worth his salt' would not favour 'safety and security' at the 'expense of opportunity and independence'. Rather, the author argues that what is needed is 'freedom to think for ourselves, to act for ourselves and to live our own lives' and that these latter two values are incompatible with 'frustration, regulations, and restrictions or with class-conscious war or any kind of dictatorship'. This 1953 example – in particular, the reference to freedom and the wish for no regulation – is an early argument for neoliberalism. Examples such as those given above also construct and help feed into the now-established stereotype that those benefiting from the welfare state are 'the idle, or undeserving poor who are morally suspect' (van der Bom et al. 2018: 40).

As established, despite being an abstract concept, the welfare state is often represented as an active agent. However, the agency of those accessing its services is also evident (see 22). Quoted directly in this example, Thatcher suggests some people are abusing the welfare state, and claims that there is a 'dependency culture'. Although *dependence* first appears in our data in 1956, it only occurs fourteen times. *Dependency*, however, appears fifty times, but is not used until 1987. It is also one of the collocates in the 1990s corpus (Table 3.4). The introduction of the term 'dependency' reflects the rise of neoliberalism and with it a neoliberalist discourse, which allowed for the discursive reframing of the welfare state. There is a move away from representing the welfare state as collective protection for those in need towards a welfare state where benefits receipt (in particular) is framed in terms of personal, social and moral failure, linked to state dependency (cf. Farnsworth and Irving 2017; Wiggan 2012). At the same time, however, it seems such a reframing is visible in our data decades before neoliberal policies were put into practice by Thatcher in the 1980s (Dados and Connell 2018: 29). The difference lies both in the frequency of reference to and in the type of terms used to characterize those who make use of (particular) welfare state services. There is no overt judgement, for example, of people who use the NHS or free education, and the majority of references to the 'idle' implicitly refer to people who are unemployed and who receive out-of-work or incapacity benefits payments. Whereas in earlier decades, emphasis is placed on people's responsibility to take care of both themselves and others despite the security net of the welfare state, in later decades the emphasis shifts to the government's (apparent) need to tackle people's dependency on state benefits. We take a closer look at the representation of these individuals under our final macroproposition.

3.4.2.3 Macroproposition III: The welfare state facilitates the creation of an underclass

Our third macroproposition relates to social class; it sums up how the welfare state is depicted as being at least partly responsible for the creation of a 'slovenly, vicious [and] idle' underclass (24) that 'sponge[s]' on the welfare system:

(24) We must get rid of the slovenly, vicious, idle wasters of the community. Unfortunately, the welfare State is only too likely to encourage their increase. (1949)
(25) The welfare state has not just an underclass of those trapped in the cycle of dependency. It has an underclass of workers. (2000)

Negative 'explicitly evaluative nominal labels' (Paterson, Coffey-Glover and Peplow 2016: 201) are used to depict a group of people who are seen to have benefitted from the welfare system or whose existence is portrayed as having been facilitated by the welfare state. Throughout our concordance lines, even as early as the 1940s (see 24), the welfare state is blamed for facilitating the proliferation of 'parasite[s]', the 'idle poor', and 'underclass[es]' of both 'workers' and 'those trapped in the cycle of dependency' (25). Many of these representations condemn those on welfare, although the fact that they are benefit claimants is rarely explicitly stated; rather, it is implied, as in 28 (see below). Some of the examples are also gendered (26–7):

(26) The mother of four children on social security was described by a magistrate yesterday as a typical product of the modern welfare state. Mrs JENNIFER ROBINSON, 31, of Stowell Avenue, New Addington, was a parasite. (1978)

(27) The only difference is the Welfare State instead of the workhouse, and most divorced and single mothers live on social security. (1991)

One mother, while being sentenced for theft, is described as a 'typical product of the modern welfare state' (27) and 'divorced and single mothers' are generalized as not being able to support themselves, with the (highly questionable) claim that most are living 'on social security' (20); see also Toolan (this volume). Such negative descriptions and generalizations about those seen to benefit from the welfare state function to construct and perpetuate the existence and 'othering' of an immoral, passive and lazy 'underclass'. Example 28 is an exemplar of this position:

(28) While the upper classes slowly wind down, there is emerging, at the other end of the social spectrum, a replacement layabout class. Not so much the idle rich as the idle poor, these are the sons and daughters of an indulgent welfare state, people whose idea of a useful qualification is knowing how to fill in a claim form. Nevertheless, they have high expectations. They harbour desires not just beyond their own pockets, but beyond most other people's, too. … They want to dress like their idols, David Beckham and Wayne Rooney, whose fortunes are based on their ability to do a job that resembles nothing like work: football. … The Chav (for it is he) looks on and thinks: 'I'll have some of that'. The money doesn't matter – it's not his anyway. It's all about priorities. Chavs would happily live in a tent if it meant their kids could wear Burberry baby-gros. (2005)

This article, written by Sarah Vine, is a review of a television documentary about a designer clothes shop in Middlesbrough. Here, the welfare state is blamed for the 'idle poor', a replacement 'layabout class' for the 'upper classes', but 'at the other side of the social spectrum'. Whereas the 'upper classes' are thus construed relatively neutrally (there is one negative depiction of them as the 'idle rich', and elsewhere they are depicted as living in 'a high-handed style of squalor'), the use of the attributive adjective 'layabout' negatively modifies 'class' when the term is used to refer to other socio-economic groups. The attitudes of this 'layabout class' are negatively evaluated; they have 'high expectations' but the implicature is that they should not, and they 'harbour desires not just beyond their own pockets, but beyond most other people's, too'. The group are labelled as 'chavs' and the example is gendered – referring explicitly to men. In line with Bennett's (2013b) findings on the use of 'chav' in British media, example (28) is characterized by boulomaic modality (Simpson 1993). Vine includes with epistemic certainty descriptions of this group's wishes, desires and fantasies, as well as *verba sentiendi* – words denoting thoughts, feelings and perceptions (Simpson 1993: 39, 48, 56). All of these descriptions serve to index the 'chav lifestyle' and link it to the provisions of the 'indulgent' welfare state, which Vine (implicitly) blames for the chavs' existence; they are the welfare state's 'sons and daughters'.

Indexicality here refers to the 'inherently dialectical character' (Silverstein 2003: 197) of language. Silverstein (2003) distinguishes between different orders of indexicality. First-order indexical items may be defined as those relatively 'value-free' (linguistic) items which may be associated with particular groups. When these items become recontextualized and ideologically imbued with meaning, a second-order indexical link is formed. Within linguistics, a large body of research has focused on how certain linguistic features index culturally salient stereotypes of particular groups of people (e.g. van Dijk 1991; see also van der Bom et al. 2018). In (28), Vine constructs a harmful stereotype of those growing up in the welfare state, presupposing certain attitudes, desires and behaviours. In doing so, she takes an all-knowing point of view despite not being part of this apparent social group. Our findings echo those of Bennett (2013b: 160), in that 'class-based inequality' is recast here as an aggregate of poor 'personal choice' and blame for one's circumstances is placed on the individual.

There are several similar examples in our corpora, many of which draw on the indices of social class identified in van der Bom et al.'s (2018) analysis of a corpus of tweets about the programme *Benefits Street*. Those in the programme were associated with 'deviant' behaviours such as smoking, drinking alcohol and spending money on high-value electrical items (such as *iPhones*), designer clothing (see 28) and spray tans. We found similar examples in our data, including (29–30) which, perhaps surprisingly, date from the 1950s.

(29)   Perhaps the popularity of bottled beer is itself a manifestation of the welfare state at any rate, there is no sign that it is diminishing. (1950)

(30)   My gambling is provided by the welfare state, a social service for which I am grateful. (1952)

Here, the popularity of a particular alcohol ('bottled beer') and addiction ('gambling') are represented as being facilitated by the welfare state. These preferences/behaviours are linked to a certain group of people who (unfairly) benefit from the welfare state. However, there are also examples in our corpora where such stereotypes are rejected.

(31)   The great majority of them came here to get work and not to 'sponge' on the welfare state. (1958)

(32)   None of my colleagues would have endorsed Dr. Friedman's wild simplistic statements about the lazy British worker and our welfare state being the major causes of the present difficulties here. (1976)

(33)   A favourite target in the stern climate of the 1980s, caricatured as privileged leeches on the body of the welfare state who guzzled the taxpayers' millions and then demanded more. (1992)

(34)   Well-educated young adults, keen for legal work. Far from being 'parasites' on the welfare state, most want nothing so much as to be prosperous tax-paying citizens. (2000)

Closer examination of those examples reveals, however, that they refer to 'coloured people' whom have immigrated to Britain (31), students (33) or potential immigrants who are 'well-educated young adults' (34). None of these examples relate to the 'irresponsible' and 'immoral' social class negatively characterized elsewhere in our data. Only example (32), in which Economics Nobel Prize winner Dr Friedman's depiction of the 'lazy British worker' is criticized, directly negates the stereotype established above. However, it is notable that this example comes from a letter to the *Times* editor and was not content produced by an employee of the newspaper.

3.5 Discussion and conclusions

In this chapter we have contributed to research on the discursive construction of economic inequality in the British media by examining how the welfare state is represented in the *Times* from 1940 to 2009. Our findings show that contrary to our expectations, the modern welfare state is consistently linked to a number of key concepts over time. (RQ2: Is the welfare state associated with any core concepts which remain unchanged over time?) Our thematic collocate analysis showed that while there is variation in the individual collocates connected with the welfare state across decades, the semantic fields these collocates are drawn from begin to stabilize in the 1970s, and are then continued to different extents into the 2000s. This trend is particularly clear with the semantic fields of *destruction/opposition, economic, idea/notion/concept* and *initialization/building*.

Although individual collocates vary across decades, there is also considerable overlap: *benefits, depends, welfare, social, structure,* occur across decades. Collocates particularly prevalent are those related to building metaphors – linked to the *foundations* or the *structure* of the welfare state – and benefits. While *benefits* is a collocate for nearly every decade, the meaning of this collocate shifts between benefits in its generic sense and the use of the term more specifically to refer to welfare payments given to benefits recipients. Thus, the answer to RQ1 '(How) do reports about the welfare state change over time?' is that key elements of the *Times*' reporting on the welfare state remain relatively static. Any changes that do occur relate mostly to an increased use of certain collocates. There is, for example, a marked increase in negatively loaded collocates relating to the destruction and/or opposition to the welfare state in the 1980s compared to earlier decades.

Further examination of our data revealed a number of macropropositions that were present throughout the decades: (i) *the welfare state is ripe for reconfiguration*, (ii) *the welfare state breeds immorality* and (iii) *the welfare state facilitates the creation of an underclass*. These also reveal that the language used to report on the welfare state indexes wider discourses on neoliberalism as well as on morality and class specifically. (RQ3: How does the language used to report on the welfare state index wider discourses about the UK welfare state from the 1940s to 2009?) The macroproposition analysis foregrounds how the welfare state is continuously depicted as in need of restructuring. There is a relatively consistent narrative which holds that the welfare state is responsible for the economic and moral shortcomings at the time of reporting. This is present not only from the 1970s onwards, as reported by some others, but right from the welfare state's inception. Moral discourse, at times linked to an underclass, also featured particularly prominently in our data. As others have noted, this is a key feature of neoliberal discourse (e.g. Bennett 2013b; Fairclough 2000; Levitas 2005). What is especially surprising, however, is that some trends indicative of neoliberal discourse are present early in the seventy-year span covered by our dataset.

Our findings also indicate that the *Times* takes a narrow view on what the welfare state actually is. There are no trends in our data which indicate that the NHS or free education was a core component of the *Times*' coverage of the welfare state. It is highly likely that the NHS and educational policies are referenced elsewhere in the newspaper, but – significantly for this paper – they do not appear to be addressed under the umbrella of the welfare state. This is despite the fact that the National Health Service Act (1946) is directly associated with the formation of the welfare state. By reducing the welfare state to merely the receipt of benefits (however implicitly expressed), it becomes possible to blame the apparent shortcomings and expense of the welfare state on a stereotypical, morally bankrupt social underclass. This apportioning of blame – moving from the collective to the individual – maps closely with the rise and promotion of neoliberalism from the 1980s onwards. This could perhaps be predicated by the fact that the *Times* is a right-leaning newspaper which has consistently supported the Conservative Party, but nevertheless serves as a foundation for future research contrasting the *Times* with alternative, left-leaning source material.

Another avenue for future work is for the UK welfare state to be compared to welfare states elsewhere. It was already noted above that the *Times* often made reference to Sweden's welfare state, for example. Additionally, one could look to welfare states elsewhere: in 2013, the newly ascended King of the Netherlands Willem-Alexander gave his first major Speech from the Throne. In it, he declared that the 'traditional welfare state is slowly but surely changing into a participation society'[5] and he outlined the government's plans to 'ask from everyone able to do so, to take responsibility for his or her own life and environment'.[6] The coinage of the term 'participation society' was picked up widely in the media and was made Dutch word of the year (NRC 2013). It represents both a political ideology and an austerity policy, and, significantly for the present paper, is said to have inspired David Cameron's reforms of the welfare state (Waterfield 2013). Thus there is scope to investigate how European welfare states are connected to each other, both economically and ideologically.

Acknowledgements

We would like to thank Professor Toolan and Dr Gómez-Jiménez for being so encouraging. This chapter is dedicated to Manuel Villagrasa van der Bom.

Notes

1 Proposals for how to deal with OCR errors are beyond the scope of this paper. However, they are problematic for historical research that draws on the methods of corpus linguistics, and we encourage further discussion of how such errors may be computationally and manually accounted for.
2 As the analysis will show, the welfare state is newsworthy insofar as it meets Potts et al.'s (2015: 151) criteria for the news value of 'impact' as it is 'discursively constructed as having significant effects or consequences'.

3 There is some overlap between the temporal and the scope categories (i.e. *cradle-to-grave* and *comprehensive*) due to wider notions about the conceptual relationship between time and space.
4 It is interesting that similar rhetoric was used by Conservative MP George Osbourne in his conference speech in 2012: 'Where is the fairness, we ask, for the shift-worker, leaving home in the dark hours of the early morning, who looks up at the closed blinds of their next door neighbour sleeping off a life on benefits?' (Osbourne 2012).
5 Translation our own. Original: '… leidt dit ertoe dat de klassieke verzorgingsstaat langzaam maar zeker verandert in een participatiesamenleving' (NRC 2013).
6 Translation our own. Original: 'Van iedereen die dat kan, wordt gevraagd verantwoordelijkheid te nemen voor zijn of haar eigen leven en omgeving' (NRC 2013).

4

What can be done about child poverty?

What the *Times* said then and what it says now

Michael Toolan

4.1 Introduction

4.1.1 Child poverty, broad trends

On 28 March 2019 the government's Department for Work and Pensions reported that the number of children living in absolute poverty in the UK had increased by 200,000 in the previous year, 2017–18 (absolute poverty being defined as living in a household whose income is below 60 per cent of the 2010–11 median income level) (see Inman and Booth 2019). In fact, the official records show that child poverty has been on the increase in the UK since 2011 (see Rahman 2019 and the Social Metrics Commission 2019). Different means of measuring are touted and contested, including absolute poverty, relative poverty and the poverty line, but whichever measure is used, the broad trends show increasing child poverty to the point that now more than 4 million UK children – a third of all children – are living in poverty (Child Poverty Action Group 2019). According to the politically centrist Resolution Foundation, the most recent increase in child poverty was linked to the freeze in the value of working-age benefits, made worse by a spike in inflation to 3 per cent in late 2017. But a longer term cause over the last several decades has been the steep rise in housing costs, especially in the south. Those were the decades in which the stock of social housing declined precipitously so that more young families had to turn to the private sector, where the lack of new building of affordable housing exacerbated the shortage and drove rents up. Analysis of Office of National Statistics data by the National Housing Federation revealed that there are 847,000 children from working families living in poverty for the sole reason that their homes are too expensive.

4.1.2 Child poverty in the newspaper

This chapter is an attempt to compare how child poverty was thought about and talked about in the *Times* in the 1970s to how it was thought and talked about in the 2000s, with a view to seeing how if at all that discourse has changed. Because the reality has changed, and for the worse: there is clear evidence of significantly more child poverty in the UK today than in the 1970s (Glennerster et al. 2004, see also Joyce 2014). Growth in child poverty is arguably the worst aspect of the growth in wealth inequality in Britain since the 1970s, media reporting and representing of which has been my research priority for several years (see Toolan 2018).

Have the centre-right press ways of talking about child poverty changed, encouraging readers to think of it as ineradicable, something simply to be lived with, or more accurately, alongside? Do the representations amount to a more distanced attitude than earlier, in which it is implied that 'life-style choice' or, bad luck, other people's hardship cannot be the responsibility of the state, and is not an unfairness the state should rectify?

4.1.3 Brief sketch of the sociopolitical background

The first UK government support for families with children in modern times was an income tax credit (1909), which in practice was a small subsidy to middle-class parents (Sinfield 2019). Following the influential 1942 Beveridge Report, Family Allowance was introduced in 1945 as a subsidy to larger families: initially, a 5 shillings (25p in the new money) per week payment for each child after the first; by 1975 the rate had risen to £1.50 for each eligible child. In the late 1970s, this allowance and the child tax allowance were replaced by Labour's Child Benefit scheme, the first universal payment, paid for every child and all mothers. By 1978 the rate was £3 per child per week, plus £2 for single-parent families. Another form of financial support was Supplementary Benefit (in 1988 replaced by Income Support), granted on a sliding scale to claimants who are justifiably working fewer than sixteen hours per week.

From 1971 onwards, families on low earnings were entitled to claim Family Income Supplement (later called Family Credit), and in time more did so; it was replaced first by Working Families Tax Credit and then by two instruments: Working Tax Credit and Child Tax Credit.

Three key means of sharply reducing child poverty in the UK, according to such research and campaigning agencies as the Bevan and Rowntree Foundations, include increasing the household income of the poorest families, supporting parents (e.g. via counselling) and supporting the educationally disadvantaged from the pre-school years onwards (see Joseph Rowntree Foundation 2019). With regard to the third of these prescriptions, one of the most significant governmental initiatives in recent decades was Sure Start. This was launched in 1998 by the Labour Government (which came to power in May 1997 after eighteen years of Tory rule), and took slightly different forms in the four nations of the UK. Sure Start's declared aim was to give children 'the best possible start in life' and 'enhance the life chances for young children growing up in disadvantaged neighbourhoods' (National Evaluation of Sure Start Team 2010: 2) through improvement of childcare, early education, health and family support, with an emphasis on outreach and community development. Two generations of government-sponsored evaluation (National Evaluation of Sure

Start and Evaluation of Children's Centres in England, NESS and ECCE), 2001–12 and 2009–15, respectively, found that local programmes of Sure Start brought significant benefits in some respects, including to the children's physical health and Body Mass Index scores, their mothers' mental health and family stability. With the emergence of the Labour Government's *Every Child Matters* initiative in 2003, what was previously a 'targeted' project (locally run Sure Start programmes but centrally funded and limited to those areas of greatest deprivation) was changed to a more widespread provision of Sure Start Children's Centres, both controlled and funded by cash-strapped local government. In the years since 2010, real-terms spending on the Centres has declined sharply, partly as a result of austerity cuts, and the Centres' benefit to the most disadvantaged families has been widely judged to have declined as a consequence.

4.2 Divergent explanatory narratives about child poverty

One way to think about the representation and discussion of poverty in the press over the past fifty years and more is to see it as fitting and refreshing two distinct cognitive scripts and 'explanations' of that poverty. One of these scripts sees the UK as an advanced, moderate, reasonable country, where the rule of law and basic rights are protected, and everyone ('within reason') has a fair chance to find work and earn enough to live decently and raise their own children to do better and go further. In this script, the continued existence of a significant percentage of the population living in poverty is explained as stemming from some dysfunctionality on their part, some failure in those affected to act reasonably by the standards of the wider community. The script exempts only the very old or seriously disabled from criticism, and accepts that the state should provide them with some assistance meeting their basic needs,[1] but it regards the poverty of all other working-age individuals and families, including their children, as the financial responsibility of no one but themselves. Charitable giving to help the unfortunate is acceptable, and respects the power and choices of the individual citizen. But it is wrong to enforce redistribution, for example through taxation of the hard-working and solvent, as if everyone were under an obligation to subsidize those who should be regarded as largely responsible for their own financial difficulties.

The other script explains things differently, beginning with a less sanguine background understanding of what life is like in the UK for many people. It sees the statistical evidence of acute income- and wealth-based disparities in terms of health, longevity, education and employment as indicating the British system is not a fair one where everyone has a chance to prosper. In this script the majority of chronically poor people are not 'work-shy' or trapped in an addiction: they are more likely to be a single mother juggling low-paid part-time work with child-raising responsibilities, struggling to afford over-priced low-quality private rented housing, aided by some state assistance (child benefit, and various means-tested benefits related to housing costs and low income, all now controversially integrated in the Universal Credit scheme) and unreliable support payments from the children's father. In these conditions, the children are more prone to illness and markedly less likely to experience the richly stimulating upbringing on offer to most of their more comfortably off contemporaries (expensive out-of-school activities, such as sports, music, ballet, riding lessons, exciting holidays and visits to attractions). Financially comfortable parents are more able to cope with the ongoing cuts in the funding of schools, public libraries and leisure centres. Schools are particularly crucial, in terms of what they can offer and how they can nurture every child's talents. Inequality is rampant here: to give one of innumerable similar trends, a British Phonographic Industry survey of teachers in England (2019) found that only 12 per cent of schools in deprived areas have an orchestra, compared with 85 per cent of independent schools. Integral to this script is the question whether the state's provisions, funded by the tax system we collectively endorse, does enough for the absolutely poor and is fair to their disadvantaged children. The Script 1 explanation of poverty fits an individualist laisser-faire ideology well; by contrast, a Script 2 account fits a communitarian interventionist ideology well.

A Comment article published in the *Times* in the later decade under scrutiny here, together with several of the readers' letters published in response to it, vividly demonstrates the two contrasting poverty scripts at work. On Tuesday 16 September 2003, the writer and journalist Libby Purves published a Comment entitled 'You have to be rich to lead a life of poverty'. The article reviewed some of the ways in which such things as high-interest-rate store-cards and payday loans, sometimes used to pay for essential items, both exploited the poor and kept them poor. Largely aligning with a Script 2 narrative, Purves asked how the state might do more to help. Some burdens the government could not prevent, she argued, but 'whenever we can see ways to level the financial playing field, we should'.

This triggered a good deal of response from letter writers, and these appeared exactly a week later and not on the Letters page but in a full-page feature on p. 36 entitled 'debate@thetimes.co.uk'. The page was headed by a reproduction of the Purves article title and the first few lines of her text, and then this sub-head, which itself moves from a Script 2 to a Script 1 perspective: 'Helping the Poor: How can society help the 13 million Britons on low incomes – or should they be helping themselves?' Some of the letters expressed sympathy and agreement with Purves, while also recommending that the poor resort more to second-hand goods and the bargains allegedly to be found at car-boot sales, more government support for heterosexual marriage and the traditional family, more use of not-for-profit credit unions and low-cost loans and more help with fuel bills for the elderly poor. These letters held closer to a Script 2 mindset. They contrast with some Script 1 responses, such as a letter (entitled 'Stop whining') that was entirely unsympathetic: 'I FIND Libby Purves's whining for the poor pretty sickening. It seems that it is no longer fashionable to stand on one's own feet, or to expect others to do so. Everyone looks for help and charity from someone else.' The longest letter, from a reader in Belgium writing in a 'nothing will help' Script 1 spirit, claimed Purves's remark that 'we all want the poorest and their children to scramble upwards' exposed a 'sad but serious' mathematical flaw in her thinking. In the reader's view, the only way the poor can create space to scramble upwards is by displacing somebody higher up and propelling them downwards towards the underclass, and it was hypocrisy to pretend otherwise.

4.3 Challenges in preparing comparable 'child poverty' corpora for the 1970s and the 2000s

How can a reliable picture be obtained of just what view the *Times* took of UK child poverty in the 1970s? The solution I adopted was to focus solely on stories in the *Times* of that decade that were categorized in the Gale Archive as appearing in the Opinion and Editorial section of the paper, a section containing just editorials (also known as 'leaders') and letters to the editor. From that section, I collected into my corpus just those stories in which *children* occurred as a keyword and *poverty* occurred anywhere in the text. My hunch was that from these stories more than any other specifiable set, a picture might emerge of what the *Times* of those years regarded as or represented to be the true situation with regard to children and poverty insofar as these intersect.

Just twenty or so stories were identified that met the above criteria, and this list was further reduced by the removal of a couple of articles whose focus was remote from that of children and poverty in the UK. The small corpus of leader articles and letters that remained was then added to by the inclusion of those leaders, articles or letters to which the items already included were direct responses. For example, a letter printed under the title 'Women in Poverty' on 5 September 1970 is in the corpus since it contains both the search terms 'children' and 'poverty', but the letter was a response to an article entitled 'Growing Points: Women in Poverty', published on 2 September 1970. So the latter article, although not containing the word *children*, was also included in the corpus. With these few added items, the corpus amounts to just 30 stories in 13,100 words. While such a corpus would be much too small to be informative for some research purposes, it is not unreasonable to regard such a targeted sample as relevant to the particular critical-discursive task at hand, namely, determining the *Times*'s articulated stance in the 1970s towards child poverty in the UK. It might be reassuring to find a larger corpus with its promise of the reliability of larger numbers and more established trends, but the onus is on the sceptic to identify a more pertinent search instruction for data-gathering from the *Times* than the one adopted.

Compiling a corpus of relevant stories from the *Times* in the decade running from January 2000 to December 2009 was in a sense easier, but less targeted. Now using the Nexis database rather than the Gale Archive, a search was made for all those stories containing the words 'children' and 'poverty' occurring no more than fifty words apart. This identified 1,837 articles. When, in the 'Search Within Results' tab, I stipulated that only those results which also included the word *UK* be returned, the number of articles reduced to 877, which reduced further to 826 after automatic similarity processing had applied. A signal disadvantage of the Nexis database is that it sub-categorizes by subject-matter, and not at all by sub-genre: thus, one cannot select stories appearing exclusively on the Sports pages, the News pages or, for that matter, in the Op-Ed section. As a consequence, the 2000s corpus includes many items from other sub-genres in addition to those of editorials and letters. I have manually removed some of the most uncontentiously irrelevant of these, plus stories concerning child poverty only outside the UK. The resulting corpus contains roughly 750,000 words. There is thus an enormous disparity in size between the two corpora, but since the aims of this study are critical discourse analytical rather than linguistic, this disparity need not be hugely disabling, if the analysis proceeds with care. It would be wrong to assume that the much smaller corpus is inevitably a less accurate representation of the *Times*'s thinking with regard to children living in poverty than the larger corpus.

Compiling a corpus for critical discourse analytical purposes assumes that the texts articulate a broadly shared ideological stance. This is postulated even though the texts come from many different authors, partly because the writers can be grouped together as 'the sort of people who wrote for or to the *Times* material that was accepted for publication', and mostly that set seems neither random nor unmanageably diverse. They are usually marked out as experts or authorities on the matter they discuss; most of the letter writers in my small corpus are sufficiently well known that all these years later their biographical details can still be retrieved from the internet: Anthony Locke (Warden, Toynbee Hall), Prof. J. E. Meade ('one of the greatest economists of his generation', according to his obituary in the *Independent* 1995), Ruth Lister (Director of Child Poverty Action Group 1979–87, made a Baroness in 2011), Prof. C. V. Brown, Mr Richard Lawson (subsequently and still today a prominent Green Party campaigner) and others. *Times* leader articles in the 1970s were not signed, but arguably anyone tasked with writing a *Times* leader is by that recognition alone a relatively influential commentator on current affairs, writing with the newspaper's endorsement.

Having gathered a small but relevant sample as my 1970s *Times* corpus, the challenge is how best to analyse this corpus so as to derive its core schema or script, the essentials of the dominant picture it assumes and projects. Some kind of sorting, some kind of selecting of 'key' words, phrases, clauses, propositions, events, conditions, is required, but complications abound. For example, editorials and letters tend to be strongly declarative or representative in mode, asserting various things to be the case and therefore some further declaration also is the case or should be done. But not all declarations are of equal opinion-shaping significance. Some simply describe an undisputed context or common ground: uncontentious facts. More important are those with an implicitly modal or evaluative inflection and these are the ones a CDA must focus upon. An example of the former comes in Prof. Meade's March 1980 letter about child benefits when he points out that 'child benefits are paid to the parents regardless of their earnings' (this remained true until January 2013, when this benefit became means-tested). An example of the latter is his assertion that 'the payment of child benefits is ... a main weapon for the relief of poverty', which is a forcefully expressed viewpoint.

4.4 Corpus-based comparisons: Keywords in the 1970s and the 2000s

4.4.1 Keywords in the 1970s

As a first analytical step, the 1970s corpus was subjected to a keyword analysis, to identify the disproportionately frequent lexical words in it, its keywords, relative to a suitable reference corpus. I have used the British National Corpus (BNC henceforth)

Table 4.1 Top Thirty Lexical Keywords in the Times 'Children + Poverty' 1970s Corpus

Item	Frequency in Corpus	Percentage of Corpus Text	Frequency in Reference Corpus	Percentage of Corpus Text	LL	Log Ratio
allowances	60	0.49	21	0.00	403	7.45
poverty	42	0.34	16	0.00	279	7.33
families	47	0.39	57	0.01	246	5.66
children	75	0.61	357	0.05	232	3.68
family	58	0.48	209	0.03	206	4.08
poor	37	0.30	93	0.01	153	4.60
child	36	0.30	110	0.01	137	4.32
benefit	33	0.27	100	0.01	126	4.33
benefits	31	0.25	97	0.01	117	4.29
supplementary	16	0.13	3	0.00	115	8.35
income	28	0.23	89	0.01	105	4.27
child-benefit	11	0.09	0	0.00	90	10.39
unemployment	21	0.17	48	0.01	90	4.74
wage	14	0.11	7	0.00	89	6.93
incomes	13	0.11	4	0.00	88	7.63
social security	13	0.11	6	0.00	83	7.05
increase	29	0.24	168	0.02	80	3.35
poorest	10	0.08	1	0.00	75	3.40
poverty trap	9	0.07	0	0.00	74	9.26
tax	25	0.20	153	0.02	66	10.10
living	21	0.17	97	0.01	66	3.73
low	21	0.17	110	0.01	61	3.55
pay	20	0.16	101	0.01	59	3.60
prices	21	0.17	144	0.02	52	3.16
parents	17	0.14	88	0.01	50	3.56
inflation	15	0.12	67	0.01	48	3.77
wage-earners	7	0.07	3	0.00	45	7.16
money	20	0.16	166	0.02	43	2.88

sample of Written Informative English, which is pre-installed in Wmatrix, a corpus analysis package available online (Rayson 2009). Table 4.1 lists the top thirty lexical keywords in the 1970s *Times* corpus.

Some of the top keywords here are fairly predictably present in the textual vicinity of one or both of the search terms (e.g. *families* and *child* expectably co-occurring with *children*; *poor* and *unemployment* as similarly with *poverty*). It is the less expected items that often prove more revealing, beginning with most key item, *allowances*, which is not ordinarily strongly associated with the words *children* or *poverty*. But before proceeding it must be noted that while, by virtue of being top keywords, the above words can be expected to co-occur in the corpus texts, we cannot assume that the co-occurrence is proximate, that is, that they are collocates. This stronger linkage remains to be determined.

Using just the above top keywords as evidence, the corpus suggests that the editorial sections of the *Times* in the 1970s saw situations in which children and poverty were involved as also situations involving allowances, families, benefits of one kind or another (including supplementary, child or social security), wages or income and unemployment. Keywords do not in themselves disclose narrative sequence (the listing above does not indicate that *children* lead to *unemployment* and that this leads to both *poverty* and *social security*: that is an imposed chronology). But drawing on real-world knowledge, some sequencing can be postulated: *children* in *poverty* is one outcome, when *benefits* and *allowances* and *wage/income* (if any: *unemployment* may apply instead) are insufficient. But the inadequacy of benefits/allowances has had to be inferred here, at this level of coarse granularity. For confirmation, a closer look at *allowances* as keyword in context (KWIC henceforth) is needed.

The concordance lines for *allowances* reveal that in thirty-eight out of sixty instances the collocate immediately to its left, known as the L1 collocate, is *family*. In several of the other twenty-two cases, the two words in the L1 position just to the left of *allowance* and just preceding L1 (known as L2) are *child* and *tax*. Thus *allowances* often occurs immediately next to two of the other top keywords. But attention should be paid also to two more of the top keywords without intrinsic connection to *children* and *poverty*: *benefit* and *benefits*. These occur thirty-three and thirty-one times, respectively, thus roughly as frequently as *allowances* (rarely used in the singular). *Benefit* often has *supplementary* or *unemployment* as its L1 collocate, while the commonest L1 collocate of *benefits* is *child*. It becomes clear, from corpus examples, that various allowances and benefits were replaced, during the decade, by child benefit, which the *Times* was strongly in favour of, as potentially especially suited to banishing child poverty.

These keywords reflect the fact that the 1970s *Times* habitually talks about child poverty in relation to financial interventions by the state (in the form of *family allowances, supplementary benefit,* or *child benefits*) aimed at mitigating the conditions faced by those living at or below the poverty line. Arguably this assumes that where children are growing up in poverty, the state should address this by means of subventions, where these can be provided without imposing an 'intolerable' tax burden on the better off.

A Leader article of late April 1970 similarly suggests that the *Times* of this earlier period supported activism in the government's interventions against child poverty – as, indeed, it did with regard to the introduction of maternity leave benefits (see Gómez-Jiménez 2018):

(1) Higher family allowances [i.e. an automatic grant to cover the costs of each child] are the best remedy for child poverty. They are the simplest means of helping the families of low wage-earners and the wage-stopped. They ought to have a higher priority at this time than a further increase in supplementary benefits [which were means-tested: MT]. ... Nearly all the objections can be reduced in essence to the crude proposition that parents should not be paid by the state to have children they cannot afford. ... [T]he nation has become far more aware of the suffering that comes from child poverty and public opinion should be more open to persuasion [concerning raising family allowances: MT] than many politicians suppose.

Here, the idea that increased family allowances amounts to paying parents to have children they cannot afford is rejected as a crude proposition, and the *Times* instead suggests public opinion may be more humane than politicians suppose. The editorial's position is directly at odds with that of a September 1970 letter to the editor, also in my corpus, which argues poverty comes chiefly from population growth: the government should stop family allowances and 'abolish poverty ... through population growth control'. In the 2000s, the *Times* sometimes carries arguments close to the latter view, in Op-Ed contributions from Jamie Whyte. In the 1970s the *Times* distanced itself from such a hard line.

The prominence of the emphasis on *family allowances* in the corpus, and the desirability of increasing family allowance payments to alleviate the poverty in large families living on low wages, continues throughout the 1970s corpus. By comparison with a more decisive intervention, such as the imposition of a minimum wage at a tolerable level, the stance could be described as 'concerned but gradualist'. A 30 May 1978 letter from Frank Field, by then the director of the influential Child Poverty Action Group, reflects the continued frustration of anti-poverty campaigners at the *Times*'s approach as too complacent. Field's immediate purpose is to correct the *Times*'s over-optimistic interpretation of a Royal Commission's findings, as reporting that the poor were not getting poorer. He points out that the Commission looked at the poorest 25 per cent as a whole, rather than the most severely impoverished (e.g. the poorest 10 per cent). He urges fuller consideration of the rights and morality of the situation in the UK, where he sees a striking contrast between the force with which *Times* editorials 'argue for other countries to put their own house in order' and 'the timorousness you show in tackling moral questions here at home':

(2) When discussing issues of poverty, we are told that our moral code of conduct must take second place to the laws of the market. Nothing must be done to improve the lot of the poor dependent on benefit because this is unfair to the poor who earn their poverty. Yet no action should be taken to tackle the issue of low wages because this will, according to you, necessarily lead to unemployment.

4.4.2 Keywords in the 2000s

When keyword analysis was applied to the 750,000 word corpus from the 2000s decade (again with BNC British Written Informative sample as reference corpus) the lexical items found to be disproportionately frequent are those listed in Table 4.2. Focusing on the fully lexical, the pronouns *I, she, her, we* and *you* (much less key in the 1970s) and the negative contraction *n't* have been excluded. So too have several personal names that appeared in the initial list of most key keywords computed by Wmatrix: *Mr Brown, Gordon Brown, Mr Blair* and *Tony Blair*. Interestingly, in the 1970s corpus the names *Sir Keith Joseph* and *Frank Field* were prominent but not top keywords.

Direct comparison of Tables 4.1 and 4.2 highlights numerous disturbing contrasts. To give one simple example, note the presence of *Britain* as a 2000s keyword (in the 1970s corpus it has an entirely normal frequency: 0.04 per cent of the text). This suggests that with regard to children and poverty, 'Britain' was not formerly but is now a prominent characterizing feature: living in Britain, being British, being subject to conditions in Britain. Here are three random examples of how *Britain* features in the 2000s '*children + poverty*' corpus:

(3) David Blunkett, the Education Secretary, cannot rely on such divine intervention to help Britain's children.
(4) The area, in the north of Sheffield, includes some of the most socially deprived housing estates in Britain where unemployment is both high and ingrained.
(5) Children from poorer families have far less chance of improving their lives in Britain than those in most other wealthy countries.

Turning to patterns of broader significance, there seem to be two noticeable contrasts with the 1970s corpus keywords: the absence of mentions in the later corpus of *allowances* and *benefits*, and instead the keyness of *charity/charities*; and the prominent mentions of *schools, education* and *pupils*. Here I turn to the second of these contrasts. While some commentary on *allowances* has already been offered, I return to the first of these topics in Section 4.5, where whole semantic domains (rather than single words) are compared and contrasted.

The keyness of *schools* in the 2000s texts is one of the most revealing contrasts between the two corpora. There is no intrinsic linguistic or logical link between poverty and schools, while the link between children and schools is primarily sociocultural rather than linguo-semantic. As for the collocates of the word *schools* in this corpus, Antconc finds that among the most numerous L1 lexical collocates of the 750 instances of *schools* are *faith, failing, grammar, independent,* primary, *secondary, specialist* and *state*. As might be expected from the presence in the keyword list, in addition to *schools*, of *school, education* and *pupils*, the semantic domain P1, 'Education in general', is also one of the most key semantic domains in the later corpus (see Table 4.4).[2]

School/schools, neither of them a 1970s corpus keyword, constitute just 0.1 per cent of that corpus; by contrast they are both keywords and combined constitute 0.2 per cent of the 2000s corpus. Interestingly, the few mentions of schools in relation to children and poverty in the 1970s involve claims about their shortcomings or failing

Table 4.2 Top Thirty Lexical Keywords in the *Times* 'Children + Poverty' 2000s Corpus

Item	Frequency in Corpus	Percentage of Corpus Text	Frequency in Reference Corpus	Percentage of Corpus Text	LL	Log Ratio
children	3,652	0.52	357	0.05	3358	3.44
poverty	1,723	0.25	16	0.00	2336	6.84
child	1,213	0.17	110	0.01	1146	3.55
says	1,035	0.15	168	0.02	750	2.71
parents	836	0.12	88	0.01	747	3.34
families	668	0.10	57	0.01	644	3.64
people	1,954	0.28	744	0.10	640	1.48
schools	597	0.09	63	0.01	533	3.33
school	762	0.11	169	0.02	446	2.26
Britain	1,011	0.14	305	0.04	444	1.82
charity	420	0.06	28	0.00	436	4.00
family	814	0.12	209	0.03	420	2.05
tax	701	0.10	153	0.02	415	2.29
poor	540	0.08	93	0.01	377	2.63
education	617	0.09	137	0.02	361	2.26
poorest	211	0.03	1	0.00	294	7.81
life	815	0.12	291	0.04	292	1.58
money	601	0.09	166	0.02	289	1.95
Labour	558	0.08	143	0.02	289	2.05
young	642	0.09	195	0.03	280	1.81
charities	207	0.03	2	0.00	280	6.78
Africa	304	0.04	30	0.00	278	3.43
pupils	239	0.03	15	0.00	252	4.08
income	409	0.06	89	0.01	244	5.16
world	1,006	0.14	470	0.06	233	1.19
spending	300	0.04	44	0.01	230	2.86
lives	374	0.05	79	0.01	227	2.33
home	756	0.11	313	0.04	217	1.34
social	532	0.08	176	0.02	210	1.69
childcare	149	0.02	1	0.00	205	7.31
global	223	0.03	22	0.00	204	3.43

to redress disadvantage, but then three of these four come in letters from anti-child-poverty campaigners.

What explains the far more pronounced attention to schools in the 2000s? I believe it reflects the *Times*'s conviction that in these years education has become far more of a problem, bearing on child poverty, than was judged to be the case in the 1970s. The intervening years saw a steadily growing tide of disquiet regarding the quality of state school education, particularly at the secondary level, with the emergence of new collocations such as *failing schools* and *sink schools*, and a greatly increased emphasis on testing, published evaluations of schools' performance and 'league tables' ostensibly aimed at 'driving up' quality. There was nothing like so extensive an overhaul or increase in funding. This all added to teacher stress and insecurity. There was widespread distrust of the existing arrangements, including local authority funding and oversight, leading to the promotion of academy schools funded directly by central government rather than the local authority. The covert message conveyed by much government policy and national press reporting of the state or public educational system (as distinct from the often elite independent schools) was that schools varied greatly in quality and that parents (mostly middle class, if *Times* readers) needed to take care over school choice. Otherwise their child might land up in one of the inadequate schools which it was implied were often all that was on offer to many of the children living in poverty.

On the basis of the list of most key keywords, the later corpus suggests that the editorial sections of the *Times* in the 2000s saw situations in which children and poverty were involved as also situations involving first-person speakers, females (the pronouns noted earlier), much talking or explaining, much negation, parents, families, people, Labour and its leaders Brown and Blair, both Britain and Africa, and schools. But state provisions in the way of benefits or allowances are not at the forefront, by mention or implication, nor represented as directly affecting child poverty, despite being frequently named in the 1970s discussions, where they were usually represented as important and in need of increased funding. The *Times* of the 2000s, comparatively speaking, seems to downplay the idea that child poverty can or should be combatted by welfare state interventions.

Why is *parents* so highly key in the 2000s (far more so than in the 1970s)? Parenting is thematized as relevant to child poverty in the 2000s in ways it was not thirty years earlier. Among the 836 instances, as many as 70 have *lone* and 30 have *single* in L1 position collocate; by contrast, there are just five instances of *married parents* (and eight of *unmarried parents*), ten of *two parents* and eight of *both parents*. A prominent message of these *lone/single-parent* sentences is that lone parents are less often in paid work than the *Times* deems appropriate:

(6) The average couple-family, where one partner has a job, is £1 a week better off than the average workless one-parent family because lone parents get so much extra support from the state, according to a study by the right-wing think tank, Centre for Policy Studies.

(7) Single parents could face tougher conditions and earlier work tests to encourage them to take jobs. At present half the lone parents in Britain work.

But whatever the detailed contextual information might reveal about the actual sense in which these phrases are used, these frequencies suggest that in the 2000s the *Times* represents child poverty as quite frequently linked to the presence of a single or lone parent (in the earlier corpus there are no instances of *single* or *lone* occurring immediately before *parent(s)* or *mother*). Arguably this emphasis moves beyond recognizing the correlation to implying a cause: if only these parents were not lone or single, their children would not be poor. Formulated thus, the implied solution is not for the state to provide lone parents with more benefits but for those parents to find a partner.

4.5 Key semantic domains in the 1970s and 2000s corpora compared

The calculation of key semantic domains in the two corpora (with BNC Written Informative as reference corpus) arguably yields even more revealing trends than a keyword calculation alone. A handful of the most key semantic domains are based on very few corpus instances (e.g. 'Degree', based on just eight instances of *relative/ly* in the 1970s corpus) or are essentially grammatical rather than lexical (e.g. 'Existing', based on many occurrences of *is, be, are* or *was*; or 'Pronouns', based on many occurrences of *it, I, that* in the 2000s corpus). When these are excluded and a frequency threshold of at least 0.2 per cent of the text is applied, the thirteen most key semantic domains in the two corpora are as listed in Tables 4.3 and 4.4, respectively, in descending order of keyness with the most frequent words instancing each category given in parentheses.

Clearly a number of these key domains are hierarchically or paraphrastically related, and tell their own story about UK childhood poverty in the 1970s and 2000s as viewed by the *Times*. In the 1970s this unsurprisingly involved lack of money, and debts. But the prominence of 'Food' as a key semantic domain is a sharp reminder that one of the most immediate reflexes of poverty is food problems: poor diet and unhealthy 'comfort' food. Sentences like the following, from an interview with one young mother of two children, are indicative:

(8) We don't go out anywhere except for Sunday dinner at my parents'. My dad comes and fetches us, we get a free meal and I do all the washing and clearing up for my mum, who suffers with arthritis. It usually takes me all afternoon but it's worth it. Before we started doing that we never had meat at all, except a tin of mince for a shepherd's pie, or a few sausages.

Not insignificantly the profile goes on to describe how the couple briefly fell behind with their council house rent because of wedding expenses but somehow managed to pay off the arrears. The story concludes:

(9) Social workers approve of Mrs. Matthews. She is one of the deserving poor, though, of course, they wouldn't say so.

Table 4.3 Key Semantic Domains in the *Times* '*Children + Poverty*' 1970s Corpus

Semantic Domain with Most Frequent Instantiations	Frequency in Corpus	Percentage of Corpus Text	Frequency in Reference Corpus	Percentage of Corpus Text	LL	Log Ratio
Money and pay (*allowances, income, tax*)	265	2.17	2,536	0.34	517	2.68
Money: Lack (*poverty, poor, poorest*)	87	0.71	152	0.02	410	5.13
Kin (*family, families, parents, mothers, wife, husband*)	185	1.52	2,123	0.28	308	2.41
People (*children, child*)	151	1.24	2,265	0.30	190	2.03
Helping (*benefit, benefits, support, services*)	157	1.29	3,796	0.51	99	1.34
Money: Debts (*poverty-trap, expenditure, pay, paid, spend*)	75	0.61	1,189	0.16	88	1.95
Unemployed (*unemployment*)	31	0.25	259	0.03	67	2.87
Government (*government, governments, income tax*)	120	0.98	3,330	0.45	57	1.14
Negative (*not, no*)	148	1.21	4,567	0.61	54	0.99
Strong Obligation (*should, need, must, necessary*)	132	1.08	3,891	0.52	54	1.05
Quantities: many/much (*increase, many, much*)	127	1.04	3,879	0.52	48	1.00
Money: Cost and price (*prices, cost*)	56	0.46	1,193	0.16	44	1.52
Food (*food, school meals, meal, cooked*)	70	0.57	2,068	0.28	28	1.05

Table 4.4 Key Semantic Domains in the *Times* 'Children + Poverty' 2000s Corpus

Semantic Domain with the Most Frequent Instantiations	Frequency in Corpus	Percentage of Corpus text	Frequency in Reference Corpus	Percentage of Corpus Text	LL	Log Ratio
People (*children, people, child*)	8,100	1.16	2,265	0.30	3,861	1.93
Money: Lack (*poverty, poor*)	2,589	0.71	152	0.02	2,780	4.18
Kin (*parents, family/ies, mother, father, mothers,* etc.)	6,070	1.52	2,123	0.28	2,238	1.61
Education (*school, education, schools, pupils*)	6,257	0.89	3,245	0.44	1,169	1.04
Money and pay (*tax, income, investment, credit*)	4,788	0.68	2,536	0.34	852	1.01
Speech: Communicative (*said, says, say, told, talk, story, speech*)	6,141	0.88	3,808	0.51	708	0.78
Government (*government, country, chancellor*)	5,374	0.77	3,330	0.45	621	0.78
Helping (*help, charity, support, aid, benefit, services*)	5,641	0.81	3,796	0.51	708	0.78
Residence (*home, living, live, homes*)	2,303	0.33	1,190	0.16	434	1.04
Knowledgeable (*news, know, known, experience*)	2,430	0.35	1,297	0.17	424	1.00
Crime (*crime, criminal*)	1,024	0.15	383	0.05	344	1.51
Disease (*disabled, AIDS, disease*)	1,639	0.24	868	0.12	286	1.00
Money: Debts (*spending, pay, spent, debt, spend, paid*)	1,937	0.28	1,189	0.16	230	0.79

Several of the top domains are predictably represented in stories that refer to children and poverty, so need little comment. 'People', 'Pronouns', 'Money: Lack' and 'Kin' are key domains in both corpora and on the basis of very similar sets of words. The prominence of 'Kin' in both periods reflects the *Times*' enduring view not only that children in poverty has much to do with their parents and family but also if children are to escape poverty, then parents and family should be principal agents of such change. The Keyness of 'Speech: Communicative' in the 2000s reflects the more extensive reporting of personal experience narratives in the *Times* and other newspapers in recent years.

Turning to other differences besides Education, discussed earlier, the 'Money and pay' domain requires comment. Like 'Money: Lack' it is present in both corpora, but in the 2000s it is represented by quite different high-frequency words (*tax, income, investment, credit*) than in the earlier corpus (*social security, allowances*). There is an intuitively clear link between the 1970s 'Money and pay' words and *poverty* (and even *children*), but there seems no obvious link between *poverty* and the 2000s 'Money and pay' words which seem rather to connect not with poverty but decent pay and prosperity. Since *tax* is by far the most frequent word in the 2000s corpus 'Money and pay' category, a few KWIC lines, harvested randomly, are presented below, to probe the tenor of this domain:

(10) However, the chancellor, who still remembers the 'tax bombshell' that destroyed Labour's general election campaign in 1992, will also want to address Tory claims about Britain's rising tax burden which were finally confirmed by Downing Street last week.
(11) And the children's tax credit, the first recognition of children in the tax system in a generation, provides up to £520 extra a year for five million families.
(12) But it is clear that thousands of households are not taking advantage of the existing tax break, either because they are unaware that they are eligible or because they simply find the forms far too confusing.
(13) This group [higher earners] has lost out as a result of Labour tax and benefit changes, the IFS estimates.
(14) They may not realize that the tax credits that boost their income are a deliberate Labour policy rather than a Revenue & Customs contrivance.

Could this be a tell-tale indication of a change of conception and representation of poverty in the later period? A closer look at how and why the word 'tax' is being used in the textual vicinity of mentions of child poverty reveals two things: one is that *tax* is often followed by *cuts* or *burden* in the corpus stories, arguably reflective of the *Times*'s general 2000s message that personal taxes were still too high and were themselves a cause of impoverishment of some families with children; the other is that *tax* is also often followed by *credit*, reflecting the fact that the Labour Government of that decade introduced the 'working families tax credit' as a means of topping up the low income of families where someone was in work, but poorly paid work. In a sense, employers were enabled to continue to pay poorly, thanks to this wages subsidy, which was created on the grounds that significantly raising the new statutory minimum wage levels might drive some employers out of business, making more people unemployed. In short, the newly prominent semantic domains in the 2000s *Times* corpus reflect a shift to a Script 1 explanatory account of child poverty and away from a Script 2 account. By implication, addressing the Money/pay dimension of child poverty still has to do with *income* and *tax* as before, but now it has less to do with *allowances* and more to do with *investment* and *credit*. And tellingly, while 'Unemployed' is a key semantic tag in the 1970s corpus it is not so by the 2000s, by which time the *Times* recognizes that in an era of zero-hours minimum wage jobs, unemployment is no longer a main cause of poverty any more than employment guarantees escape from it.

The 1970s corpus stories link child poverty with *social security* (as Table 4.1 confirms) and *allowances*, implying that both of these are 'naturally' involved where child poverty arises.[3] In the 2000s corpus, instead, the semantic domain of 'Helping' is prominent: where there is poverty there may well now be *help, charity, support* and *aid* – but these are far from necessarily state aid or statutory benefits, funded by the general tax take from individuals and companies. And, as the presence of 'Residence' among the key semantic domains suggests ('Alive' is also key, but falls just below the 0.2 per cent frequency threshold), there is more emphasis in the 2000s on the living conditions for children living in poverty, the kind and cost of the home they are being raised in, and what they or their parents – their mothers especially – say or tell about their lives (reflected in the sixth most key semantic domain).

4.6 From idleness to feckless?

Comment that is explicitly critical of the poor is infrequent in either the 1970s or 2000s corpus, but that is not to say that it is not powerful and telling when it does appear. Searching through the 1970s keyword list, the highest keyword with a prima facie critical colouring is the sixtieth, *idleness*. It is the only exemplar in the corpus of an item assigned to the Semantic domain of 'Unused' (A1.5.1–), and there are four instances (making it 0.03 per cent of the text, LL 28). Until one examines their use in context, there is no knowing quite how *idleness* is being related to child poverty or by whom, but the keyness of this evaluative term (low frequency, admittedly) made it of interest. If the word 'idleness' is one that is contentiously associated with a Script 1 attitude to poverty, then certainly another is the more negative near-synonym, *feckless(ness)*. I accordingly searched for this word, too, in the 1970s corpus, and then looked for all instances in the corpus of words classed in the same Semtags as *feckless*, namely A1.5.1–'Unused' and S1.2.5–'Weak', respectively.

The four 1970s corpus instances of *idleness* occur in just two texts, two letters. The first two come in rapid succession in a letter from Mr Ralph Howell, Conservative MP, September 1975:

(15) It [our crazy tax and benefit system] is a system which rewards idleness as effectively as it penalizes effort.

(16) Not only are increasing numbers of the low paid unable, by their own efforts, to escape dependence on the state but the taxes which they pay are used to maintain others in idleness, whose income can often exceed the take-home pay of those at work.

And the second pair come in equally rapid succession in a letter from Dr Richard Lawson on 6 September 1977, protesting at the complacency with which a *Times* leader on 24 August had opined that the then high unemployment level was a reality to be accepted:

(17) In the second place enforced idleness and poverty is inevitably going to drive a proportion of jobless teenagers into crime, which quite apart from the social disruption costs the economy in insurance, police, courts, prisons and probation services.

(18) Thirdly unemployment is in itself a severe psychological stress, through idleness, boredom, purposelessness, loss of self-respect and abuse from misinformed neighbours.

In short, use of *idleness* is very limited in the 1970s corpus, and comes in the comments of just two correspondents.

As for Semtag S1.2.5–'Weak', there are just three uses in all, only one of which has the relevant critical inflection, *feckless*, the others being *vulnerable* and *susceptible*. This single use of *feckless* comes in an editorial on 8 September 1970, in which the *Times* urges an increase in family allowances on the new Conservative Government. It acknowledges that their recommendation 'will not appeal to those people, and there are more of them than well-meaning social reformers sometimes appreciate, who regard family allowances as an encouragement to feckless breeding'. Thus, *feckless* is a judgement attributed to those opposed to increased allowances for poor families, an opposition which the editorial explicitly rejects, going on to say that letting children remain in acute poverty to punish the parents is 'barbaric and futile'.

In the much larger 2000s corpus the use of *idleness* or other A1.5.1– words is even more scarce, proportionately: only two instances of *idleness* and only fourteen words in the Semtag A1.5.1–'Unused' semantic category, thus of negligible frequency, and overwhelmingly words without any bearing on poverty: *untapped, disused, write-offs*. Of the *idleness* cases, one is irrelevant as it relates to the Nauru islanders, while the other comes in a compassionate commentary from (again) Libby Purves, where she reaffirms the principle that the able-bodied should earn their keep while she also understands the entrenched pessimism and dependency in many of the UK long-term unemployed. *Idleness* is not a fair judgement on them:

(19) That [fatalism and nihilism in some of the British long-term unemployed], not simple idleness, is the difference between a second-generation British refusenik and an ambitious Pole who still believes, owing to his very different national history, that life's natural path leads upwards.

What, finally, of *feckless* and *fecklessness*, and other items from the Semtag S1.2.5–'Weak' category in the 2000s corpus? In this much larger corpus, Semtag S1.2.5–'Weak' comprises 0.3 per cent of the corpus, but overwhelmingly the most frequent item here is *vulnerable* (84 of 192 instances), that is, weakness of a non-culpable kind. Of these 192 items, only the 12 instances of *feckless* and 1 of *fecklessness* carry the negative judgement of relevance here. Here are the thirteen uses in their sentential contexts:

(20) 'It is definitely time we exploded the popular myth that most lone parents are feckless teenagers trying to get council flats.' [Joanne K. Rowling]

(21) Back in the Fifties, Ohio housewife Evelyn Ryan supported her ten children and feckless husband by entering contests for advertising jingles. [Lisa Kennedy]

(22) There is one other inescapable conclusion from the book – it is the women's addiction to unstable relationships with feckless men that is to blame for most of their problems. [Daniel Finkelstein]

(23) For other campaigners the principal enemy is made up of feckless, grasping fathers, who cannot be persuaded by argument to support their own kids, and who therefore must be compelled to do so. [David Aaronovitch]

(24) '[Families living in poverty] are people who we work with. They're not A. N. Other group that we don't see who are feckless or cut away from the mainstream of society', she says. [Fay Schopen]

(25) Here you are struck by the feckless lack of ambition among children in working-class areas. The problem we face is not simply a matter of money. We are dealing with a poverty of the heart and the mind and spirit, a poverty that saps all ambition and initiative. [letter from Brian Davis, 14 December 2007]

(26) 'They are helping to bust the myth that poverty is just down to feckless parents.' [headline to article by Dame Elisabeth Hoodless of Community Service Volunteers]

(27) They are helping to bust the myth that poverty is just down to feckless parents. [in body-text of same article as no. 24]

(28) One pervasive caricature is that of 'feckless people on benefits', he says. Half the children living in poverty have a parent who works. [Emily Ford, interviewing Martin Narey of Barnardo's]

(29) Poverty? In modern Britain? Yeah, yeah, we all know what that's really about, don't we? Feckless parents who waste all their money on widescreen TVs and booze and don't have enough left for the children. We know the type. But the truth is, we don't have a clue what modern social deprivation means. [Melanie Reid]

(30) [The Government's capital gains and inheritance tax benefits for affluent married couples are] Not exactly the sort of incentives that might encourage a feckless absent father on a sink estate to enter into the bliss that is holy matrimony. [Andrew Ellson, Personal Finance editor]

(31) This is always a tale of mutually assured redemption, the poor and their charities become richer financially, and the millionaires richer emotionally

as they realise that the poor are not always feckless and some even deserving. [Andrew Billen, reviewing the weekend's TV]
(32) Sooner or later, fleeting relationship will be followed by pregnancy, single parenthood and a plunge into a benefits culture designed to reward fecklessness. [Andrew Norfolk, on deprivation passed from parents to children, as in the Shannon Matthews case]

These various instances confirm that 'feckless' is very much in use, as a description of the inadequacy of the poor or the unemployed. In addition, the feckless are usually men, fathers or parents, never explicitly women (although no. 20 is likely to be referring to a *female* teenager). While several of the contributions clearly emphasize that the idea is myth or caricature, at least as many use the term evidently believing it contains a kind of truth (items 21, 22, 23, 25, 30, 31 to some extent and 32). Even if partly denied, the fecklessness of the poor is also partly acknowledged and presupposed: the poor are *not always* feckless (but yes, sometimes they are); poverty is not just down to feckless parents (but it is in part). And indeed, if one looks again at the quotation from Libby Purves, denying that the British long-term unemployed are in thrall to idleness, there is more than a hint, in her diagnosis of 'fatalism and nihilism', that they are prone to fecklessness. Evaluating the poor as *feckless* is a Script 1-advancing stereotyping which the *Times* of the 2000s is unashamed to adopt, whereas the *Times* of the 1970s inferably shuns such an evaluation.

4.7 Conclusion

Children growing up in poverty was a far more widespread problem in Britain in the 2000s (and since then) than it was in the 1970s. In both decades, the *Times* represents child poverty as regrettable and a cause of many numerous undesirable consequences. But what does the newspaper implicitly advise its voting readership they should ensure be done about it? The evidence from the 1970s corpus suggests that in that decade the newspaper endorsed state intervention along lines broadly consonant with Script 2 thinking: a generously funded universal child benefit was commended, as was more state investment in social housing and schools: doing less was judged unfair. But the 2000s corpus evidence suggests that by and in the later decade the *Times* was largely of the view that a Script 1 story was appropriate, in which poverty is largely the personal responsibility of the individual just as their children are. Trying to make everyone responsible for solving the problems of the poor and their children (e.g. through high taxation) would be to impose an unreasonable burden on the majority: it would be doing more than was fair. Two elements, within the power of the state to provide and instrumental in the eradication of cross-generational poverty, are decent housing and decent schools. The *Times* 2000s corpus represents these as beyond the power of the modern state to guarantee for all children. Most parents can provide them for most children; for those impoverished parents who cannot, it is unfortunate but simply in the nature of harsh reality that their children must accept inferior housing and schooling. There is no reasonable and affordable alternative.

Notes

1 A persistent embarrassment for this Script's ostensible compassion for the disabled is the strong correlation between disability and poverty, with nearly half of all families living in poverty containing a member who is disabled. See the Social Metrics Commission (2019: 4).
2 No great significance attaches to the alphanumeric labels for the semantic domains identified by the automatic tagger used in Wmatrix (the UCREL Semantic Analysis System) (Rayson 2009). Distinct semantic areas are distinguished by the letters of the alphabet, up to three levels of numbering, and suitable use of + and − signs. For example, S1.1.3+ is the specific domain for words relating to 'Participating' (e.g. *meeting, conference*), while S1.1.3− is the tag assigned to words concerning 'Non-participating' (e.g. *absence, truancy*).
3 The fact that *social security* is identified as a keyword (phrase) in Table 4.1 but does not reappear among the key semantic domain instantiations in Table 4.3 (or Table 4.4) reflects a difficulty with automated semantic analysis. For purposes of semantic categorization Wmatrix notes the many uses of the word *social* and only classifies half of those concerning social security or benefits as I1.1 (Money and pay), the other half being classified as S1.1.1 (Social Actions).

5

Inequality, accountability and responsibility in UK Press reporting on corporate fraud (2004–14) and modern slavery (2000–16)

Ilse A. Ras

5.1 Introduction

Over the past few years, I have been collecting data on how UK newspapers report on crimes that relate to wealth inequality, specifically looking at how reporting of these crimes maintain such wealth inequality and are made possible through it. I first focused on corporate fraud, as this is an explicit instance of an economically powerful party using its economic power to retain its advantage and to disadvantage less economically powerful parties; I have also, more recently, concentrated on modern slavery (which includes human trafficking), as non-exploitative work is a key factor in enabling economically disadvantaged people to challenge economic inequality. Corporate fraud and modern slavery are referred to as 'sets of crimes' here because, as I will explain in Section 5.2, both are umbrella terms that cover a range of behaviours outlawed under UK law. Whereas the stereotypical view of crime is that of volume crimes, for example vandalism and pickpocketing, or violent crimes, taken to have been committed by those belonging to less (or under-) privileged or marginalized communities, modern slavery and corporate fraud instead tend to be 'crimes of the powerful' (see Sutherland 1949). These are crimes committed by (or on behalf of) and/or primarily benefiting those belonging to a (global, economic) elite community. Both crimes externalize the costs of doing business, thereby further entrenching these beneficiaries' powerful positions and increasing the precarity of the already precarious. While corporate fraud benefits some among the global corporate elite, with little attention paid to the effects on those less economically powerful, modern slavery more directly oppresses some among the global poor.

This chapter aims to explore how newspapers neg(oti)ate and understand (in) equality, responsibility and accountability in the context of reporting on these sets of crimes that perpetuate global *unfairnesses*. These neg(oti)ations are read as techniques of neutralization (Sykes and Matza 1957; Thompson 1980). Techniques of neutralization are those arguments used by, as termed by Sykes and Matza (1957), delinquents, to render an act of delinquency less unacceptable to themselves and others in their direct social environment.

I will first set out what 'corporate fraud' and 'modern slavery' mean (in a criminological sense) and what they have in common (Section 5.2). I will then explain the techniques of neutralization that are relevant to my analysis (Section 5.3), as well as the methods used to collect and analyse my corpora (Section 5.4). I will finally show how the concepts of (in)equality, responsibility and accountability are used in the context of British newspaper reporting on corporate fraud and modern slavery (Section 5.5), with some concluding remarks at the end of this chapter (Section 5.6).

5.2 Corporate fraud and modern slavery

Corporate fraud and modern slavery are similar in a number of ways. Beyond the idea that they are unfair exploitations of a flawed system (in that they maintain, create and depend on (global) wealth inequality that leaves victims even more vulnerable to that exploitation), both rely on deception, benefit relatively powerful offenders and come at an enormous economic and social cost.

Let us first focus on deception. The UK Fraud Act 2006 suggests that fraud is the failure to enable the victim to give informed consent to a decision (usually financial) from which the offender intends to profit and which exposes the victim to (financial) loss. Similarly, the UK Modern Slavery Act 2015 prohibits inducing a person 'to provide services of any kind, ... to provide another person with benefits of any kind, or ... to enable another person to acquire benefits of any kind' through 'force, threats or *deception*' (emphasis mine). The majority of instances of modern slavery and human trafficking occur when someone is deceived about the exploitative conditions of a job, for instance about the kind of work that is done (see Darbyshire 2000) or about the debt that is incurred to obtain the job in the first place (International Labour Office and Walk Free Foundation 2017).

That corporate fraud and modern slavery are 'crimes of the powerful' (see Sutherland 1949) is most clear when considering corporate fraud, which, by definition, is committed by, or on behalf of, a corporation (Fraud Act 2006). While certainly not all corporations are rich and powerful, many are. Babic, Heemskerk and Fichtner (2018) noted that, according to 2016 revenues, of the top 100 economic entities in the world, 71 are corporations. Similarly, it is the globally privileged who benefit from modern slavery, although 'globally privileged' here indicates a rather wider group of actors/perpetrators, including, again, corporations, but also, more broadly, Western consumers, the latter of whom benefit, for instance, from low prices. These actors benefit, primarily, through externalizing the costs of doing business, as forced and low-wage labour keep salaries low, and a disregard for labour conditions (such as health and safety) enables employers to keep other labour-related costs low. Furthermore, a lack of secure labour relations, which is a marker of exploitative labour also without going to the extremes of modern slavery, enables the company to lay off workers in times of limited production, and re-hire them when production picks up, thereby externalizing business risks by increasing worker precarity. In other words, forced labour in the private sector often entails a transfer of wages and security that labourers would have had if their employment had been more secure and paid at a non-exploitative rate, from labourers to employers and employment agents. It must be noted here that the ultimate responsibility does not necessarily lie with the direct employer or agent, but may also be attributed to the company delivering a product to the end-consumer – who can play off suppliers and thus force suppliers to reduce production costs even further – and may even be attributed to the consumer, whose primary criterion for selecting a product is also often the price.

5.3 Discoursal techniques of neutralization

It is important to consider what equality, responsibility and accountability mean, in the first place, in the context of a particular crime or unfairness, in order to address where responsibility and accountability lie and to tackle that unfairness and the systematic factors that allow for that unfairness to persist. When we ask the question of how we decide what (criminal) responsibility is, and where it lies or should lie, we must also refer to Sykes and Matza's (1957) theory of techniques of neutralization. According to this theory, people use certain arguments both before and after their committing a deviant act to mitigate their sense of guilt and shame, which would otherwise keep them from committing that act and/or damage their self-image (1957). These arguments are, they argue, generally learnt through interactions rather than invented (1957). In this regard, this theory draws on Sutherland's (with Cressey 1955) theory that one cannot commit a criminal act without learning both the techniques and justifications for committing that act. Sykes and Matza describe five of these arguments or techniques of neutralization: 'denial of responsibility', or the defence that the accused should not be held responsible for that act (due to not having done it, not having done it intentionally or not having a choice but to do it); 'denial of harm or injury', or the argument that it cannot have been wrong to commit the act, as no party was adversely affected; 'denial of the victim', which is victim blaming by the offender; 'condemnation of the condemners', which is the defence that those condemning the act have no grounds for doing so; and 'appeal to higher loyalties', which is the defence that the criminal act serves a higher cause (Sykes and Matza 1957).

These techniques may be used by both 'stereotypical' criminals and non-traditional offenders, such as corporate criminals (Stadler and Benson 2012). Similarly, Piquero, Tibbetts and Blankenship (2005) suggested that MBA students, presented with a hypothetical case that allowed for corporate offending, would generally suggest that the pursuit of profit justified that offending. The use of such defences is not limited to individual corporate offenders; Fooks et al. (2012) showed that corporate social responsibility (CSR) documents are used to defend potentially questionable corporate behaviour. Thompson (1980: 907–8) noted that institutional denials of responsibility often occur through the blaming of external circumstances (1980: 907), thereby transferring the blame, or by blaming the collective without reference to the responsibility of an individual person who is part of it (1980: 908), thereby diluting it.

The current study contributes to this body of work by not examining the texts directly produced by corporations, like CSR documentation is, or arguments directly presented by (those being trained to be) executives, or the views communicated by those negatively affected by these crimes, but by examining how these topics are covered by a supposed third party, being British newspapers. These, in turn, may be taken to affect and reflect the views of a broader population that may have the power to ignore, approve of or take measures against these kinds of acts, for instance through investment and consumption decisions and through pushing for (either directly or through electoral choices) legislation and the enforcement thereof.

5.4 Method and data

5.4.1 Data

My interest in this regard is in the understanding of the words *equality, inequality, responsibility* and *accountability* in the contexts of reporting on corporate fraud and modern slavery; explorations of how corporate fraud and modern slavery are reported on by UK newspapers in general may be found in, respectively, Ras (2017) and Gregoriou and Ras (2018). The corpora used in this study cover reporting on corporate fraud and modern slavery in British newspapers in recent years.

5.4.1.1 Corporate fraud corpus

The corpus on corporate fraud (hereafter CFC, for corporate fraud corpus) was collected manually through Nexis database and includes articles, without restriction of newspaper section, published between January 2004 and December 2014 by the *Daily Mail*, the *Daily Telegraph*, the *Guardian*, the *Mirror*, the *Sun*, the *Times*, the *Financial Times*, *Mail on Sunday*, the *Sunday Times* and the *Sunday Telegraph*. This corpus was initially collected to analyse and compare how major (defined by circulation numbers) UK daily and Sunday newspapers write about corporate fraud, per newspaper, rather than how UK national newspapers write about corporate fraud as a collective; this is why specifically these newspapers, rather than all UK national newspapers as categorized by Nexis, were selected. The time period selected covers four years prior to the 2008 global economic crisis (2004–07), the three years that may be considered as the peak of the global economic crisis (2008–10) and four years of the aftermath of the crisis (2011–14). December 2014 was furthermore a natural cut-off point for this corpus as data collection began in 2015. The query term initially used was 'corporate fraud', as well as the names of certain companies tried in the United Kingdom and the United States for fraud, including Enron, as covered in Rosoff, Pontell and Tillman's case studies of white-collar and corporate crime (2010). US cases were included in the queries, too, as US cases are also likely to be of interest to British readers (due to cultural proximity; see Jewkes 2011, 54–5, and thus likely to also be featured in British newspapers). Subsequent search terms were generated by qualitatively assessing the search results, that is reading the recovered articles and selecting potential search

Table 5.1 Articles, Types and Tokens per Year in the Corporate Fraud Corpus (CFC)

Year	Articles	Types	Tokens
2004	8,473	52,656	4,568,865
2005	7,105	52,928	3,848,977
2006	12,577	55,835	7,609,680
2007	6,888	54,847	4,054,348
2008	7,102	54,908	4,448,648
2009	7,350	56,784	4,780,530
2010	6,825	64,018	4,038,959
2011	6,893	58,316	4,249,610
2012	9,959	64,880	6,483,916
2013	9,775	59,450	5,563,421
2014	7,496	58,074	4,594,969
Total	90,443	632,696	54,241,923

terms from these articles. A full list of used query terms is included as an appendix to Ras (2017). Each article recovered using these query terms was then examined for relevance, defined as covering any aspect of a case of corporate fraud, which was in turn defined as an act of fraud committed by someone in the corporation on behalf of and for the benefit of the said corporation, from the point of allegation onwards (see Ras 2017: 23); articles that were recovered using the search terms that did not relate to corporate fraud were not included in the corpus. For instance, when searching for the name of a company accused of corporate fraud, articles about other goings-on at this company, such as acquisitions and the hiring/firing of executives, were also recovered, but not included in the final corpus. Table 5.1 details the number of articles, types and tokens in each year of the corpus in the CFC.

5.4.1.2 *Modern slavery corpus*

The corpus on modern slavery and human trafficking (hereafter MSC, for Modern Slavery Corpus) was also collected through Nexis (Gregoriou and Ras 2018), using the method set out by Gabrielatos (2007). Gabrielatos (2007) suggests first selecting a number of core search terms.[1] The following core search terms were selected: 'human trafficking', 'human trafficker', 'trafficking (in/of) human being/s', 'slavery', 'sexual exploitation', 'sex trafficking', 'sexual trafficking', 'sex slave' and 'forced labour'. The aim was to collect articles published between January 2000, as the UN Protocol to Prevent, Suppress and Punish Trafficking in Persons, Especially Women and Children was adopted in 2000, and December 2016, as data collection began in the last quarter of 2016; this also allowed the corpus to contain reporting on the debates in the UK Commons and Lords leading up to the adoption of the 2015 Modern Slavery Act, as well as its direct aftermath. Keyword lists for each of these sample corpora were subsequently generated through comparison with the BNC Written Sampler, after which the potential of each keyword to serve as an additional search term was evaluated through Gabrielatos's (2007) Relative Query Term Relevance (RQTR) score, which indicates the relevance of a potential search term relative to a baseline established by the relevance of the core search terms. The relevance of search terms is calculated based on the number of results each core and potential search term generates. The resultant list of search terms was then used to collect news articles from Nexis over the period from January 2000 to December 2016, limited to those sources Nexis marks as 'UK national newspapers', as the aim of this corpus was to consider how UK national newspapers as a collective write about modern slavery and human trafficking. The newspapers labelled as such by Nexis were Business, the *Daily Edition*, the *Daily Mail*, the *Daily Star*, the *Daily Star Sunday*, the *Daily Telegraph*, the *Express*, the *Guardian*, the *Independent*, the *Independent on Sunday*, the *Mail on Sunday*, the *Mirror*, the *New Review*, the *Observer*, *People*, the *Saturday Magazine*, the *Sun*, the *Sunday Business*, the *Sunday Express*, the *Sunday Mirror*, the *Sunday Times* and the *Times*. Table 5.2 details the number of articles, types and tokens in each year of the corpus in the MSC.

Whereas the CFC covers reporting over the years 2004–14, the MSC covers a longer period, 2000–16. Furthermore, due to differences in the selection criteria for the newspapers to include, the MSC also includes reporting by sources labelled by Nexis as being UK national newspapers that are not included in the CFC. That said, there is a substantial overlap between the two corpora, both in terms of time frame and in terms of sources included. As this chapter examines overall linguistic trends, rather than more granular aspects of the data, these differences in corpora are perhaps less problematic than they would have been otherwise.

It would be worth expanding the CFC in future to include reporting from all UK national newspapers in the period 2000–03, and to change both corpora from being

Table 5.2 Articles, Types and Tokens per Year in the Modern Slavery Corpus (MSC)

Year	Articles	Types	Tokens
2000	3,233	67,084	2,782,086
2001	3,836	68,787	3,079,180
2002	3,419	66,055	2,732,868
2003	3,582	68,225	2,852,935
2004	3,755	71,571	3,109,448
2005	3,953	72,075	3,259,880
2006	4,481	72,288	3,348,225
2007	5,455	75,074	3,844,481
2008	4,523	72,155	3,350,278
2009	4,719	73,840	3,472,340
2010	4,670	83,163	3,438,550
2011	4,765	77,125	3,551,722
2012	5,207	77,427	3,913,563
2013	6,241	78,956	4,314,405
2014	6,121	82,279	4,393,221
2015	7,361	89,057	5,909,450
2016	6,448	81,981	5,194,704
Total	81,769	1,277,142	62,547,336

static samples to being monitor corpora, that is to continue collecting news articles by UK newspapers on these topics.

5.4.2 Method

First, it was determined which words in these corpora specifically indicate accountability, responsibility and the states of being accountable and responsible, as well as *inequality* and *equality*. This was done by generating corpus outputs for the search terms *accountab** and *reponsib** in AntConc (Anthony 2019), whereby the asterisk serves as a wildcard for multiple characters. The relevant target words became *accountability, accountable, equality, inequality, responsibility, responsibilities, responsible,* and *responsibly*. I considered and compared some relatively simple relative frequencies on the usage of these various target words in the two corpora, examining also whether these differences were statistically significant by generating a log-likelihood value (see Table 5.3). This was done following Rayson (n.d.), who indicates the following correspondences between log-likelihood and p-value:

- '95th percentile; 5% level; $p < 0.05$; critical value = 3.84'
- '99th percentile; 1% level; $p < 0.01$; critical value = 6.63'
- '99.9th percentile; 0.1% level; $p < 0.001$; critical value = 10.83'
- '99.99th percentile; 0.01% level; $p < 0.0001$; critical value = 15.13'

Secondly, c-collocates were obtained for each of these target words. C-collocates, or constant collocates, are those words that collocate with one (or more) of the target words with a frequency above a certain threshold, across a certain number of pre-determined years (Gabrielatos and Baker 2008). Rather than setting an absolute frequency threshold, I set a relative frequency threshold of 0.1 per cent of the total number of collocates for a particular target word (rounded to the nearest positive integer). In other words, only those collocate types with a frequency above $1/1000^{th}$ of the total number of collocates would be counted as 'present' among the collocates for that target noun in that year. The relative number of years in which a collocate had to

Table 5.3 Relative Frequencies and Log-Likelihood Values for 'Equality', 'Inequality', 'Responsibility' and 'Accountability'

Target Noun	MSC Relative Frequency (%)	CFC Relative Frequency (%)	Corpus with Higher Relative Frequency	Log-Likelihood Value
Equality	0.00507	0.00057	MSC	2351.34
Inequality	0.00239	0.00067	MSC	582.49
Responsibilities	0.00184	0.00322	CFC	223.13
Responsibility	0.00957	0.01285	CFC	281.57
Responsible	0.01033	0.01303	CFC	181.62
Responsibly	0.00031	0.00060	CFC	3410.29
Accountability	0.00117	0.00248	CFC	282.52
Accountable	0.00104	0.00205	CFC	196.84

have a high enough frequency (i.e. about 0.1 per cent) to be counted as 'present' was set to 60 per cent, meaning that, as the MSC covers seventeen years, the collocates for each of the target words had to occur with a relative frequency of 0.1 per cent of all collocates (per year) across eleven years. For the CFC, a collocate had to occur with a relative frequency of 0.1 per cent in seven out of eleven years. Function words were excluded from the resultant lists of c-collocates for each target word and the remaining content words were manually categorized into semantic domains. Where further examination was necessary, concordances for certain 'target noun + c-collocate' combinations were generated to examine a particular collocational pattern in more depth.

5.5 Inequality, responsibility and accountability in the corpora

5.5.1 Frequencies

What Table 5.3 shows is that there is a significant difference between the corpora in the use of the selected target words. *Equality* and *inequality* are substantially overused in the MSC, whereas the items relating to responsibility are overused in the CFC. This difference in the prevalence of these terms indicates that responsibility and accountability are less often discussed, relatively speaking, in the context of news reporting on modern slavery. It must be noted here, however, that (corporate) responsibility is not entirely absent from the agenda on measures against modern slavery. For instance, section 54 of the Modern Slavery Act 2015 asks all commercial organizations doing business in the UK that have an annual turnover greater than £36 million to publish an annual statement of the measures taken to prevent and remediate modern slavery in their supply chains. However, this legislation was introduced towards the end of the corpus, whereas the US Sarbanes-Oxley Act 2002, which focuses on the accountability of corporations for the veracity of corporate financial statements, was introduced before the start of the CFC. As such, it is perhaps not surprising that items relating to responsibility are less prevalent in the MSC.

Given that there is such a difference in the prevalence of these topics in the respective corpora, we may also expect that the c-collocates will be equally varied; for example, we may expect a greater variety of c-collocates for *equality* in the MSC than in the CFC, but for *responsibility* and *accountability* in the CFC than the MSC. A glance at Table 5.4, Table 5.5, Table 5.6 and Table 5.7 shows that this intuition bears out.

5.5.2 C-Collocates

5.5.2.1 *Equality and inequality*

Table 5.4 shows the c-collocates for the target word *equality* in, respectively, modern slavery and corporate fraud news reporting. What both corpora appear to have in common is an understanding of equality as something of which relates, particularly,

Table 5.4 C-collocates for 'Equality' in the Modern Slavery Corpus (MSC) and Corporate Fraud Corpus (CFC)

	MSC	CFC
Material actions	Act, work, struggle, fight, achieve	
Increases	More, greater, some	More
Types	Racial, gender, race, sexual, gay, economic, political	Gender, racial, race
Boulomaic	Need, like	
Deontic	Will, would, should, must	Will, would
Geography	Up, world, out	
Justice	Justice, freedom, equality, opportunity, liberty, fairness, equal, diversity, respect, rights, true	Rights
Time	Before, when, now, still	New
Negation	No, not	
Actors	Commission, women, human, men, society, people, minister, party, labour, government, public	Commission, women, human
Verbal/written actions	Law, said, says, say, bill, promote	Law
Possession	Have, has, had	Has

Table 5.5 C-collocates for 'Inequality' in the Modern Slavery Corpus (MSC) and Corporate Fraud Corpus (CFC)

	MSC	CFC
Material actions	Tackle	
Increases	More, some, growing, levels, high	Rising
Types	Gender, racial, racism, sexual, poverty, economic, income, wealth, poor, rich	Income, poverty
Deontic	Will, would	
Geography	Global, world, out	
Justice	Injustice, power	
Time	When, still	Time
Negation	Not, no	Not
Actors	Women, people	
Verbal/written actions	Said	
Possession	Has, had, have	Has

to gender and race (rather than social class), as suggested through c-collocates such as 'gender' and 'racial', and which is something to continue to strive for, as suggested by c-collocates relating to increase ('more', 'greater').

This desire for greater *equality* is especially pronounced in the MSC, also through the inclusion of material actions ('achieve') and verbal actions ('promote'). Concordances show that *equality*, in the MSC, is 'fought' for and 'achieved':

(1) No one needs a history degree to know the *fight for equality* and popular democracy did not end, with the American Civil War, in 1865. (emphasis mine)
(2) But perhaps the biggest victim of this hagiography is the anti-slavery movement itself: one of the greatest popular political movements in British

Table 5.6 C-collocates for 'Responsibility' in the Modern Slavery Corpus (MSC) and Corporate Fraud Corpus (CFC)

	MSC	CFC
Material actions	Do, actions, work, act, bear, face, caring	Actions, do, ensuring, behave, act, acted, behaving, bear, making, protection
Business	Corporate, business	Corporate, business
Money	Investments	Financial, market, investments, losses, credit, fiduciary
Actors	People, children, collective, minister, individual, others, other, man, men, group, child, police, government, companies, company	Management, bank, board, banks, directors, executive, firms, authority, FSA, people, shareholders, regulators, chairman, consumer, group, minister, individuals, body, customers, lenders, government, powers, public, companies, company
Increase	More, some, much, many, very, most	More, full, some, very, additional, many, fully, well, most
Time	New, now, when, after, before	Ultimately, new, when, now, after
Geography	Up, Britain, out, world, way	Up, office, out, directly, way, UK
Adjectives	Social, personal, socially, moral	Social, personal, seriously, legal
Negation/lack	Not, no	Not, no
Verbal/written actions	Said, says, state	Regulating, regulation, regulatory, said, lies, says
Visibility		Oversight, overseeing, visible
Possession	Have, take, has, had, accept, own, taking, took, claimed, share, rights, given, takes, assume, held	Take, has, have, had, taking, accept, took, accepted, own, given, takes, share, rights, taken, include, held, hold

history, and in many ways the prototype of every reform movement since – from the campaigns over suffrage and factory hours, to anti-apartheid and *the fight for racial equality and gay rights* – with its combination of legal challenges, parliamentary lobbying and popular agitation. (emphasis mine)

In the CFC, material actions such 'fight' simply do not recur sufficiently often enough to count as c-collocates to *equality*.

Additionally, the MSC appears to understand *equality* as a much broader concept than the CFC does. In the context of modern slavery, *equality* does not just refer to economic equality, but also to concepts such as *justice, freedom, opportunity, liberty, fairness, diversity, respect* and *human rights*. Furthermore, c-collocates for *equality* in the MSC include a greater number of actors who are either affected by or work to affect *equality*, including *men, society, minister*, the *Labour Party*, the *government* and the *public*, beyond the *commission* and *women* that both corpora have in common.

Table 5.5 shows the c-collocates for the target word *inequality* in, respectively, modern slavery and corporate fraud news reporting. Both corpora discuss increases in types of *inequality*. There is, again, a greater recognition of the dimensions of *inequality* in the MSC. Whereas the MSC focuses on multiple types of *inequality*, the CFC only recognizes, here, again, income inequality. Furthermore, the MSC again explicitly notes efforts to tackle *inequality*, which is again largely absent from the CFC.

Table 5.7 C-collocates for 'Accountability' in the Modern Slavery Corpus (MSC) and Corporate Fraud Corpus (CFC)

	MSC	CFC
Material actions	Actions, make, made, making	Actions, performance, efforts, make, made, making
Business	Corporate	Corporate
Money		Financial
Actors	Companies, people, police, government, public	Companies, management, board, directors, executive, banks, bank, company, office, shareholders, investors, executives, regulators, institutions, people, boards, managers, individuals, FSA, government, law, parliament, system, public
Improve/increase	More, greater, some	Greater, more, better, improve, increase, some, fully, properly
Time	New	New, last, now, while, when
Geography	Local, way	Way, local
Adjectives/adverbs	Democratic	Independent, personally, political, democratic, responsible
Negation/lack	No, lack, not	Little, lack, not, no
Verbal/written/mental actions	Said	Decisions, regulation, Sarbanes-Oxley, said, says, report
Visibility	Transparency, transparent	Transparency, clear, openness, open, transparent
Possession	Have, has, held, hold, holding	Has, have, had, held, hold, holding

Reporting on corporate fraud does not, in general, seem to recognize the links between (in)equality and corporate fraud, whereas modern slavery is much more explicitly linked to various types of (in)equality, beyond the simply economic.

5.5.2.2 Responsibility

Table 5.6 shows the c-collocates for the target words *responsibility*, *responsibilities*, *responsible* and *responsibly*, together indicating the concept of responsibility in, respectively, modern slavery and corporate fraud news reporting. Both corpora appear to understand *responsibility* as something that one has/accepts/takes, or does 'not' have/accept/take, and again something of which more is needed. 'More', in this regard, appears to mean not just more of one type (multiple varieties, such as 'social', 'personal' and 'legal', are mentioned) but also the taking up of additional responsibilities (as in 'new'). Furthermore, in both corpora, mention is made of CSR, which is not surprising given the tendency for CSR reports to often cover topics such as the anti-fraud and anti-slavery measures taken by the company.

However, there is a much greater sense of urgency in taking up and assigning *responsibility* in the CFC than in the MSC, as indicated through such c-collocates as 'ensuring'. This urgency is also illustrated by the sheer number of actors who are linked to *responsibility* in the CFC, which suggests that a key element of reporting on corporate fraud remains that question of where *responsibility* lies; for example, does it lie with those companies actually committing fraud or with the agencies tasked with regulating and examining corporate behaviour?

What concordances show is that while there is an acknowledgement that corporations and their executives should bear at least some *responsibility* for corporate fraud (their *actions*), there is also a constant emphasis on other responsible parties, specifically regulators. This may imply that corporate fraud is not (just) the fault of the corporate fraudsters but also of those parties tasked with monitoring and enforcing regulations for failing to prevent it. This corresponds to Thompson's (1980) category of *transfer of responsibility*, which allows those executives responsible for the actual act of corporate fraud to neutralize or minimize their perceived responsibility. Examples of these tendencies are the following:

(3) At the end of the day, rogues are still *the responsibility of the company*. (emphasis mine)
(4) Under an agreement between AIG and the justice department, the company *accepted responsibility for the actions of its employees* in the General Re and Capco transactions. (emphasis mine)
(5) This lawsuit is an attempt by Barclays to avoid taking *responsibility for its own actions*. (emphasis mine)
(6) But, *as a regulator, you have a responsibility* to point out the vulnerability you see in the industry. (emphasis mine)

Note in example (5), however, the euphemistic nature of a word such as 'actions', which downplays the gravity of the actual crimes of which Barclays is accused. In other words, where corporations *do* assume responsibility, they downplay the thing for which they take responsibility, which corresponds to Sykes and Matza's (1957) *denial of harm and injury*.

While the question of *responsibility* is much more urgent in the CFC, that does not mean it is absent from the MSC. In the MSC, however, *responsibility* is diluted, rather than transferred, by linking it primarily to organizations in the plural or in list form, and through the concept of 'shared' *responsibility*:

(7) Kailash Satyarthi, founder of the Bachpan Bachao Andolan child rescue movement which helped free the girls, said *the tea companies had to take responsibility* for the conditions that have led to the trafficking scandal. (emphasis mine)
(8) She said that consumers, as well as Western retailers, Bangladeshi manufacturers and the government, *all shared some responsibility* for conditions in the industry, which employs four million people in Bangladesh. (emphasis mine)

Note, however, that there is a greater acknowledgement of the groups of people for whom responsibility must be taken, such as 'children', in the MSC compared to the CFC:

(9) The main *responsibility* of governments towards *children* is to protect them as subjects with human rights. (emphasis mine)

In the CFC, those negatively affected by corporate fraud, such as customers, are barely mentioned, and when they are, are also expected to shoulder some part of responsibility in ensuring they are well informed before engaging with a potentially fraudulent company. In other words, while there appears to be a slight tendency to victim blame in the CFC, this tendency is absent from the MSC:

(10) But despite the move away from the ancient principle of 'caveat emptor' – let the buyer beware – and towards placing more responsibility on the vendor, *customers still have to take responsibility for their decisions*, the FSA says. (emphasis mine)

(11) Government actuary says tougher regulation *encourages consumers to duck responsibility* for their own mistakes. (emphasis mine)

A further difference is the mention of 'regulation' as a response to (the threat of) these crimes, which is emphasized in the CFC:

(12) If the Government refuses to take *responsibility for this debacle*, why should anyone believe in its willingness to take *responsibility for the proper regulation* of the industry in the future? (emphasis mine)

The discussion of whether to bring in additional regulation and legislation to respond to modern slavery and human trafficking, however, appears largely absent from newspaper reporting.

5.5.2.3 *Accountability*

Table 5.7 shows the c-collocates for the target word *accountability*, together indicating the concept of accountability in, respectively, modern slavery and corporate fraud news reporting.

Again, as with *responsibility*, the number of actors linked to *accountability* in the CFC is substantially larger than in the MSC, suggesting again some debate over who is to be held accountable for corporate fraud. While both corpora agree that *accountability* for their respective sets of crime must be increased (and is currently lacking) and that *accountability* is closely linked to transparency and clarity, only the CFC indicates the potential measures that are to be taken. The measure it proposes is introducing regulation, as the United States has done through the Sarbanes-Oxley Act 2002 which, broadly, introduced stricter measures for guaranteeing the validity and veracity of corporate financial statements.

5.6 Discussion and conclusion

This chapter has examined the use of words relating to (in)equality, responsibility and accountability in two corpora of UK newspaper stories: one of items reporting on modern slavery (2000–16) and one of items on corporate fraud (2004–14).

My analysis suggests that reporting on these crimes tends either to ignore the question of where responsibility lies or to imply that regulatory bodies and governments should take responsibility and enforce accountability rather than corporations. Additionally, the far-reaching impact of corporate fraud is underplayed through the lack of reference to (wealth) inequality.

The frequency data suggest that discussing responsibility and accountability is only a very recent development in discussions of modern slavery, which may be taken, also, to signal a historical reluctance of the press to assign responsibility in the case of modern slavery. This can be identified with what Sykes and Matza (1957) call a technique of neutralization, and more specifically, a *denial of responsibility*. A denial of responsibility is not a denial of the crime itself or the defendant's involvement, but it implies they had no choice over their involvement and that it was beyond their control.

The c-collocate data similarly show that there is much more discussion of responsibility in the CFC than in the MSC. This suggests that there is limited attention to responsibility in the MSC or, alternatively, that responsibility for modern slavery is more readily taken up, whereas responsibility for corporate fraud is up for debate. This latter tendency can dilute the sense of responsibility, even transferring it entirely to another party (see Thompson 1980). On the other hand, however, this collective sense of responsibility may also suggest an acknowledgement that multiple parties should be held responsible for the system that enables both corporate fraud and modern slavery.

The overall tendency to link modern slavery and human trafficking to inequality suggests that UK newspapers tend to understand and communicate how the exploitation of vulnerable people is the result of, and sustains, inequality. Compare this to the lack of consideration inequality given in the CFC, which suggests that there is perhaps less of an understanding of how unfair behaviour by large multinational corporations creates and sustains inequality. Given the seriously detrimental effects of corporate fraud (see Punch 1996), the fact that these newspapers either fail to grasp, underplay or simply are unconcerned by the links between corporate wrongdoing and wealth inequality is highly problematic.

In short, there is an increasing discussion of responsibility in cases of modern slavery, albeit still limited. However, the fact that modern slavery is linked to various forms of inequality is clearly understood and communicated, and there is, compared to the CFC, little to no victim blaming. Conversely, the locus of responsibility remains hotly debated in cases of corporate fraud, and is often transferred. However, it is less clear in this reporting that corporate fraud contributes to (and is the result of) various forms of inequality, and there is certainly a sense that the defrauded have some sort of co-responsibility to be aware (in the sense, perhaps, of caveat emptor). In terms of neutralization, this suggests that the responsibility for modern slavery is denied or diluted, whereas the responsibility for corporate fraud is transferred; furthermore, corporate fraud is suggested to be a less grave crime than it truly is. In other words, this newspaper coverage generally only covers what is already pretty clear and over the whole fails to dig into the structural factors that continue to allow these corporations to 'get away' with exploiting people and market vulnerabilities, thereby allowing the already economically powerful to continue enriching themselves to the detriment and at the expense of those less economically powerful and less well informed.

Note

1 This method could not be used for the CFC, given that many newspapers also label acts of fraud committed by individuals, victimizing corporations, as corporate fraud; as such, it was not possible to select a satisfactory set of core search terms. It should be acknowledged here that this ambiguity requires further examination. Where possible, Gabrielatos's (2007) method for selecting query terms is preferable, given its relative objectivity and hypothetical ability to be exhaustive. However, as the MSC contained substantially more 'noise' than the CFC, it would also be advised to introduce the step of manually discarding blatantly irrelevant articles to Gabrielatos's (2007) method.

6

Health inequality and the representation of 'risky' working-class identities in obesity policy

Jane Mulderrig

6.1 Introduction

In this chapter I argue that through its current anti-obesity policy strategy, the UK government helps reinforce, rather than challenge, the inequalities which underlie this classed social problem. In particular, I use critical discourse analysis (CDA henceforth) to examine how the government constructs particular, psychologically profiled, 'at risk' social groups at which policy is targeted through a social marketing campaign, Change4Life (C4L henceforth). Now in its tenth year, this commercially sponsored policy strategy draws on practices from the private and public sectors in order to transmit a behaviour-change message aimed primarily at children. The chapter combines corpus-aided methods with qualitative, multimodal methods to investigate the government's use of market research and social marketing as its primary policy intervention. The findings highlight the subtly normative, emotive, classed and gendered patterns of representation used to construe the problem of obesity and its subjects. Following Schneider and Ingram (1993), I argue that these adverts textually realize the social construction of working-class *disadvantaged* and socially deviant policy targets on the one hand while on the other hand reinforcing the position of the food and drinks industry as an *advantaged* policy stakeholder. This policy construal is, I argue, ideologically aligned with a neoliberal political settlement which eschews market regulation in favour of enterprise, individual responsibility and extrinsic rewards. The chapter concludes that despite outward appearances and a discourse of enablement, C4L does little to address the pro-business balance of power which underpins the political economic conditions that produce obesity. It positions the commercial sector as powerful partners and pedagogues, while placing ultimate responsibility on the individual to adopt 'smarter' consumer behaviours.

The chapter is organized as follows: I begin by outlining my interdisciplinary theoretical framework, which brings the principles and methods of CDA into dialogue with ideas drawn from Foucault's work on governmentality. I contextualize the data in terms of the government's historical framing of obesity as a policy issue, and then outline the corpus-aided, multimodal methods used. I then move onto a detailed examination of the linguistic and visual strategies through which C4L construes and communicates with particular 'at risk' policy targets.

6.2 CDA, governmentality and the role of policy targets

In order to investigate this policy intervention, I drew on Fairclough's discourse-dialectical approach to CDA (Fairclough 2003, 2015), which combines an analytical focus on semiosis (primarily language, but also images, gesture, sound, etc.) with a critical investigation of its *interconnectedness* with the wider social order. The approach assumes a dynamic and mutually constitutive relationship between discourse and other non-discursive elements of social practices. It follows from this that the critical analysis of policy must attend to the socially structuring potential of policy discourse, while guarding against reducing practices (and their analysis) to 'mere' signification (Mulderrig et al. 2019). Policy texts are specific instantiations of social practices (relatively stable, conventionalized forms of social activity which shape organizations and help structure social life). Because of this social embeddedness, texts are vehicles for both social stability (reproducing distinctive ways of acting, thinking and being associated with a particular social practice) and social change ('interdiscursively' introducing different modes of signification from other social practices). CDA therefore seeks out dialogue with other disciplines in order to arrive at an adequate explanatory account of the social problem under investigation (in this case the construal of obesity policy targets).

In the present case I suggest that Foucault's work on governmentality (2007) is helpful in conceptualizing C4L as a strategy of governance, highlighting the political rationalities and specific constitution of social subjects which underpin this 'behaviour change' approach to obesity policy. Governmentality refers to a distinctive form of political power comprising the array of institutions, relations and practices through which the social and economic well-being of a territory and its population are managed. It is also a means of explaining, through historical analysis, how expertise-led control over individual behaviour emerged in the eighteenth and nineteenth centuries as a dominant technique of political rule in Western states.

In coining the term 'governmentality' Foucault deliberately exploits certain semantic ambiguities. The word combines 'gouvernement' (government) and 'mentalité' (mentality). The former, which he characterizes as 'the conduct of conduct' (Foucault 2007: 192–3), invokes a range of meanings: (i) to lead or guide, (ii) self-direction or self-discipline (with all its ethical overtones) and (iii) behaviours, actions and comportment. As Dean (2010) reminds us, these meanings carry a certain normative impetus, suggesting a set of ideals to which individuals or groups should aspire. They presuppose it is possible to regulate (others') behaviours and that it is the legitimate responsibility of certain (government?) agents to ensure this regulation occurs. In this sense, government is an intensely moral activity in which policies and practices are premised on expert claims to know what constitutes good, desirable, beneficial goals and behaviours.

This function of policy is particularly apparent in C4L, a policy strategy whose primary and explicit goal is self-directed behaviour change. The accumulation of this expert knowledge is made possible through biopolitical techniques of calculation and surveillance like, for instance, the demographic profiling and statistical modelling of obesity trends which underpin government health policy and the National Child Measurement programme whereby children are weighed in schools. The dissemination of this knowledge, on the other hand, is realized through biopedagogical strategies like health education campaigns (Mulderrig 2017). Pre-emptive health policies of this kind typify techniques of liberal governmentality, managing and securing 'at a distance' a population of free, self-steering individuals. Consequently, the 'self' is a key instrument of (self)regulatory control, adapting one's own behaviours (and that of one's family) to prescribed norms and shared values.

It thus follows that policy initiatives like C4L are fundamentally hegemonic rather than coercive, and success is contingent on being able to affect the way target audiences construct their own identities, goals and behaviours. Indeed, Schneider and Ingram (1993) argue that the social construction of various target audiences is an integral part of public policy. They posit a typology of more or less advantaged policy targets (e.g. entrepreneurs versus welfare dependents). Their model shows how policy helps (re) produce normative subject positions for these targets: 'Policy teaches lessons about the type of groups people belong to, what they deserve from government, and what is expected of them' (Schneider and Ingram 1993: 340). Secondly, it demonstrates that precisely because of the different levels of power and esteem enjoyed by these target groups, public policy will tend to disproportionately favour those who are already favoured. What their model does not reveal, however, are the actual policy processes by which such targets are discursively construed.

In this chapter I therefore examine the linguistic representation of target groups in UK obesity policy. As with other chapters in this volume, I also consider these findings in relation to the wider question of how public discourse represents social inequality. Specifically, I ask: (1) By what linguistic processes was a target population construed and assigned a normative, symbolic identity? (2) By what linguistic processes does the government attempt to encourage audience identification with this target profile in order to secure policy compliance? To answer this, I examined the policy documents which surround this intervention as well as the marketing campaign through which this symbolic identity is textually realized. I begin with a consideration of the historical policy context which set the conditions of possibility for constructing obesity as a policy problem, with a particular focus on the question of social inequality.

6.3 Political context

6.3.1 Inequality and obesity

Social inequality is a highly complex and contested matter. It has inspired some of the key political struggles of the past two centuries, reflecting the diverse forms that inequality can take. Two fundamental concepts underpin the idea of equality: the distribution of societal resources and the relations which hold between people. Its relevance extends across the range of human activities, including political, economic, social, legal and cultural domains. It is also a perpetually moving target: the changing historical landscape produces not only new forms of inequality but new political conditions in which strategies for addressing them take place (Mulderrig 2007). The creation of the post-war welfare state, for example, was welcomed when a majority of the British population were on low incomes or in poverty. However, as living standards increased for the majority, support for this high-tax system dwindled. Since the 1980s, neoliberal governments have scaled back spending on redistributive welfare in favour of market-based policy solutions to social, as well as economic, problems.

Different forms of inequality intersect with one another in complex ways. The historical persistence of health and income inequalities is starkly illustrated in infant mortality rates. In the 1931 census, the rates were twice as high for the poorest classes as for the rich. Perinatal health has since improved, but the inequality gap has remained largely the same (Office for National Statistics 2015), perhaps reflecting widening gaps in income inequality. The UK ranks seventh out of the thirty OECD countries for income inequality: the richest 20 per cent enjoy seven times the income wealth of the poorest 20 per cent (Wilkinson and Pickett 2010: 17). The issue of obesity adds further complexity to this picture of social inequality.

On the one hand, there are clear links between obesity prevalence and social inequality. UK has among the highest levels of obesity in the EU, with children from the most disadvantaged backgrounds more than twice as likely (26 per cent) to be obese as the least deprived (11.7 per cent) (Guy's and St Thomas' Charity 2018). However, as these figures indicate, obesity is by no means confined to the poorest sections of society, suggesting that its increasing prevalence is the result of a complex set of factors beyond purely social deprivation. Indeed, this complexity is clearly stated in a government-commissioned report on obesity (Foresight 2007), which blames obesity on modern 'obesogenic environments', including the overproduction and marketing of cheap, unhealthy foods. Despite this evidence, as I argue below, government policy persists in foregrounding the role of individual lifestyle choices, and it does so in the name of social justice. The links to social inequality are cited as the driving force behind policy (Public Health England 2018), but in a neoliberal policy environment, individual behaviour-change solutions represent the most politically expedient diagnosis.

6.3.2 Obesity policies: 1991–present

Obesity was first recognized as a key issue for health policy in 1991: the Department of Health's (DOH henceforth) publication 'The Health of the Nation' (DOH 1992) included the reduction of obesity among its goals for improving the overall health of the nation for the very first time in the UK. Since then, successive task forces have been created to accumulate scientific evidence and formulate policy strategies. However, as Ulijaszek and McLennan argue, 'UK obesity policies reflect the landscape of ... political pressures and values, as much as, if not more than, the landscape of evidence' (2016: 397). By 2001 the National Audit Office criticized the government's response as inadequate, citing a trebling of obesity rates in the previous twenty years. In 2003 damning reports from the Chief Medical Officer (who described obesity as a 'health time bomb') and a parliamentary health committee inquiry added fuel to an escalating public discourse of 'crisis', the latter again framing the issue as an individual rather than societal problem: 'Should obesity be blamed on gluttony, sloth, or both?' (House of Commons Health Committee 2004: 23).

Meanwhile, prevalence rates continued to increase annually. Faced with pressures to formulate a policy response, the Labour Government (1997–2010) brought obesity back onto the political agenda, commissioning various expert inquiries. Among these were the 2007 Foresight report and the 2010 Marmot report. The respective remit of these commissions was to synthesize broad-ranging scientific analyses of obesity prevalence and to identify the most effective strategies for tackling health inequalities. Both reports are notable for the extent to which they embrace a much more complex, society-wide framing of obesity and other health inequalities. Marmot explicitly acknowledges the ethical dimensions: 'We do have an ideological position: health inequalities that could be avoided by reasonable means are unfair. Putting them right is a matter of social justice' (2010: 3). Foresight begins by shifting the focus of agency away from the individual:

> Unhealthy weight is often seen as a result of individual choice on diet, exercise, and lifestyle. However, this report maps the complex web of societal and biological factors that have, in recent decades, exposed our inherent human vulnerability to weight gain.
>
> Foresight 2007: 3

Indeed, it argues that policies which focus on the individual are unlikely to address the full complexity of the problem:

> Solutions to address the obesogenic environment such as changes in transport infrastructure and urban design ... can be more difficult and costly than targeting intervention at the group, family or individual. However, they are more likely to affect multiple pathways within the obesity system in a sustainable way.
>
> Foresight 2007: 11

Foresight is cited as the key source of scientific evidence underpinning the government's policy response, the 'Healthy Weight, Healthy Lives' (HWHL henceforth) strategy (DOH 2008b). The document sets an ambitious target of reducing, by 2020, childhood obesity levels to those of 2000. While some progress towards this has been made, this is only at the top end of the socio-economic spectrum, with the result that the inequality gap has widened further (NHS 2019).

This is conceivably due to a significant curtailment by subsequent governments of the investment in schools and regional infrastructure pledged in HWHL. Notwithstanding its wider ambitions, HWHL is dominated by a managerial discourse of 'enabling', a key grammatical device for achieving the rather vague, attenuated government agency of neoliberal governance (Mulderrig 2011). Its policy proposals thus lie firmly in favour of enabling behaviour change rather than direct regulatory interventions.

The main strategy to emerge from HWHL was the child-focused C4L social marketing campaign, launched in 2009 at an initial cost of £75 million, and now largely funded by commercial partners in return for advertising. Social marketing makes use of commercial marketing technologies in the public sector to influence the voluntary behaviour of target audiences. This has ideological implications, since it recontextualizes in public health the discourses, relations and values of the commercial sector. Corporate partners of C4L include the supermarkets Asda and Tesco and manufacturers PepsiCo, Kellogg's and Unilever (all of whom have a very large stake in profiting from some of the unhealthy products censured in this campaign).[1]

C4L's stated aim is to target 'at risk' families (mainly clustered in poorer urban regions), whose 'problematic' lifestyle behaviours and attitudes were diagnosed using market research. To do so, it commissioned the market research companies 2CV and TNS (a subsidiary of Kantar) to carry out 'audience segmentation' analysis, the results of which were set out in the document 'Healthy Weight, Healthy Lives: Consumer Insight' (hereafter Consumer Insight) (DOH 2008a). In Section 6.5, I analyse how particular 'at risk' policy targets are construed in this document and then examine how the C4L campaign attempts to represent and persuade this same target demographic.

6.4 Method

The data examined in this chapter take two main forms: policy documents issued on behalf of the UK government's DOH and a corpus of adverts broadcast on TV and social media as part of the C4L social marketing campaign. Through intertextual analysis of the launch policy document (DOH 2009) I was able to identify the range of discourse practices which informed this policy intervention (see Mulderrig 2019). Healthy Weight, Healthy Lives: Consumer Insight Summary (DOH 2008a) (hereafter Consumer Insight) (DOH 2008a) was found to have played a key role in identifying and behaviourally profiling 'at risk' family types to be targeted through a communications campaign. This document is analysed in Section 6.5.1. The marketing company M&C Saatchi was commissioned to design the campaign, including the 'Change4Life' brand logo to be used across a range of genres, including the centrepiece of the campaign, a series of cartoon adverts. These are analysed in Section 6.5.2.

The analysis is concerned with how these data (normatively) represent policy targets and how a range of semiotic modalities intersect in the adverts to produce distinctive ideational and interpersonal meanings. To operationalize these questions in text analysis, I draw on frameworks within, or inspired by, a systemic functional view of language as social semiotic. In particular, I examine transitivity patterns (Halliday and Matthiessen 2014), appraisal (Martin and White 2008), social actor representation (van Leeuwen 1996) and multimodal analysis (Kress and van Leeuwen 2001). Although not primarily a corpus-aided study, insights from the qualitative analysis were occasionally 'sense-checked' using corpus software tools, in particular when investigating the historical policy context which informed this campaign. I used Sketch Engine (Kilgarriff et al. 2014) in order to examine keywords and collocates,[2] although my remarks in the ensuing analysis are mainly confined to raw frequencies.

6.5 Findings

6.5.1 Consumer Insight

Consumer Insight's market research surveyed attitudes and behaviours in relation to diet and physical activity among 883 sample families with children under the age of eleven, mapping these against various demographic variables (DOH 2008a). Cluster analysis was then used to identify six types of target family, with three isolated as being the most at-risk. The document summarizes the behaviours and attitudes of families under three categories: health, weight and parenting (focusing in particular on awareness of weight status and health risks), healthy eating (including shopping and cooking habits) and physical activity. In a process it describes as 'audience segmentation', it then categorizes the families into six types, the first three of which are assigned 'priority at-risk' status. These are summarized in Table 6.1, including the dispositions (attitudes and behaviours) attributed to them (DOH 2008a: 46–50).

6.5.1.1 Normative classification of families

It is readily apparent from the demographic information included in Table 6.1 that those designated most 'at risk' are at the bottom end of the socio-economic scale. These classifications are also sexist and ageist, with mothers used as a proxy through which to socially profile the family type as a whole (age and socio-economic status are clearly correlated). Each cluster is assigned a description (column two) and 'pen portrait' (column four) summarizing its key characteristics. This typology is used to classify the population into 'normal' and 'deviant' groups. This classification is realized in part through the language of evaluation.

Evaluation can be either inscribed (realized through explicitly evaluative semantics) or evoked, relying on the audience to infer evaluative meaning based on shared values or contextual knowledge (Martin and White 2008). As with all implied language (Fairclough 2003), the latter can be a powerful resource for (re)producing ideologies and shared cultural values. The evaluation in Consumer Insight takes both forms.[3] Explicitly negative evaluative semantics (underlined) represent the three most 'at risk' family types in terms of deficit (money, knowledge, motivation and parental control) and (dietary) excess, in contrast with positive representation (double underlined) of the remaining three family types. However, much of the evaluation is implicit – it relies on, and helps construct, a discourse of 'good' and 'bad' dietary and lifestyle behaviours with which the policy issue of obesity is framed and policy targets differentiated. 'Deviant' groups are thus obese or overweight; are poor working class or aspiring middle class; enter motherhood early or are single parents; lack self-awareness, lack control over either their children's behaviour or over their food consumption; eat the wrong things and do not exercise. Indeed, the evaluation works in large measure through negation and opposition, realized either syntactically ('don't enjoy'; 'it's not safe') or semantically ('in denial'; 'lack'). This is juxtaposed with the remaining three 'normal' groups (4–6 in Table 6.1) who exercise discipline over their diet and activity levels and that of their children; buy culturally valued organic and Fairtrade foods; and exercise judgement about shopping and food content. In short, the latter manifest

Table 6.1 Typology of Family Clusters in C4L Campaign

	Type Description	Demographics	Dispositions
1	'Lacking time, money and knowledge'	Class C2, three-person household, mothers (aged 25–34) and most likely to be obese	'Find buying, cooking and getting children to eat healthy foods difficult; don't enjoy preparing or cooking well-balanced meals; would pay to make life easier; believe exercise is costly, time-consuming and not enjoyable; believe it is not safe for children to play outside'.
2	'Lack the knowledge and parenting skills to improve their family's lifestyle'	Class DE, typically single parents on low incomes, very young (aged 17–24) mothers	'Lack the experience and resources to develop good parenting strategies. Children are difficult to manage, and tend to dictate their own diet and activity levels. Food can be a battleground. Parents often find it easier to 'give in' and let children have the processed foods and fizzy drinks they want.'
3	'Affluent, overweight families who over-indulge in unhealthy foods'	Class C1, mothers aged 35–44, most of the family overweight	'Cluster 3 families are proud of having "bettered" themselves. Dad is likely to work in middle management; mum may have a part-time job to earn extra money for luxuries. Their children's educational attainment and material possessions are key priorities. They enjoy food, and believe themselves to be well informed about healthy eating. Although the whole household is likely to be overweight, cluster 3 parents don't recognise the problem. They are often in denial about the healthiness of their children's diets and their true activity levels.'
4	'Living Healthily'	Class AB, affluent, older mothers (aged 45–64), keen on exercise	'Cluster 4 families take food very seriously. They are interested in organic, environmentally-friendly and Fairtrade products, and check labels for additives and E-numbers. They work hard to feed their children healthy food, and successfully limit their consumption of processed foods and carbonated drinks.'
5	'Strong parenting skills but need to make changes'	Mixed demographics, High adult obesity levels, high consumption of snacks and processed foods	'Cluster 5 parents are great believers in traditional family values and think children should eat what they're given … barriers to healthy eating are rooted in beliefs'
6	'Plenty of exercise but too many bad foods'	Class C2, typically lives in London or South-East, relatively affluent	'Mums are the driving force behind cluster 6 families' active lifestyles, and are often keen joggers and cyclists. Food fuels their high levels of physical activity. … They are open to ideas about improving their diet and incorporating more exercise into their lives.'

The document uses the Office for National Statistics 'Social Grade' categories for classifying the families by socio-economic status. These are AB (higher/intermediate managerial and professional occupations), C1 (supervisory/junior managerial professional), C2 (skilled manual) and DE (semi-skilled and unskilled, unemployed).

the operation of what Foucault calls 'biopower', wherein advanced liberal governance encourages citizens to inculcate messages about what is 'normal' and then monitor and control their behaviours accordingly. This negatively evaluative construal of at-risk policy targets is mirrored in the corpus findings.

6.5.1.2 Representation of children

Looking at the distribution of the most prominently represented social actors in this document, the lemma *child* has the most frequent occurrences (420), followed by *parent* (227), then *mother* (76), *mum* (11), *father* (23) *grandparent* (2) and *grandmother* (2). The child is thus clearly the principal focus of this policy, and is further categorized through L1 collocates (first word to the left of the search word) as *obese, overweight, happy, Muslim* and *Black*. Transitivity patterns (Halliday and Matthiessen 2014) for this search word reveal a mixed picture of agency: by far the most frequent verbal collocate where *child* is the subject is *be* (70), with the next two most frequent being *consume* (co-occurring with references to unhealthy food) and *do* (references to physical activity), revealing a clear preoccupation with children's lifestyle behaviours. The copula verb performs a variety of functions, with relational processes and passive structures by far the most frequent (thirty-one and nineteen, respectively).

Relational processes semantically construe processes of being (rather than doing) by means of a logical relationship between the subject and another entity or attribute. In effect, they are a linguistic means of classifying actors; in the data they are primarily used to categorize children in terms of attributes related to well-being (*healthy, happy, active, overweight*) and behaviours (*difficult to manage, fussy eaters*). The most frequent pattern involved dependent clauses in which mental processes construe parents as misrecognising their children's well-being, for example 'many parents <u>assumed</u> their children were 'healthy' as long as they seemed happy'. Indeed, many of these examples account for the fact that mental processes (*believe, feel, agree*) are the most prominent type of process collocating with parent. I return to this point below.

Passive structures are also prominent in the representation of children. However, these are managing actions (Mulderrig 2011) and thus do not imply a lack of agency but instead a transfer of agency from parents to children. Thus, children are given excessive licence and '<u>allowed</u> to choose what they [eat]'; '<u>allowed and encouraged</u> to be sedentary'; '<u>given considerable choice</u> over what they eat'; '<u>given the freedom</u> to eat large amounts of convenience foods' and 'strongly <u>encouraged</u> to clear their plates'.

6.5.1.3 Representation of parents

The second most prominent category of actor in the corpus is *parent(s)*. L1 collocates most frequently (11), quantify them (*many*), or categorize them by demographic status (*black Caribbean* (6), *black African* (4), *young* (3), *single* (2)) or as *priority cluster* (Types 1–3 in Table 6.1). Each represents problematic behaviours or attitudes, for example 'many parents <u>underestimated</u> the risks'; 'many parents also <u>claimed to believe</u> that their children were getting enough exercise' or 'black Caribbean parents <u>were more concerned</u> about their children being underweight than overweight'. These examples illustrate the most common transitivity patterns through which parents' actions are represented.

The most frequent verbal collocate (with *parent* as subject) is *believe* (12), representing parents' failure to recognize their children's health needs: (parents believe) 'that happy children are healthy children'; 'that their diets were healthy'; 'that their children were already sufficiently active'. The next most frequent R1 verbal collocate is the copula followed by predicates which quantify (*often, more likely, generally*) their (problematic) behaviours and attitudes (*afraid, concerned, reluctant, unaware*). For example, parents were 'afraid to let [children] go out alone'; 'concerned that their children have enough energy [and therefore overfeed them]'; 'reluctant to evaluate their children on the basis of weight' and 'preoccupied with getting their children to clear their plates'. Semantically, these patterns construe a negative, mental-affective set of processes for *parents*, revealing a textual preoccupation with their misguided attitudes and beliefs. However, the document does not explicitly state that these beliefs are wrong; instead this is presupposed, by classifying these beliefs as characteristics of 'at risk' family types. L1 verbal collocates help represent the policy solution, in which parents are the object of *help, given, tell, lead, motivate* and *encourage*, where initiatives like social marketing are the grammatical agent.

Cumulatively, collocation patterns for (Types 1-3) *parents* and *children* thus reveal a prominent representation of parents as lacking control and poor judgement in relation to their children's health, contributing to the overall construal of 'at risk' policy targets as deviant. Throughout the document, the representation of problem behaviour is interspersed with quotations from parents (usually mums) as a means of exemplification. For instance, on page 11, the report argues that 'the desire to make their children happy often led parents to embrace unhealthy behaviours'. Immediately below this claim the following quote is highlighted in bold typeface: 'They love it when we go to McDonald's once a week, because there are never any arguments and everyone's happy. We all have a good time there, so why not go back?' Mother, Birmingham. There are fifty-four of these quotes throughout the document, representing the voices of mothers from London, Birmingham, Newcastle, Oldham and Leicester. Rhetorically, these quotes play an important role in enhancing the perceived legitimacy of this document, by intertextually offering the reader direct access to the source of evidence for the claims it makes. However, in some cases, we might question their authenticity; some appear fake or staged, like this excerpt in which the mother, surprisingly, has to ask what her child's favourite food is:

Mother: So what do you want to eat? Do you want your favourite?
Child: Yeah.
Mother: Well, what's that?
Child: Fish fingers, waffles and beans.
Mother and child, Birmingham (DOH 2008a: 21)

Finally, a key point highlighted in this document is that 'at risk' families considered healthy eating to be the preserve of the middle classes: 'Adopting a healthy lifestyle was seen as hard work, stressful and unrealistic. It was also strongly linked to "middle class" values and activities – yoga classes, gym membership, buying organic food.'

(DOH 2008a: 18). This claim is supported with the quote 'We're not like that, you know, like organic types and mums that have the time to cook all day because they don't have to work' (DOH 2008a: 46). Interestingly, this quote does not explicitly use the term 'middle class', nor does it appear in any of the other quotations from mums throughout the document. Instead, it is represented through material and cultural proxies of implied affluence ('don't have to work') and lifestyle choices ('organic types'). Indeed, despite little evidence of a preoccupation among the participants with links between healthy eating and 'middle-classness', this is strongly emphasized in the document's recommendations for policy intervention.

6.5.1.4 Strategic design of government communication

Following focus group research with parents who looked at examples of government health messages, the document ends by offering insights into the strategic design of government communications. In this section, I briefly examine the document's key recommendations, before assessing the extent to which these are realized in the C4L social marketing campaign. It states that 'engaging families, particularly priority cluster families, with messages about diet and activity and persuading them of the benefits of changing their behaviour will mean developing a new language and tone of voice' (59), clearly indicating the need for quite explicit stylistic design. Moreover, this should aim to secure audience identification among a working-class target population: 'Target Specific Clusters: families in clusters 4 and 6 already have high levels of awareness of healthy behaviours. The inclusion of messages designed to appeal to cluster 4 in particular may alienate families from lower socio-economic groups' (DOH 2008a: 60).

The emphasis on language design is evidenced by the organization of this section under three 'What works' headings, focusing on key messages about diet and activity; the use of language; and imagery. The second section on language calls for a focus on 'future dangers' rather than explicit reference to 'obesity' and 'weight'. Its overall goal is to maximize audience identification 'as if written by another parent'. Language should, it advises, be empathetic ('Use "we", rather than "us" and "you" … acknowledging their concerns and reflecting them back by using phrases such as "it's hard to say no to your kids"'), avoid judgement and 'use the kind of colloquial phrases that parents use themselves, like "bags of energy"'. In summary, the government is advised to downplay overtly authoritative language in favour of a more personal, informal style.

The advice for imagery follows a similar theme of mirroring the target audience's presumed identity, values and circumstances, implying but not explicitly stating social inequality. It thus recommends using images of happy, healthy children playing in everyday settings which are not 'too aspirational or middle class'.

6.5.2 The C4L campaign

In this final section I examine how this strategically designed communication was realized in the corpus of thirty-three C4L adverts (the average duration is thirty seconds). Each advert features a narrative about an unhealthy lifestyle habit, which is problematized using a scientific discourse of health risk or nutritional content, and then concludes by advocating a healthier 'Change4life'. This is animated by colourful plasticine figures who represent the C4L family (age and gender are signified by colour and size).

6.5.2.1 Multimodality

In most of the adverts the government authorial voice is backgrounded, its message ventriloquized by a child who in each case has a marked northern English accent and dialect features. This corresponds with some of the regions which have the highest levels of social deprivation and obesity (Yorkshire, Lancashire, Sunderland).[4] In line with recommendations in Consumer Insight, the language is colloquial and childlike ('that's loads of calories!' 'we're right little monkeys'). The overall tone of the ads is fun, happy and optimistic. This is achieved through a combination of visual and linguistic modalities. Highly saturated, bright primary colours are used, with yellow being the most prominent colour, conveying positive affective meanings (Kress and van Leeuwen 2002).

Humour also plays an important role in these adverts, helping to off-set the face threat of negatively evaluating the depicted lifestyles as problematic, excessive and risk-laden. It is realized through typical cartoon devices like visual metaphor, anthropomorphism, hyperbole and technical modality. For example, a drinks straw 'periscope' reveals the sugar content in a can of coke, fat inside the body takes the form of a cackling ghoul, mum's over-indulgence is comically exaggerated and biological processes of fat storage are simplified through cartoon medical cross-sections (see Figure 6.1, left to right).

In this way humour is used to soften quite serious and alarming messages about disease risk. In fact, the mood and visual modality of the adverts is phased, reflecting the content of the message.

6.5.2.2 Move structure

Each advert has four main moves, three of which are typically narrated by one or more of the child characters. The first move involves a confession about an unhealthy lifestyle ('we love pop'; 'mum gives me enough to feed a horse'; 'we're always hunting down the

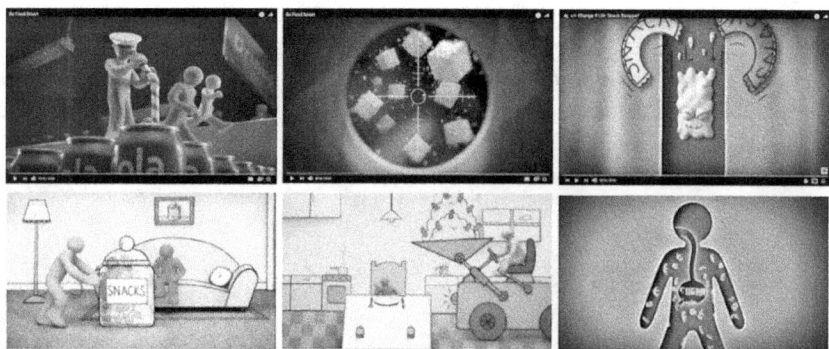

Figure 6.1 Visual tropes used to achieve humour and evaluative health warnings in the C4L campaign.

sweet stuff'). Simple present tense and progressives with time adverbials (underlined) convey the idea that these are entrenched, habitual behaviours.

The second move introduces bioscientific discourse to evaluate this behaviour as out of control and posing serious health risks ('too much food gets stored as fat in the body'; 'that could mean heart disease, cancer, or type 2 diabetes'; '9 out of 10 kids growing up with dangerous levels of fat in their bodies'; 'every ten minutes a kid like me has a tooth removed in hospital'). The shift in register is framed using reported speech ('my teacher says …'; 'mum says …'). It is in this section that we also see the greatest use of inscribed evaluation, realized through a combination of adult-like scientific discourse ('dangerous levels of fat') and childlike reactions ('yuk!', 'Nasty!', 'Terrible!') which add affective meanings to these warnings. Visually, the mood changes to darker, sombre colours as metaphor and technical modality are used to emotively translate these rather esoteric messages. In some adverts the visual modality also changes from low to high: children receive a warning about sugar content of drinks in a much more realistic-looking kitchen setting, and later adverts include a real boy brought face to face with his own annual sugar and snack food consumption (Figure 6.2).[5]

The third move returns to the bright, idealized, cartoon-scape in order to give the viewer specific guidance on how to change their behaviour. This is typically realized through memorable slogans and benchmarks ('now I eat me sized meals'; 'just remember, choose less red go more green instead';[6] 'we turn the dial and swap some of our snacks for healthier stuff we like';[7] 'now we look for healthy sugar swaps'). At this point the lively signature theme tune phases in for the first time, boosting the illocutionary force of this message with a rapid 2/4 'march time' rhythm. In a final closing move a disembodied government voiceover exhorts the viewer to make a C4L. This move borrows from the genre of product advertising in soliciting a response from the viewer, frequently offering free merchandise ('get your snack swapper now', 'search Change4Life', 'download the sugar smart app' and 'get a free Disney stopwatch').

6.5.2.3 Actor representation

The visual and linguistic representation of actors in these adverts mirrors their distributional prominence in Consumer Insight. Children are present in every advert and mums in all but the three most recent adverts. Dad, on the other hand, appears far less frequently (in a third of the adverts) and only peripherally in opening and closing sequences. He neither speaks nor is he talked about. Visually, he is represented

Figure 6.2 Visual modality in health warnings in C4L campaign.

only as eating junk food in front of the TV or joining the family in the recommended behaviour change (eating a healthy meal at the dining table or exercising in the park). By contrast, the dynamic between children and mums in terms of agency plays a key role in construing the deviant behaviours of 'at risk' policy targets.

The adverts reflect the poor parenting skills attributed to target families in Consumer Insight by representing children raiding the cupboards for snacks, swinging on the curtains and emotionally manipulating mum into supplying sweets. Perhaps reflecting parental resignation to this behaviour, the children characterize their own 'naughty' behaviour using parental language ('we're right little monkeys', 'we're always hunting down the sweet stuff' and 'I'm a little monkey'). For mum, agency is an index of her educational transformation during these adverts. At the beginning of the adverts her agency, in the form of control over her children's behaviours, is marked in its absence. This is most often implicit: mum is absent from the scene while children help themselves to snacks; mum stands with hands on hips in frustration and confusion. The adverts do not explicitly blame mum, but rather represent her as lacking knowledge ('it's hard to know what to buy; eating healthily can be confusing'). Indeed, mum's love for her children is a prominent theme, but one which ultimately leads to poor parenting ('mum loves me, but she gives me enough to feed a horse'; 'mum loves me, but I know how to get around her and get the things I like'; 'I think she really loves me'). These patterns echo the parent–child power dynamic represented in Consumer Insight: 'Looking after children is mum's job, but she finds it hard and lacks the confidence to enforce the rules' (DOH 2008a: 46). Indeed, her lack of domestic authority is an opportunity for some commercial product placement. Thus, in a 2014 advert the solution to mum's confusion in the supermarket is solved intertextually, whereby a cooking lesson from commercial partners Asda functions as the 'solution' move in the ad's problem-solution narrative (Figure 6.3), implicitly reinforcing the powerful position of the food, drinks and retail industries as obesity policy stakeholders and lifestyle pedagogues.

Having inculcated the C4L message, mum then becomes principal agent of change, a 'smarter consumer' with the help of various pedagogic devices (rules of thumb like 'green is good' and '100 calorie snacks' and aids like recipe books and apps).

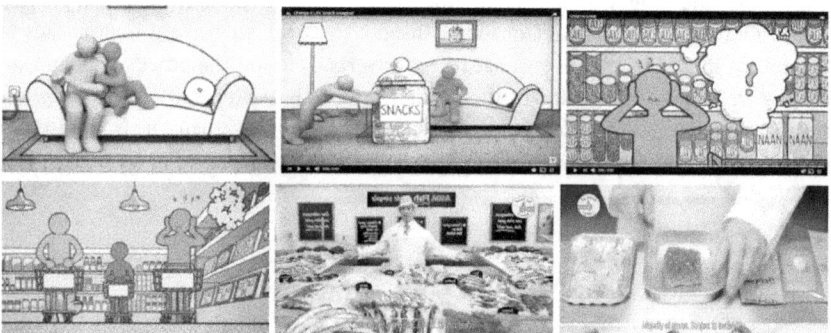

Figure 6.3 Cooking lesson from Asda: Representing mum as lacking parental control and domestic skills.

Through these patterns of visual and linguistic representation, the C4L ads reproduce the 'at risk' policy targets construed in Consumer Insight. These are predominantly mothers who, by subtle multimodal implication rather than explicit representation, are northern, working-class, full of love and good intentions, but nutritionally ignorant and lacking in basic parenting skills.

6.6 Conclusions

Current obesity policy is formulated in the context of competing political and social forces. On the one hand, governments are under increasing pressure to tackle the threat to societal well-being which obesity poses. More than a decade ago, HWHL stated that this issue is as complex and urgent as climate change, requiring a transformation of the environment we live in and action by schools, the food industry, employers and government, as well as individuals. It pledged a significant amount of money to achieve this, importantly including investment in urban planning, as well as school meals, physical education and compulsory cooking classes. However, obesity policy must also contend with a neoliberal political landscape which eschews welfarist and regulatory governance in favour of market liberalism and individual choice. Such an environment militates against the kinds of interventions which would be required in order to address the full causal complexity of obesity. This is illustrated in the difficulties in tackling the supply side of the problem. The 2013 Public Health Responsibility Deal calls for action by industry to reduce the production, retail and marketing of unhealthy foods, although to date it has received only a tiny percentage of signatories, while the growth of fast food outlets in (deprived) urban areas continues (Public Health England 2018).

Matters were further complicated by the spread of a global financial crisis nine months after the publication of HWHL. The UK's response to this was a cross-party consensus on a neoliberal default of public retrenchment through a prolonged programme of austerity. As a consequence, promised investment in schools and urban infrastructure was curtailed, while obesity policy returned to a primary emphasis on individual behaviour change. Support for C4L continued but responsibility for funding it shifted to commercial partners. While social marketing can disseminate valuable health advice, it is also ultimately a market-derived discourse practice, reinforcing rather than challenging the consumerist forms of social engagement which sustain our 'obesogenic environment'. C4L draws on market research to profile the population and construct demographically specific 'at risk' policy targets, whose problem behaviours are reflected back to them in cartoon form. In essence, C4L operates as a calculative technique of governmentality by which the population is classified into 'normal' and 'deviant' groups, and rendered governable by inculcating more middle-class, self-disciplinary subjectivities.

Throughout the policy discourse and C4L intervention, social inequality is the elephant in the room. It is everywhere implied, for example in the social classification used as a basis for policy design, yet nowhere is it explicitly foregrounded as a policy problem in its own right which must be addressed. In this sense obesity policy addresses the symptoms (unequal health), not the disease (social inequality). The C4L policy strategy goes to extraordinary lengths and great expense to target government help at those considered to be most at risk. Laudable though this goal is, the consumerist mechanism for achieving this covertly blames them for their poor life choices. Consumer Insight called for messages which avoided alienating the target audience by appearing too middle class, and we saw how this was realized linguistically in C4L by subtly projecting a (northern) working-class identity. This target population is acknowledged to be at the most deprived end of the social spectrum (DOH 2008a; Foresight 2007). Indeed, this is apparent in the evidence C4L offers as a health warning: 'Every ten minutes a kid like me has a tooth removed in hospital.' This statistic points to the systemic complexities which underlie health inequalities. In 2005 the National Audit Office reported that oral health among twelve-year-olds was the best in Europe. The following year, the government introduced a new (cheaper) system for funding NHS dental care, paying dentists by 'unit of dental activity'. This was framed as a means of encouraging more preventive health, but in fact had the opposite effect because in order to maintain revenue, less time was available for preventive care. Children in particular suffered because dentists no longer had adequate resources to devote to early years oral health care (Armstrong 2018). Since 2006 rates of emergency hospital procedures have increased exponentially, with a 13 per cent gap in hospitalization rates between the most and the least deprived areas (Appleby, Merry and Reed 2017).

Obesity policy rests on a precarious irony. Recognizing the socially uneven distribution of the problem, the population is profiled to identify the most 'at risk' groups, a defining characteristic of which is their socio-economic disadvantage. However, this is seen as beyond the scope of government intervention, while the material barriers they face to sustainably adopting healthier lifestyles are brushed aside as a form of consumer deficit to be addressed by re-educating them, through social marketing, into 'smarter' lifestyles. It has been the aim of this chapter to reveal, through critical multimodal analysis, the role that current obesity policy plays in perpetuating a political status quo designed to favour the advantaged commercial stakeholders while entrenching the disadvantaged policy targets by characterizing their attitudes and beliefs as deviant and in want of consumerist remedies.

However, this state of affairs is neither inevitable nor necessarily permanent. Indeed, there are hopeful signs that government is prepared to intervene in the political economic conditions which have created this problem. After years of delays, in 2018 the government finally introduced a tax on the soft drinks industry for sugar content over 5 g per 100 ml, and is now considering extending this to chocolate. While this does inevitably encourage greater use of some harmful sugar substitutes, evidence from other countries (notably Mexico) suggest the strategy has an impact on obesity. There is also currently a government consultation to ban junk food advertising on TV, streaming and social media sites before 9.00 p.m., while Labour MP Tom Watson has called for a ban on the use of cartoon mascots used to market sugary cereals to children. It remains to be seen whether such regulatory interventions can offer a counterweight to the neoliberal default framing of obesity as a matter of individual choice, rather than a barometer of societal well-being, equality and justice.

Notes

1. For example, Kellogg's has been a long-standing sponsor of the Amateur Swimming Association, which until recently used its Tony the Tiger cartoon mascot on merit badges. The mascot belongs to Frosties cereal, which according to an NHS survey (2012), ranks the highest for added sugar among those marketed at children.
2. EnTenTen within Sketch Engine (Kilgarriff et al. 2014) was used as a reference corpus. L1 collocate is the first word to the left of the focus word; R1 collocate is the first word to the right.
3. Precisely because of the variable cultural values upon which evaluation works, the distinction between inscribed and evoked evaluation is not always clear cut. It is, in fact, more accurate to talk of a 'cline' running from words/phrases whose semantic content is purely attitudinal ('obesity is terrible') to those whose semantic content is ostensibly experiential but which triggers evaluation based on a set of cultural ideas or values ('low calorie').
4. Notable exceptions are Wolverhampton and parts of East London, both of which have high concentrations of (child) obesity and deprivation.
5. Kress and van Leeuwen (1996) apply the semantic function of modality (degree of commitment to propositional content) to the visual mode, in which higher modality would be more realistic, detailed images (e.g. photos) and lower modality would be more generic and idealized (e.g. cartoons).
6. The 'traffic light' nutritional labelling system on foods uses 'green' for a healthy choice and 'red' for an unhealthy one.
7. On a cardboard C4L 'snack swapper' offering alternative snack ideas.

7

We are NOT all in this together

A corpus-assisted critical stylistics analysis of *Austerity* in Print News Media 2009–10 and 2016–17

Lesley Jeffries and Brian Walker

7.1 Introduction

Since at least the period of Margaret Thatcher's premiership in the UK (1979–90), the idea that the nation's finances were analogous to the budget of an average family has been naturalized as common sense.[1] Some see this 'household budget' philosophy as also linked to the Conservatives' resurgence in 2010, after the New Labour years, when their avowed aim was to 'balance the books'. There followed a slimming down of government spending, often labelled *austerity*, which coincided with an increasing inequality of wealth between the richest and the poorest in the country. Many have argued that these two trends are not coincidental, but related by causation. One of the major discourses of inequality, therefore, is the discourse that presented austerity to the electorate in a way that made it an attractive option and persuaded people to vote for it across three general elections in a way that has been likened to turkeys voting for Christmas (see 'Turkeys Voting for Christmas' 2017). In this chapter, we investigate the evolving meaning of the word *austerity*,[2] as used in the national press to discuss government policy, and we draw some conclusions as to how naturalizing the ideology of austerity may have influenced our perceptions of inequality.

Our research focusing on the development of corpus stylistics in relation to current affairs and politics has led us to favour the analysis of small-to-medium-sized corpora using a combination of computational and qualitative methods to trace the changing semantics of certain key lexis in political debates. Although much corpus linguistic research in recent years has focused on the ever-increasing power of computers to search incrementally growing data sets, we see a place for the use of corpus tools to investigate the language of particular periods, topics or contexts in greater detail than is possible using big data and algorithmic analysis alone. After examining the behaviour of certain keywords of the newspaper reporting of the Blair years (Jeffries and Walker 2018), we started to investigate austerity as a concept through the behaviour of the word form itself.

Our research on this topic has so far considered how *austerity* is used in Hansard (the UK parliamentary record) in 2006–15, compared with the war and post-war period of the 1940s (see Jeffries and Walker 2019), and we have also examined the origins of the recent resurgence of this word in a speech given by David Cameron (as the leader of the opposition) at the Conservative Party conference in Cheltenham in 2009 (see Evans and Walker 2020). Here, we aim to assess the contribution of austerity to the prevailing political climate by comparing newspaper usage of this term from 2009 to 2010, just after the financial crash of 2008, with similar newspaper usage from 2016 to 2017 when austerity as a political strategy in the UK was reported to be coming to an end.

The chapter will begin with a discussion of some of the most important concepts underlying this work (Section 7.2), notably the idea of 'sociopolitical keywords' and some semantic background to the lexical item we examine in this chapter: *austerity*. Section 7.2 will finish with an outline of the research questions we are aiming to answer. We will then (Section 7.3) explain the process of compiling the corpora for this investigation and of analysing them using the tools of corpus stylistics and the framework of critical stylistics (Jeffries 2010). In Section 7.4 we will report the results of our analysis which aims to ascertain what kind of semantic differences (if any) exist between the earlier and later uses of the word, first using statistical keywords (7.4.1) and then in relation to the immediate clausal co-text (7.4.2), using a critical stylistic approach. Section 7.5 will discuss these findings in the context of greater inequality.

7.2 Background to the research

Our aim in this chapter is to carry out rigorous and timely research into the behaviour of a significant sociopolitical keyword of our times, but we are also interested in both the wider political context of our data and the wider theoretical implications of this kind of work. Here, we start by introducing some key ideas and set out the methods we are using in this project.

7.2.1 Sociopolitical keywords

The notion of sociopolitical keywords takes inspiration from Raymond Williams's influential book ([1976] 1983) *Keywords*, which tried to both capture and challenge the prevailing ideology of the post-war years via an exploration of his chosen cultural keywords. Like Williams, we wish to identify specific words which characterize periods in British political history and in doing so question and sometimes challenge the ideology that they represent. We use the term 'sociopolitical keywords' in preference to 'cultural keywords' because in this and other studies that we have carried out on individual word forms, our emphasis is on those keywords which have both social and political significance.

Our work is thus founded on a general hypothesis that some words will be important indicators of the ideologies and culture of different political times as they wax and wane both in use and sociopolitical importance over time (see Demmen, Jeffries and Walker 2018; Jeffries and Walker 2019). We are also interested in looking at the way that words might take on political or cultural significance in a time-limited period, particularly where their use and reuse may have some ideological influence on the outlook of the electorate. Additionally, in this and other studies, we also see a pattern demonstrating that sociopolitical keywords become paradoxically emptier of meaning as their representativeness of the prevailing ideology becomes more established in the period concerned. Although there could be some very short-lived buzz words which hardly have time to be of great impact, we nevertheless suggest that the investigation of lexical items over relatively short periods can be insightful (see, for example, Jeffries 2003, 2011).

Other studies have combined corpus linguistic approaches with the investigation of cultural keywords (see for example Stubbs 1996; Jeffries and Walker 2018), and Durant's (2006) article suggests that 'the development of electronic search capabilities applied to large corpora of language use ... encourages renewed attention to cultural keywords' (Durant 2006: 19). We agree with Durant's suggestion, though we use purpose-built, relatively small corpora, rather than large ready-made general corpora, to study lexical items over a relatively short, focused period of political history. This, it seems to us, is closer to the spirit of Williams's original work, which was interested in the keywords of a historical period.

7.2.2 Austerity

In the context of other work on sociopolitical keywords, there are many reasons to consider *austerity* as one such keyword, not least, perhaps, because of its explicit adoption by politicians in favour of 'a programme of government measures designed to reduce public spending and conserve resources, esp. during a time of economic hardship; the conditions resulting from such measures' (*Oxford English Dictionary* 2019) and its rejection by opposition politicians and campaigners for social justice.[3] Note, however, that our previous work on this word has demonstrated that the definition given above does not accurately reflect the post-war use of this term which did not refer to a general restriction of public spending across the board: 'While the consumption of food and goods was restricted, the Attlee government was simultaneously investing in infrastructure and the new welfare state, amongst other things' (Jeffries and Walker 2019: 58).

Our research into the use of this word in Hansard in the post-war and recent (2008–15) periods teases out a subtle difference in its usage, and therefore in its meaning, in the two sets of data. In this chapter, we seek to look in more detail at the beginning and end of the recent period of austerity to see whether there are further changes in usage to be mapped out.

7.2.3 Austerity and (in)equality

In a speech given by David Cameron in South Korea in 2017 (when he was no longer prime minister), he asserted that opposing austerity was selfish because it meant 'spending money today that you might need tomorrow'.[4] Cameron's assertion rests on the ideological premise that it is necessary and financially sound to balance the books, not just in the short term, but continuously. This opinion runs counter to the borrow-and-pay-back basis of most modern financial processes (e.g. credit, bank loans, mortgages, student loans, pensions) which are nevertheless usually accepted in practice by the very same people who portray government debt as verging on the immoral.

The kind of austerity practised in recent years has affected society unevenly, unlike that of the post-war years in which governments subjected the rich and the poor to the same laws of rationing, and invested money to create the welfare state, including the National Health Service. The UK Conservative Party's policies on reducing public sector funding are widely documented to have disproportionally affected the poor and increased inequalities, particularly wealth inequality, prompting 'an unprecedented decline in British living standards' (Tepe-Belfrage and Wallin 2016: 390). Powell states that the 'impact on the poor was brutal' and that some of the measures associated with austerity contributed 'directly to increasing debt, hunger and homelessness' (Powell 2017: 230) and in 2014 Credit Suisse reported that the United Kingdom was the only G7 country 'recording an increase in inequality this century' (Stierli et al. 2014: 37). Similarly, Tepe-Belfrage and Wallin (2016: 390) note that 'the monetary policies of austerity have furthered a form of regressive redistribution in which wealth has been transferred to the upper-income decile whilst spiking inequality and entrenching low pay and precarious work', and Nunn argues that state interventions and policies, such as that known as 'fiscal consolidation', have 'accentuated rather than curtailed ... income inequality' (Nunn 2016: 472). Furthermore, due to government passing the responsibility for austerity to local authorities and local communities 'the material-economic burden of austerity' has also spread 'unevenly across the United Kingdom', with the '[m]ore deprived and socially excluded regions, localities, social groups and individuals' suffering the most (Strong in press).

In practice, then, rather than balancing the books (which remain in deficit), the policy of austerity in the early twenty-first century has meant the permanent shrinking of public services and a consequent increase in inequality which is the exact opposite of the effect of austerity under Atlee.

7.2.4 Aims and research questions

In the context of this evidence that austerity has produced more wealth inequality since 2009, our aim was to investigate the textual construction of the concept of austerity by analysing how the word *austerity* behaves linguistically in newspaper commentary on budget statements and election campaigns in recent years. We especially wanted to identify any differences in the usage of the word in news reporting when austerity began as a political policy and when, a few years later, some were reporting a possible end to austerity. In the next section we describe in more detail our beginning and end points of austerity and the data we collected. With our research aims in mind, we ask the following research questions: What can co-textual analysis tell us about the meaning of *austerity* in print news data from 2009 to 2010 and from 2016 to 2017?

And also, are the usage and meaning of *austerity* as revealed by this analysis different in the two periods?

7.3 Data and methods

In this section, we explain our data collection and analysis processes in as much detail as we have space for, in the hope that it will help readers to see where our results and conclusions come from.

7.3.1 The corpora

To address our research aims, we built two corpora of print newspaper data, both made up of news stories containing the word *austerity* collected from two periods of time which we refer to as the Start of Austerity (SoA) and the End of Austerity (EoA). For the purposes of this research, SoA is the fifteen-month period from April 2009 to June 2010 and EoA is from November 2016 to November 2017. The word *end* in the latter label should be seen as being enclosed in 'scare' quotes and followed by a question mark, since it is highly debatable whether austerity as a policy was coming to an end at that point. While these start and end points are somewhat arbitrary, we offer justification for our decisions below along with some essential background context.

During the period April 2009 to June 2010 there was a change in UK government from the (left of centre) Labour Party, under the leadership of Gordon Brown with Alistair Darling as chancellor of the Exchequer, to a Conservative-Liberal Democrat coalition, with David Cameron as prime minister and George Osborne as chancellor. We chose April 2009 as the opening point for the SoA period because two important political events stimulated debate and speculation about austerity in the press. First, on 22 April 2009, Alistair Darling presented a budget that, in response to the country's budget deficit and a global recession, included increases in some taxes and decreases in some public spending. Some newspaper reporting of the budget used the word *austerity*, prophesying austerity as an inevitable economic policy, for example, 'Austerity or inflation. That's the choice for the next government' (Reece 2009). Secondly, on 26 April 2009, at the Conservative Party Spring conference, David Cameron (the party leader of the opposition) gave a keynote speech about the beginning of an 'age of austerity' (a noun phrase we discuss further in Section 7.4.2.1). We chose June 2010 as the closing point of the SoA period because this coincided with George Osborne delivering his first budget as the new chancellor, putting into practice the austerity policies proposed by the Conservatives during the election campaign.

The EoA period is when austerity policies had been in place for a number of years and it was becoming apparent that they had failed to reduce the budget deficit. The opening point of this period is the chancellor Philip Hammond's autumn budget statement in 2016, while the closing point is Hammond's first budget following the Conservatives' narrow general election victory in June 2017, when some sections of the media were debating whether austerity was coming to an end.

130 The Discursive Construction of Economic Inequality

Table 7.1 Focal Points for Data Collection for the Start of Austerity (SoA) Period

Date	Event
22/26 April 2009	Darling's Spring Budget / Cameron's 'age of austerity' speech
24 March 2010	Darling's final Budget
6 May 2010	Election – Cameron Prime minister; coalition with Liberal Democrats
22 June 2011	Osborne's first budget

Table 7.2 Focal Points for Data Collection for the End of Austerity (EoA) Period

Date	Event
23 November 2016	Hammond's Autumn statement
8 March 2017	Hammond's Spring Budget
8 June 2017	Election – Theresa May Prime Minister
22 November 2017	Hammond's Autumn Budget

In order not to be overwhelmed with data, we identified key political events (i.e. budget statements and general elections) from our SoA and EoA periods where we expected there to be intensified debate in the newspapers about UK economic policy. The key events can be found in Tables 7.1 and 7.2. We searched an online database for articles containing the word *austerity* on the days of these events in any of the UK national daily newspapers, including Sunday editions, whether popular (sometimes referred to as tabloid, for example, *Daily Mail*, *Daily Mirror* and the *Sun*,) or serious (sometimes referred to as broadsheet, for example, the *Daily Telegraph*, *Financial Times*, the *Guardian*, the *Independent* and the *Times*). Since reporting of important scheduled political occurrences are often discussed before and after the event, we also searched one day either side of the chancellors' budget address to the Commons, and a month before and the day after the two general elections. From the list of articles returned by the search we filtered out any articles that were about austerity in countries other than the UK or concerned austerity in a non-political/non-economic context (such as football management). We also removed duplicate articles (from second or regional editions). In this way we obtained newspaper articles that were highly relevant to the topic of austerity in a UK economic and political context.

The resulting two corpora were 423,284 words for SoA and 363,541 words for EoA. Although small from a corpus linguistic perspective, these corpora were suitable for our purposes since they were well focused and eminently manageable for the analysis we wished to carry out.

7.3.2 Analytical approach

Our corpora centre on the word *austerity* and in order to establish how it was characterized in this data, we carried out two different analyses: one based on semi-automated corpus techniques (namely, keyword analysis) and the other using corpus methods to organize the data in such a way that qualitative analysis of relatively large numbers of examples becomes possible, through concordance lines. Our qualitative analysis is informed by linguistic (specifically syntactic) information but focuses on the textual meaning of the word under scrutiny, through its place and function in the surrounding co-text using the 'textual-conceptual functions' proposed by a critical stylistic approach (Jeffries 2010).

While keyword analysis often leads directly to more detailed examination of (some of) the resulting keywords in their context, it can also give 'robust indications' of the 'aboutness' (Scott 2010: 43; see also Scott and Tribble 2006: 58) of the texts in a corpus. We use keywords and the notion of 'aboutness' here to establish the broader semantic context of our focus term *austerity* as this is one way to find out what discursive context the term is being used in. Our more detailed concordance-based analysis of the word itself gives us a finer-grained sense of how it is being used and which nuances of its meaning are changing to adapt to its wider context. More detail regarding how these approaches were used can be found below, alongside our findings.

7.4 Analysis and results

This section sets out what we have been able to establish about the usage – and thus the meaning – of *austerity* in the two corpora outlining the start and end of recent austerity policies, respectively. While we find the overuse of the term 'discourse' troublesome in many ways because of the vagueness of its referent(s), one general way to characterize the idea of 'a discourse', which is at least transparent and replicable, is to consider the keywords produced when comparing two corpora.

7.4.1 Keyword analysis

Keywords are those word forms with frequencies that are statistically significant in one corpus when compared with another corpus. Keyword comparisons can be routinely carried out using corpus analytical software which assesses differences between word frequencies using measures of statistical significance such as log-likelihood (Dunning 1993). A recent criticism of keyword calculations is that statistical significance does not give an indication of the scale of difference, usually known as effect size, between word frequencies. Some social scientists (see, for example, Kelley and Preacher 2012; Thompson 2007) have argued that calculating effect size is crucial for deciding the importance (or otherwise) of results. A number of corpus linguists have also called for keywords analysis to take into account both statistical significance and effect size (see Gabrielatos 2018). As a result, some corpus tools now provide the option to use both statistical significance and effect size to generate keywords.

We used AntConc (Anthony 2019) to calculate the keywords in our data, comparing SoA with EoA and vice versa. We used log likelihood (LL) to evaluate statistical significance and Log Ratio (LR) (Hardie 2014) to evaluate the effect size. LL indicates the confidence with which we can infer that any keywords are a result of the datasets being different in some way. It depends on the notion of a null hypothesis (usually denoted by H_0), which states that there is no difference between the two datasets or, more precisely, no difference in the populations from which the datasets were drawn (see McIntyre and Walker 2019, chapters 4 and 5 for further explanation). LL provides an indication of the probability of getting the results (in this case keywords) if the H_0 were true (i.e. no difference). The higher the LL value, the lower the probability that the results would be obtained if H_0 were true, and so the more confidently H_0 can be rejected. Probability is usually presented as a p-value, where the lower the value the lower the probability. A p-value less than 0.05 ($p<0.05$) indicates that there is a 5 per cent chance that the results would be obtained if the null hypothesis were true; $p<0.01$ indicates a 1 per cent chance; $p<0.001$ indicates a 0.01 per cent chance and $p<0.0001$ indicates a 0.001 per cent chance. LR is a descriptive statistic for calculating effect size developed specifically for keyword research. The higher the LR value the bigger the scale of difference between frequencies: a LR of 1 means that the frequency in the target corpus is twice as much as the frequency in the reference corpus; a LR of 2 means that the difference is four times as much; a LR of 3 means an eightfold difference and so on. LL can be said to answer the question, 'Can we infer that there is a difference?' (i.e. Do we have the required amount of evidence to reject the null hypothesis?), while LR can be said to answer the question, 'How big is the difference?'.

It is usual practice to set a level of significance at which the null hypothesis is rejected and below which results are ignored. Using the settings in AntConc we applied a statistical cut-off of LL 15.13 which although an arbitrary threshold is an established cut-off in linguistics and social sciences more generally and one that equates to a low probability ($p<0.0001$) that our results would have been obtained if H_0 were true. Our resulting list therefore contained keywords with a LL score of 15.13 and above. We then sorted the results by LR and applied another (arbitrary) cut-off of LR=1 in order to eliminate keywords with small differences in frequencies.

The statistical cut-offs we used highlighted 131 keywords in the SoA corpus (when compared against the EoA corpus) and 316 keywords in the EoA corpus (when compared against the SoA corpus), thus presenting us with very many possible avenues for further exploration. Not all keywords will be interpretatively important as there can be a range of reasons why words are over or under-used in corpora and a next step in a rigorous approach is to find a principled way to eliminate keywords from further investigation (see Jeffries and Walker 2018, chapter 2 for discussion of such a process). One way to do this is on the grounds that they are unlikely to help in answering research questions. Many of our keywords were proper nouns and pronouns relating to people, places, institutions, groups and currencies. While such keywords are not without interest, reflecting as they do the different participants in the narratives that contained the word *austerity*, they do not help our research in relation to the semantics of *austerity* or its discursive connection with inequality. We therefore removed such keywords from further consideration, leaving 73 keywords for the SoA period and 159 for the EoA period.

In order to ascertain the discursive context of austerity within the corpora, we arranged the remaining keywords into ad hoc, data-driven groupings suggested by the words themselves and their immediate co-text. This involved assessing each keyword in turn via concordance lines and establishing the smallest lexical unit of meaning that it was part (e.g. noun phrase) that enabled us to judge the semantic function(s) of that keyword. We then designed appropriate categories that enabled us to group the keywords.

For example, the top keywords in the SoA corpus ordered by LR were *consolidation* and *unavoidable*. We assigned *consolidation* to what we called an 'international/national finances and economics' grouping because, without exception, it was used to refer, rather vaguely, to some sort of process relating to (we assume) improving the nation's finances. A noun itself, it was premodified twenty-two times (out of fifty-six instances) by *fiscal*, a further three times by *budget* and post-modified by *of £X billion(s)* (where X was either 7, 83 or 113). It also occurred as a postmodifier in prepositional phrases: *£X billion(s) of consolidation*. We assessed the adjectival keyword, *unavoidable*, in a similar way by looking at the nouns it pre- and post-modified in noun phrases (e.g. *unavoidable budget*; *budget of unavoidable cuts*) as well as those it complemented in copula constructions (e.g. *retrenchment is unavoidable*; *the scale of spending cuts was unavoidable*). From this analysis we established that, similar to *consolidation*, *unavoidable* was connected with finances but more specifically with public sector spending cuts associated, in particular, with the 2010 budget. We therefore chose to group *unavoidable* with other keywords that related to (sometimes euphemistically) public spending cuts, job losses and taxation (e.g. *pain, painful, axe, savings*) in a category we called 'public money matters'.

In this way we assigned each keyword to a group; the results can be found in Tables 7.3 and 7.4 (keywords are ordered by LR within their groupings). The tables show all our keywords so that readers can judge our analysis for themselves, although without access to concordances it is not always clear why some keywords belong to a group (e.g. *van* always refers to *white van man*, so was placed in our 'people' category). The categories, while inevitably fairly loose, helped to highlight differences in the focus of news articles from the two periods under consideration (all of which contained the word 'austerity').

Table 7.3 Keyword Groupings for the Start of Austerity (SoA) Corpus

Grouping	Keywords
National / international finances and economics (33)	*consolidation, rebalancing, contraction, sovereign, departmental, exports, recovery, agencies, gilts, recession, ratings, levy, yield, gold, bonds, rating, sterling, monetary, structural, optimistic, banks, sales, reduction, vat, confidence, banking, sector, quarter, markets, deficit, pounds, pound, management*
Public money matters (spending cuts, wages) (23)	*unavoidable, efficiencies, thrift, medicine, painful, axe, hardest, efficiency, tightening, pain, expenditure, reductions, savings, tough, scale, frozen, departments, cutting, cut, measures, jobs, cuts, generation*
Benefits (5)	*credits, allowances, child, unemployment, benefit*
Politics and political goings on (4)	*incoming, debates, expenses, debate*
People (2)	*servants, earning*
Other (6)	*aircraft, seem, although, cup, clothes, emergency*
Total	**73**

Table 7.4 Keyword Groupings for the End of Austerity (EoA) Corpus

Grouping	Keywords
(Groups of) people (23)	councillors, mayors, jams, firefighters, infants, self-employed, van, bosses, scots, female, elderly, mayor, employed, fire, father, officers, buyers, women, police, nurses, older, struggling, pensioners
Elections (20)	mayoral, launching, manifesto, results, councils, launches, landslide, elections, draft, campaigns, manifestos, seats, launch, launched, seat, local, pledge, pledges, stand, elected
Britain leaving the EU (17)	brexit, membership, clause, discussions, negotiating, voted, negotiations, border, exit, deal, leaving, leave, vote, security, deals, migration, immigration
Politics and political goings on (15)	leak, committees, preference, apologize, update, wipeout, leaked, suspended, quit, statement, chaos, campaigning, autumn, authority, leader
Public money matters (pensions, taxation, etc.) (15)	jam, lock, diesel, premiums, triple, stamp, funding, giveaways, wage, wages, boost, extra, receive, million, duty
Social/welfare/state provision (13)	dementia, visits, delays, inequality, childcare, care, universal, fit, improve, standards, homes, social, free
Terrorism (8)	terrorism, terrorists, bombing, suicide, terrorist, terror, attack, attacks
Crime / law (8)	investigation, shoplifting, violence, penalty, court, legal, powers, law
Economics and finance (7)	headroom, long term, expenditure, productivity, crash, infrastructure, levels
Media / discourse presentation (7)	grilling, radio, mention, interview, confirmed, questions, saying
Scottish independence (6)	independence, nationalist, referendum, Scottish, nationalists, devolved
Industry/business (4)	merger, nationalize, corporations, car
Education (3)	curriculum, literacy, pupil
Other (13)	networks, ignoring, hunting, pro, fox, globalization, foot, challenges, sea, oil, seven, across, continued
Total	**159**

As Table 7.3 shows, two groups account for most of the 73 keywords in the SoA corpus: 33 keywords (45 per cent) concern national and international finances and economics; 23 keywords (31 per cent) concern public money matters. Both groups suggest that the articles in the SoA corpus not only contain the word *austerity* but are also *about* austerity, with the former group suggesting a discursive focus on the global financial backdrop and the latter on the implementation of austerity.

By contrast, Table 7.4 shows that in the EoA corpus there are just seven keywords oriented to economics and finance. Instead, with twenty-three keywords, the largest category is '(groups of) people'. The corresponding category from the SoA corpus contains just two keywords: *servants* and *earning* (where *earning* forms a participle adjective clause modifying human entities, for example *people earning £x*). These differences in keywords suggest differences in the narratives surrounding austerity in the two corpora. The texts in the SoA corpus are focused on abstract economic concepts and social actors appear to be absent from the discussions, whereas in the EoA corpus people and different sections of society are more visible in the discussions of election campaigns and budgets during this period. The EoA keywords reflect that the UK was entering different times in which balancing the books was not the only issue being discussed and suggest the news articles in which *austerity* occurs do not focus solely on austerity but mention austerity in the course of discussions of other political issues (e.g. Scottish independence; Brexit). This suggests that by 2017 austerity is an established part of the UK political landscape.

One lexical connection between austerity and equality that is readily apparent from the keywords is that *inequality* is key in the EoA corpus. This suggests that part of the discussions of *austerity* during 2017 (as represented by the EoA corpus) involve reference to inequality to a greater extent than in the SoA corpus. We might describe this as a discursive link insomuch as the word *inequality* occurs significantly frequently in newspaper articles that also contain the word *austerity*.

Our keywords provide a snapshot of our two datasets and indicate the differences in the news stories that contain the word *austerity*. From these results we might characterize the SoA data as being about austerity, while the EoA data discusses other topics in the shadow of austerity. Perhaps most striking is the shift from austerity as a series of financial manoeuvres (*rebalancing, consolidation, contraction*) to being a policy that has a human cost (*firefighters, police, nurses, jams*).[5]

7.4.2 Austerity in co-text

Our aim in the second strand of analysis is to identify textual features that demonstrate the nature of the world being created by textual means and to ascertain how these choices may influence our understanding of the sociopolitical keyword *austerity* that is at the centre of our study. The method for achieving this part of the analysis is necessarily dependent on the potential for organizing concordance lines for *austerity* in different ways to find patterns of behaviour in relation to its co-text. There are some textual features, therefore, that are easier to identify by such means than others.

It has been a feature of our prior work (e.g. Jeffries and Walker 2018) in combining corpus searches with stylistic analysis to consider how the meaning of lexical items can be influenced in a particular body of data by the way in which it is combined with other lexis within local syntactic structures, rather than simply looking at the statistical collocational habits alone. Although the automated search for collocations which corpus software makes available can be a starting point for this kind of investigation, we would argue that the behaviour of a word in its structurally related co-text is more closely linked to the specific semantic character of its usage. This can be particularly important where collocational patterns obscure other factors such as contextual negation where an apparent link between two words may actually be the opposite of what it seems.[6] While we use concordancing functions of the software to simplify the task, it is essentially a manual qualitative process of considering the co-text of each occurrence of the word form and finding out what patterns of occurrence there are in the dataset. These patterns, in turn, indicate ideational meaning in the texts in a dataset and two or more datasets can be compared to see how the behaviour of a sociopolitical keyword alters between them. While we use syntactic structuring as a means of organizing the co-text, it is the textual meaning delivered by such structures that is of interest to us, as it tells us whether the keyword has a subtly and/or ideologically different meaning in the datasets under scrutiny. For this reason, we will consider the results of this project under headings relating to the two main 'textual-conceptual functions' of critical stylistics (Jeffries 2010): naming and transitivity.

7.4.2.1 Naming

One of the clearest indicators of how a word is influenced by its co-text is in its behaviour in noun phrases. Once a label has been assigned, via a noun phrase, to some concept or artefact, its existence is difficult to challenge and in some cases (usually definite noun phrases) there is a hard-and-fast presupposition about its existence. Our keyword in this chapter, *austerity*, is a noun itself, so we would expect it to occur in all the usual places that nouns occur in English, as the head of noun phrases, as premodifiers to other nouns, and in the postmodifying element of a noun phrase after a preposition. We find *austerity* in all of these functions in our datasets, and so the questions that arise here are to what extent the proportions of such functions are similar in the two datasets and whether the co-text in each subset of tokens is semantically similar. The first of these questions is answered by looking at the raw figures, and percentages, for each function, as seen in Table 7.5.

Given our expectations from earlier work on sociopolitical keywords, we would anticipate that a word which starts to carry a specific semantic load in a particular political climate would increasingly be used on its own, with little modification to indicate what it means. In other words, the meaning of such a keyword is increasingly assumed to be known by the community of users while at the same time it is emptied of specific semantic content. In the case of *austerity*, we can see from Table 7.5 that there is an increased use as a head noun of top-level NPs (category 1) at the expense of its premodifying use (category 2) and to some extent also at the expense of more subordinate uses (category 3).

If we unpack these categories a little more, we can see in Table 7.6 that the head noun use of *austerity* (category 1) rises more dramatically in its unmodified (bald) state (category 1a) than when it is premodified (1b), and falls still further from a relatively low start for the post-modified structure (1c).

Though the numbers are too small for significance testing, we can break down the figures still further, since we looked at every occurrence, and see (in Table 7.7) that the premodification of *austerity* (category 1b), almost completely loses its connection with

Table 7.5 Broad Function Categories of 'Austerity' in SoA and EoA Datasets

Functional Category	Examples	SoA	EoA	Change
1. Head of NP	*all this promised austerity*	154 (27%)	208 (44%)	Up
2. Premodifier of another noun	*austerity package* *austerity measures*	178 (32%)	80 (16%)	Down
3. Head of subordinate noun phrase in postmodifying prep phrase	*dire political warnings on austerity* *the wintry theme of austerity*	225 (40%)	163 (33%)	Down

Table 7.6 'Austerity' in Head Noun Function in SoA and EoA Corpora

	Function	Examples	BoA	EoA	Change
1a.	Head of NP with no modification	Austerity vanishes when imposing austerity on	41 (7%)	95 (19%)	Up
1b.	Head of NP with premodification only	severe austerity axe-swinging austerity	97 (17%)	118 (23%)	Up
1c.	Head of NP with postmodification only	austerity of low wages and cuts	16 (3%)	6 (1%)	Down

Table 7.7 'Austerity' in Head Noun Function with Premodification in BoA and EoA Datasets

	Function	Examples	BoA	EoA	Change
1bi	Head of NP with evaluative / quantitative premodification	more austerity; grinding austerity; damaging austerity	63 (11%)	111 (22%)	Up
1bii	Head of NP with economic premodification	fiscal austerity; economic austerity; Tory austerity	34 (6%)	7 (1%)	Down

economics between the two periods (category 1bi) despite the data being concerned with budget speeches by the chancellor of the exchequer, and becomes much more strongly associated with negative evaluation (category 1bii), including the superficially neutral, but clearly critical, *Tory austerity*.

As we saw in Table 7.5, where *austerity* functions as a nominal premodifier to other head nouns (category 2), the frequency of such structures halves as a proportion of the overall tokens from SoA to EoA (32 per cent > 16 per cent). Most of the nouns premodified in this way by *austerity* in both corpora are general, and somewhat vague, terms for processes relating to the governing of the country. It is possible that this reduction in use as a premodifier is connected to the increasing use of *austerity* as an unmodified (bald) head noun (see below). Once there is deemed to be less need to explain what *austerity* actually is, the already referentially vague head nouns like *measures* fall away and we're left with the stark mass noun alone.

Where *austerity* occurs within the postmodification of another noun (category 3), there is a striking sub-category of cases where this higher level head noun refers to a period of time, most often denoted by the word *age*. There is an overall reduction (39 per cent down to 20 per cent) in the proportion of *austerity* tokens occurring in the postmodification of other nouns (e.g. *politics of austerity*) but this conceals a much bigger fall (28 per cent down to per cent) in the specific semantic combination of a time noun (*age, years,* etc.) with *austerity*. There is in fact a slight rise in other structures (7 per cent rising to 12 per cent).

What this demonstrates is a falling off of the representation of austerity as inevitable between the SoA and EoA datasets. The effect of seeing austerity as unavoidable follows from seeing it as produced by forces beyond the control of a mere national government. In an earlier project (Jeffries and Walker 2019), where we were comparing the behaviour of *austerity* in Hansard in the immediate post-war period (1940s) with

Table 7.8 Head Nouns Premodified by 'Austerity' in SoA and EoA Datasets, where Figures in Brackets Denote Number of Tokens Greater Than 1

SoA (178 tokens)	EoA (84 tokens)
age; alert; autumn spending review	agenda; aspect; axe
bill; Britain (8); budget(s) (32) 6%	budget; burden
chic; city; cuts (3)	chancellor; cost-cutting programme; cutbacks; cuts (12) 2%
drive(s) (4); economics; era; fashion; fear; games; government; leader; London	drive (4); economic; England; era
meals; measures (55) 10%; message (x 6); muesli	measures (18) 4%; merchants; message; narrative
package(s) (11); period; plan(s) (6); pledge; policy(ies) (5); politics (2); programme(s) (13); promises	plan (2); policy(ies) (11); programme(s) (5); project; public spending
regime (2); reshuffle; rules; saga (2); snacking; summit; tack; talk; upside; years	reforms; regime; rhetoric; road-map; tax(es) (2); thrust; times

Table 7.9 'Austerity' in Prepositional Postmodifier Following Time Nouns / Other Nouns in SoA and EoA Datasets

Function	Example	SoA	EoA	Change
1. Head of subordinate noun in postmodifying prep phrase following time reference	age of austerity; era of austerity; decade of austerity	158 (28%)	42 (8%)	Up
2. Head of subordinate noun in postmodifying prep phrase following other nouns	Climate of austerity; politics of austerity	42 (7%)	59 (12%)	Up

the recent financial crisis period (2005–16), we found that *age of austerity* (and similar phrases) was absent in the post-war period, and only became seen as epochal after the 2008 financial crisis. In the current data, we can see a more nuanced picture whereby the reporting and commentary on budget speeches reflects enthusiastic uptake of policies of austerity by the Conservative leadership in the SoA dataset through the high frequency of *age of austerity* (28 per cent) at the outset and its relative scarcity in the EoA dataset (8 per cent).

Having established the ways in which *austerity* participates in naming practices in these two corpora and observed that it has increasingly been used as an unmodified head noun in the later period, we turned our attention to how *austerity* is linked to transitivity processes (Halliday and Matthiessen 2014) in the data.

7.4.2.2 Transitivity

One of the challenges of combining corpus methods with qualitative analysis is that some of the textual meaning we may want to consider is not easily searchable with existing software. This is particularly so for textual features such as transitivity, where the syntactico-semantic categories of verb are not identifiable in any formal way. In order to get information from our datasets on the behaviour of *austerity* in

Table 7.10 Unmodified 'Austerity' Acting as Participant in Transitivity Patterns in SoA Corpus

Role	Examples
Actor in Material Action	As austerity looms for the rest of us; austerity vanishes when it comes to the prestige (…); when austerity hits; as austerity bites.
Goal in Material Action	Osborne has been openly promising us all austerity for months; extending austerity via state intervention was not…; the government's success in imposing austerity; two full parliaments of intensifying austerity.
Carrier in Intensive Relation	Austerity is a serious problem; austerity is the talk of the moment; austerity has a new champion.

relation to its co-text as the argument of a verb, we therefore limited ourselves to those bald unmodified cases which occur as participants in a clause, with a direct relationship to the verbal element. We annotated the data with participant labels from Halliday's model of transitivity to see whether there were differences in the two datasets.

In the SoA dataset, *austerity* acts in relatively equal numbers of cases as the Actor (10) in Material Actions; the Goal of Material Actions (11) and the Carrier of Attributes (10) in Intensive Relational clauses.[7] The examples in Table 7.10 show some of the variety within these roles.

When *austerity* is functioning as an Actor, it can be seen as personified in some cases where the verb appears to be an intentional action (e.g. *austerity bites*). In other cases, where the process seems to be outside the control of the Actor (e.g. *austerity vanishes*), it could appear to belong to the sub-category of unintentional Material Actions termed 'Supervention' and since both animate and inanimate things can vanish, there is not a strong sense of personification here. In the final set of cases, known as Event processes, austerity seems least personified because these verbs normally occur with inanimate Actors (e.g. *as austerity looms*). As a Goal, *austerity* appears to refer to an abstract condition which is promised or pledged on the one hand and a more tangible set of actions which are intensified or extended on the other. In neither case nor when it is followed by an intensive relational verb, does the transitivity enlighten us as to what austerity actually is. There is no intensive relational usage in this dataset which might be construed as defining the concept.

In the EoA dataset, *austerity* acts as the Goal in Material Actions (50) and less frequently as the Actor (23). Very small numbers of other transitivity patterns occur in this corpus. Table 7.11 demonstrates the variety of verbs in these two categories.

As Actor, in the EoA corpus, *austerity* is also found in a by-Agent phrase after a passive verb (e.g. *the damage caused by austerity*). The effects of this are linked to the process of naming in these texts, whereby the main noun (e.g. *damage*) is one of negative evaluation, making the topic of the clause more about the problems than about austerity itself. Many of the verbs are similarly negative in evaluation (e.g. *fail, ravage, shackle*) and where they are seemingly more neutral (e.g. *cause, continue*), these are usually followed by another noun phrase (Goal) which is negative (e.g. *is causing widespread hardship*).

Table 7.11 Unmodified 'Austerity' Acting as Participant in Transitivity Patterns in EoA Corpus

Role	Examples
Actor in Material Action	Mr Osborne said cuts and austerity would eliminate the deficit by 2015; ... have been hollowed out by austerity; a budget that has been ravaged by austerity; austerity is failing; austerity will extend well into the 2020s; austerity will continue to drive down government spending.
Goal in Material Action	He will reject calls to abandon austerity; Retailers blamed austerity; 'plan to end Tory cuts' by ditching austerity completely; He has resisted pressure to end austerity; was a massive opportunity to end austerity; Mr Hammond was forced to extend austerity; by promising to oppose austerity.

In the larger group featuring *austerity* as Goal, the EoA corpus still has the occasional mention of extending, imposing or necessitating austerity; however, by far the majority of cases relate to opposing, ending or blaming it, demonstrating again the largely negative evaluation of austerity in this later period.

7.5 Discussion and conclusions

This chapter has explored the word *austerity* in two corpora, one representing the start of the recent period of reduction in government spending and the other covering a period when commentators and politicians began to claim that austerity was at an end. We used a combination of corpus investigations (keywords) and qualitative analysis based on the critical stylistic framework to establish the discoursal context of the word *austerity*, its links (or not) with (in)equality and the usage/meaning of the word in the two sets of data.

Finding *austerity* alongside different keywords in the texts it occurs in tells us in general that it was usually the main topic of the texts we collected for SoA, but it was more peripheral as a negative background to other concerns in the EoA corpus. However, keyword analysis does not tell us how a persuasive discourse of austerity or inequality is constructed linguistically. For this, we needed the more focused analysis which examined the word in its relevant co-text surroundings. And here we found that austerity had become more negatively evaluated, less epochal sounding and thus less immediately obvious as the way forward by the EoA period.

One problem with this kind of research is understanding and establishing what a *discourse of X* actually means. We hope that on the basis of this project we can argue that one particular *discourse of inequality* is that which constructs austerity as a viable and (three times) electable policy. Since the 1970s, when Margaret Thatcher first introduced the idea of the nation as a family trying to put into its shopping basket only what it could afford, there has been an increasing inevitability associated with the need for austerity. Since then, and particularly after the financial crisis of 2008, the world has been increasingly textually constructed in this way by the press and other media, contributing to three election successes (albeit not strong ones) by the Conservatives.

The UK electorate voted repeatedly and in large numbers for measures that would worsen inequality because they saw the logic of austerity and were presented with no alternative plan.

In our decision to investigate the word *austerity*, we anticipated that it would link strongly to inequality, the focus of this volume, since it is clear to many of us living through these times that the decision of three Conservative-led governments (including one where they were in coalition with the Liberal Democrats) to make austerity their primary goal was producing unprecedented poverty levels. However, what the investigation reported here found was that, like *choice* in earlier times (Jeffries and Evans 2015), austerity by this time was seen not only as a different kind of concept from the post-war years but it had also become an *a priori* virtue akin to democracy, freedom and equality. While it may be obvious to most that austerity has contributed to the worst levels of inequality we have seen in the UK in decades, it is now defined in such a way that it is difficult to argue against as a strategy to get us back onto the road to prosperity. We may be able to see in practical ways that the metaphor of the nation's finances as a family budget where we are morally bound to balance the books is illusory. Nevertheless, the means to argue against this appear so far to be eluding us and are largely absent from the national debate where the image of austerity as an unpleasant-tasting medicine which will solve our fiscal problems remains even when politicians of all stripes are now arguing for an end to austerity.

Notes

1 The following quotation is attributed to Thatcher during her 1979 election campaign: 'Any woman who understands the problems of running a home will be nearer to understanding the problems of running a country.' See for example 'Margaret Thatcher: A Life in Words' (2013) and 'In Quotes: Margaret Thatcher' (2013).
2 We are using italic *austerity* to indicate the word and non-italic to indicate the concept. It is not always easy to separate these, but we have attempted to be consistent.
3 See 'Thousands attend anti-austerity rallies across UK' (2015) for report on anti-austerity rallies in June 2015.
4 The speech (for which Cameron was paid an undisclosed amount) was given at a leadership event in Seoul, South Korea, and was reported widely in the press; for example the *Guardian*'s coverage at Asthana and Mason (2017).
5 In this context, *jams* refers to those who are 'just about managing'.
6 For discussion of this issue, see Evans (2016).
7 A small number of additional examples (3) have *austerity* occurring as the attribute (usually after an existential verb BE) and another small set have it occurring in minor structures (3), for rhetorical effect (e.g. Austerity or inflation. That's the choice …).

8

More inequality, but less coverage

How and why TV news avoided 'The Great Debate' either side of the financial crisis 2008–14

Richard Thomas

8.1 The evolving landscape of inequality

In the 1980s, British comedian Harry Enfield developed two characters whose profiles, intentionally or otherwise, highlighted increasing income inequality. With his reliance on benefits, alcoholism, violence and his dysfunctional family, 'Buggerallmoney' emphasized one extreme. Meanwhile self-made 'Loadsamoney' bragged about his 'wad' of cash, exemplified an era of 'personal greed' (Butterick 2015: 80) and emphasized the other. Since then, income inequality has gained traction as a social issue, and is frequently viewed through the prism of the financial crisis 2008–14. The biggest crisis of capitalism 'since the crash of 1929' (Atkinson 2014: 472), however, contains conflicting narratives. While bank executives continued to enjoy high salaries, for example, the fall in real wages in the UK was much higher than that experienced by citizens in other nations (Machin 2015). Indeed, the economic crisis can be summarized as having a dramatic impact on citizens, while seemingly complicit financial sector actors did not suffer so obviously (Butterick 2015).

The bail-out of the Northern Rock Bank in mid-September 2007 is considered the first British manifestation of the unprecedented economic conditions that followed. In a report on the BBC on 26 March 2007 about the multi-million pound pay award to Barclays CEO Bob Diamond, Robert Peston, who was an influential commentator business matters (Hulbert 2015), described income inequality as 'fast becoming one of the great debates of our age'. The Conservative-dominated administration in power since 2010 had pursued policies closely associated with austerity, and yet between 2010 and 2015 the number of UK billionaires had doubled (Clarke-Billings 2015). The trend has continued in that while there were 134 billionaires based in the UK in 2017, 'fifteen years ago, there were 21' (Monaghan and Elgot 2017). Furthermore, top executive salaries have increased far faster than average pay and inflation (Topham 2013), income inequality in the UK being rated as 'well above the OECD average in the last three decades' (Organisation for Economic Co-operation and Development 2015: 1).

In sum, the nation was by then 'the most economically unequal state within Europe' (Dorling 2016b).

Alongside the growing number of billionaires, increasing numbers of people in the UK became reliant on foodbanks and pay day loans to cover their basic daily needs (Poverty and Social Exclusion 2013). One month into the new Conservative administration in 2015, and amid plans for further cuts to welfare and public services, Julia Unwin of the Joseph Rowntree Foundation declared that 'thirteen million people in poverty is still too many in the world's seventh richest country' (Joseph Rowntree Foundation 2015). In 2018, the same organization reported that the figure had since risen to over 14 million (Joseph Rowntree Foundation 2018). With the UK simultaneously claiming both record numbers of billionaires and of citizens living in poverty, it is unsurprising that the causes and consequences such disparity have gained wider recognition through seminal and accessible empirical works by Wilkinson and Pickett (2010), Piketty (2014), Dorling (2014), Sayer (2014) and others.

Even so, some with a pro-business world view have been unashamedly explicit about inequality and its potential justifications. In 2013 for example, then London Mayor Boris Johnson hailed greed as a 'valuable spur to economic activity' and called for the 'Gordon Gekkos of London' to display their avidity for economic growth (Watt 2013). Wealth, however, had become tarnished; executive salaries and perks were still considered unjustifiably high (Colvile 2014) and were often associated with greed and a lack of conscience. Most critical of all, Wilkinson and Pickett (2009: 502) suggested that 'inequality is highly predictive of health' and tangible links have long since been found between income inequality and life expectancy across a range of demographics (see inter alia Idrovo, Ruiz-Rodriguez and Manzano-Patino 2010, Torre and Myrskylä 2013).

However, the analysis of the news coverage of income inequality cannot simply polarize into the differential between wealth and poverty. The poorest and wealthiest in our societies, for example, are outnumbered by those who are neither rich nor poor but who during the financial crisis found their pay frozen, their savings reduced, their pensions delayed and their weekly shopping less affordable. Far from being a matter only for the wealthy or those professionally involved in it, business and financial news, in the words of SKY's TV Business and Economics editor Michael Wilson was happening 'in a town near you', and had 'marched right in through the front door, to you and your family' (Wilson 2008: 61). The wider focus of this research therefore is the coverage of poverty, wealth, the squeezed middle and income inequality (PWSIE issues).

There are sound reasons for examining the coverage of these issues on TV news in particular. First, information about poverty and income inequality generally emanates from the media (McCall 2013), and it not only provides a forum for debate but also shapes attitudes towards such issues (McKendrick et al. 2008). Furthermore, despite the exponential increase in internet use, more British adults use television as a news source than any other platform. Indeed, Ofcom (2018) reports that BBC and ITV are the two most used news sources in the UK. In sum, amid 'the proliferation of audio-visual devices', TV remains central within our cultural landscape (Lewis 2013a). As such, citizens might justifiably expect that such seismic financial changes are debated in useful and informative ways by a range of social actors within news reports adhering to noble journalistic principles. The core issue, therefore, is whether such expectations are met by the UK's two major TV news providers (BBC and ITV), and if not, why not? Since they are funded by a licence fee paid for by the public, it seems reasonable to expect that the BBC, for example, should serve the people paying for its output by properly scrutinizing issues such as increasing inequality and others connected with it in appropriate detail. In sum, one might imagine that given the BBC's obligation to be impartial, it would provide high-quality journalism irrespective of the political and ideological dimensions associated with such contentious and polarized societal issues such as poverty and wealth.

British broadcasting's wider regulatory system applies to both BBC and ITV, among others, and dictates that they adhere to the ethos of public service. The benchmark against which any coverage of PWSIE issues should be considered is that the journalism they produce should act in the public interest. More specifically, normative models of economic, business and financial reporting expect it to reliably and impartially explain complex issues (Schifferes and Coulter 2013). One would expect this to be especially pertinent during the financial crisis 2008–14. By looking in specific detail at the year before the crisis began, and what is commonly recognized as the last year of the crisis, it will be possible to see not only what this coverage consisted of versus a normative model but also how it evolved.

8.2 Quantifying the news, income inequality, poverty, wealth and the squeezed middle

This research consisted of a content analysis to establish the locations and basic details about news items containing traces of PWSIE issues. Thereafter, a finer grained, textual analysis established embedded meanings within news reports. The 10.00 p.m. bulletins on weekday evenings on both the BBC and ITV were chosen on the basis that they both attracted the largest audience, were comparable in length (thirty minutes) and enjoyed the status as 'flagship' news broadcasts (Barnett and Gaber 2001). Only weekday bulletins were included in the sample, since weekend bulletins are considerably shorter, are often preoccupied with sport and generally offer less detail. The 2007 bulletins were accessed through a DVD archive at Cardiff School of Journalism, Media and Cultural Studies,[1] while the 2014 bulletins were accessed through the Box of Broadcasts (BoB) database, an academic resource provided by the British University Film and Video Council (2018). In order to capture news data accurately, non-news elements such as idents, mid-bulletin summaries and warnings of forthcoming stories were not coded (Brunsdon and Morley 1978). Table 8.1 shows the details of the full research sample and the general data relating to the volume of all news within the chosen sample period.

News items containing any references to PWSIE factors were coded in detail. A news item is defined as a self-contained element within a wider story, and might include an edited package, a live interview, an anchor introduction and so on. References to income inequality, for example, are often nested in a wide range of stories (McCall 2005). There was no 'double coding' (Kalogeropoulos et al. 2015) in that items were

Table 8.1 Summary of TV News (BBC and ITV) Wider Content Analysis

	BBC		ITV	
	2007	2014	2007	2014
Total bulletins logged	212	245	171	244
Percentage of all weeknight bulletins broadcast	81.5	94.2	65.8	93.8
Total number of news stories logged	2,054	2,350	1,882	3,048
Average number of stories per bulletin	9.7	9.6	11.0	12.5
Total news time in seconds	300,483	370,304	222,400	373,715
Total news time in hours and minutes (to nearest minute)	83h 28m	102h 52m	61h 47m	103h 49m

deemed to concern wealth, poverty, the squeezed middle or income inequality, but not more than one of these. In other words, the most dominant issue was coded. While in practice this was quite straightforward, 'borderline' items were classified according to their main thrust: these were often about a range of issues, and in such cases, a judgement was made about the central and most prominent element. Captured variables included the wider story subject containing the PWSIE element, and whether the element was the substantive within the news item, or just mentioned in passing. Intercoder analysis on a sample of data was carried out by a third party.[2]

Numbers, of course, only tell part of the story. Following the content analysis, selected news items containing a good example of a recurring theme were subjected to CDA in order to identify how these key issues were linguistically addressed. CDA is useful in that it accommodates meaning that is often implicit rather than explicit (Hansen and Machin 2013) while also revealing how power and ideology are propagated and preserved (Georgakopoulou and Goutsos 1997). As such, CDA seems eminently suitable for studying the reporting of issues such as poverty and inequality. Furthermore, CDA is an established analytical method within TV news (see Thomas 2016, 2019; Ekström 2001; Johnson et al. 2010; Joye 2010), since the 'reflective commentary' of broadcast news considers 'bias, (mis)representation, inaccuracy, distortion, ideology ... dumbing-down' and 'selective construction' (Montgomery 2007: 20). More critically here, CDA has emancipatory objectives (Mautner 2010) moving towards the call for intervention (Tenorio 2011). It is difficult to conceive, for example, how one might attempt to reveal potential injustice without accompanying such analysis with the wish to inspire some solutions. Essentially, the content analysis provided a 'blueprint' of typical modes of reporting PWSIE issues, and example reports fitting these blueprints and containing multiple characteristics were selected from the wider sample of 9,334 news stories.

8.3 Shifts in coverage patterns 2007–14

Ahead of both content and critical discourse analyses, there were some assumptions that the quality of the news reporting might leave something to be desired. *A priori*, a case can be made that financial reporting falls short of its ideals amid concerns about the narrow backgrounds, outlooks and training of journalists themselves (see, inter alia, Fahy, O'Brien and Poti 2010; Merrill 2012). Furthermore, there are compelling arguments that the specialism promotes big business and the accumulation of wealth (McChesney 2003; Lewis 2013b) but that it has failed to anticipate notable financial scandals and crises (Doyle 2007; Tambini 2010).

Given that only 410 (4.3 per cent) of the total 9,334 news stories that were logged contained identifiable traces of PWSIE issues, it seems reasonable to think that these issues were not a major preoccupation for BBC and ITV news. There were reasonably encouraging signs however, in that across both bulletins in both years, between 79.5 per cent and 83.6 per cent of those stories carrying PWSIE issues did so within reporter packages. While 'live' news – reporters in the field or in the studio giving their reports or speaking live to a news anchor – is more interpretive and assists in providing up-to-date or breaking news (Cushion and Thomas 2013), logically, reporter packages are more likely to supply background and context. In sum, therefore, serious, balanced discussions about the key issues in focus are most likely to occur during the longer, more considered and generally factual reporter packages and it is here, without the breathless urgency of live coverage, that these issues are most likely to be reported in cerebral, purposeful ways.

Table 8.2 demonstrates, first, that PWSIE issues were generally more prominent on the BBC than on ITV, suggesting that in the first instance, the corporation's more demanding public service obligations are actually meaningful in this context. It is also clear that PWSIE issues were found in what are commonly recognized as hard news categories such as Politics and Foreign Affairs. In sum, it seems reasonable to infer that the core issues in focus here were located within the stories and conventions most likely to provide the greatest potential opportunities for serious discussion.

By 2014, PWSIE stories were more likely to be found in stories about the economy, business and finance. One typical example included a story on the BBC on 26 January 2014 which speculated that if the Conservatives won the general election 2015, there would be more spending cuts which would more likely disadvantage those with lower incomes. Another BBC story on 23 January 2014 covered Prime Minister David Cameron's claims that the economic recovery would benefit everyone and that wages would recover. As another example, a story on ITV the previous day described how a tiny property for sale for a comparatively large sum in London accentuated the lack of affordable housing in the capital.

Notably, apart from the issue of wealth, all PWSIE issues were usually reported thematically, meaning that the issue was covered in general terms, without relying on an example or personal story to define it. The squeezed middle and income inequality in particular were both presented almost entirely thematically. One interpretation of this is that TV news misses the opportunity to increase its impact since focusing on those with personal experience of poverty (in other words, episodically), for example, is often an effective means of engaging wider audiences (Robinson et al. 2009). However, thematic framings describe more general elements such as quantification, geographical differences, statistics and wider explanations. Accordingly, this can be seen as a positive sign, since episodic framings – which concentrate on particular personal stories and narratives – are thought to simplify issues to the level of 'anecdote' (Lyengar 1990), meaning that

Table 8.2 Types of News Story Associated with Poverty, Wealth, the Squeezed Middle and Income Inequality (PWSIE) Themes

	BBC		ITV	
	2007	2014	2007	2014
Total number of stories	2,054	2,350	1,882	3,048
Total number of stories containing wealth, poverty, income inequality and squeezed middle stories	110	133	50	117
Relative number of all stories containing wealth, poverty, income inequality and squeezed middle stories (%)	5.3	5.7	2.7	3.8
Types of News Story	Percentage of Stories	Percentage of Stories	Percentage of Stories	Percentage of Stories
Economy, Business	23.6	20.0	48.1	45.2
Foreign Affairs	29.0	38.0	12.0	12.0
Politics (inc. process, policy, scandal, people)	10.0	4.0	14.3	12.0
Sport	3.6	6.0	7.5	6.0
War / Conflict / Terror	4.6	4.0	6.8	5.1
Immigration	6.4	2.0	—	4.3
Crime	3.6	8.0	—	—
Home Affairs	9.1	—	—	—
Health/Medical/ Disease/Research	—	—	0.8	4.3
Others (all very small numbers)	10.1	16.0	10.5	11.0
Total	≈100.0	≈100.0	≈100.0	≈100.0

understandings of such issues are 'disorganized, and isolated' (De Vreese 2003: 38). So, at first glance, by virtue of their general embeddedness within longer, reporter packages about hard news stories and thematic framing, it seems as though there are some important prerequisites in place for PWSIE items to be reported both seriously and in depth.

However, such high hopes do not last long. Indeed, as Table 8.3 shows, the numbers of items involving what might be considered as the most acute issues involving the greatest levels of suffering – poverty and income inequality – actually decreased over the period defining the financial crisis. Stories about wealth and the squeezed middle increased, most likely explained by an emphasis on unusually remuneration and reward, and the fact that the financial crisis – by way of its impact on wages, prices, mortgages, public spending and pensions – was of general concern to those who considered themselves neither wealthy nor poor. This is despite a reasonable expectation that such issues might attract considerably more media scrutiny after a financial crisis lasting several years. It is possible, of course, that those determining news agendas might have felt that the public might have been grown tired, for example, of stories about banks, but such 'bad news' stories continued throughout 2014 (Thomas 2019).

Even more inexplicably, within those stories where PWSIE issues were present, the issues were actually less prominent. In other words, these issues were less pivotal

Table 8.3 Change in Number of Poverty, Wealth, the Squeezed Middle and Income Inequality (PWSIE) News Items 2007–14

	2007		2014		
	BBC	ITV	BBC	ITV	Change
Total items containing **POVERTY**	51	16	30	31	−6
Total stories	2,054	1,882	2,350	3,048	
Percentage of stories containing POVERTY	2.5	0.9	1.3	1.0	−1.1
Total items containing **WEALTH**	23	18	35	31	25
Total stories	2,054	1,882	2,350	3,048	
Percentage of stories containing WEALTH	1.1	1.0	1.5	1.0	0.4
Total items containing **SQUEEZED MIDDLE**	14	4	49	46	77
Total stories	2,054	1,882	2,350	3,048	
Percentage of stories containing SQUEEZED MIDDLE	0.7	0.2	2.1	1.5	2.7
Total items containing **INCOME INEQUALITY**	22	12	19	9	−6
Total stories	2,054	1,882	2,350	3,048	
Percentage of stories containing INCOME INEQUALITY	1.1	0.6	0.8	0.3	−0.6

within the stories that carried them. Figure 8.1 shows the percentage of items where PWSIE elements were a substantive issue within the item carrying them. It is clear that across both TV news channels, such issues were less central to the news reports in 2014 than they were in 2007.

Taken together, these are worrying findings for those who feel that as the most consumed news platform, TV news should be at the forefront of reporting such social issues, especially given that the global financial crisis accentuated their impact. The inevitable conclusion is that across years and channels, despite proper discussions about these important social issues having been given every opportunity to develop, PWSIE issues were less evident and less prominent within news agendas in 2014 than they were in 2007. While there is no data showing what happened between these years, given the severe global financial disturbance it seems reasonable to imagine that PWSIE issues might have become more prominent within news agendas by the time comparative normality returned. As it was the news focus seemed to be elsewhere, and these human conditions look to be increasingly marginalized.

8.4 Discourses of suffering, corpulence and inequality

While content analysis determines the components of a news text, qualitative analysis 'rehumanizes' statistical findings (Gephart 2004: 455). In isolation, descriptive

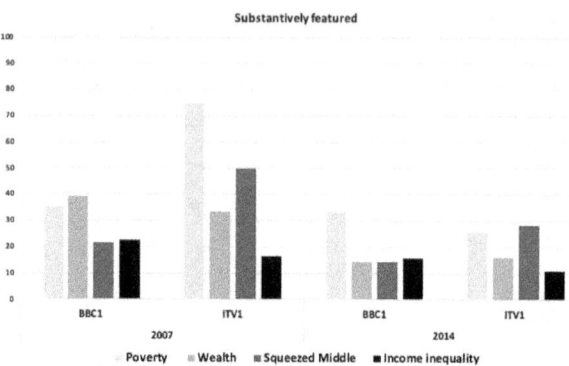

Figure 8.1 Prominence of poverty, wealth, the squeezed middle and income inequality (PWSIE) issues in the news.

statistics may be unsatisfactory (Ackroyd and Karlsson 2014) since they often ignore, for example, the language used in news reporting. Scrutiny of the particular discursive presentations of these issues via commentaries, sound bites and interviews provides a much fuller picture.

In the case of poverty, the decrease in coverage is harder to understand, since stories about international poverty in 2007 – mainly focusing on Zimbabwe's economic implosion – had, by 2014, given way to a more UK-based news focus. Hare (2014) notes that news can often be conceptualized like a hurricane, since the nearer you are to it, the more notice you take of it; it seems reasonable to imagine therefore that, as poverty came closer to home, this fact alone might have generated more stories than before. In reality, though, 106 more bulletins and over 60 hours of extra news in the 2014 sample versus the 2007 sample actually produced less coverage of poverty rather than more.

In 2014, the spotlight fell on reports about increasing poverty levels, how people are increasingly reliant on food banks, how church leaders took to criticizing the prevailing welfare system and so on. ITV's bulletin on 16 April 2014, for example, describes how an unemployed young father had become reliant on foodbanks to feed his family. The man – Steven Jones – starkly defined his financial situation as a bleak daily choice where 'either the kids go without, or I go without, and I'd rather the kids have food before I have anything to eat'.

When, albeit less often than in 2007, the news focus became more international, the ITV example in Figure 8.2 underlines the diminishing prominence of poverty within such news reports. As was made clear by anchor Mark Austin's introduction, the thrust of the story about the deteriorating conditions within a refugee camp in the Lebanon was not the plight of those forced to live there but concentrated instead on the experience of actress Sienna Miller when she visited. The story (made up of a very brief anchor introduction and an edited package) both begins and ends with details of Sienna Miller's 'narrow escape'. Closer analysis of the language used, however, suggests that this might not have been as close as suggested.

Correspondent Nina Nannar refers to an explosion at the checkpoint that they 'had come through that morning'. This actually appears considerably less close than the

Figure 8.2 ITV's report about Sienna Miller's trip on 23 June 2014.

'narrow escape' indicated by Mark Austin. The report concludes with another reminder of the apparent danger to Sienna Miller, and her appearance resonates with notions that while celebrities attract media attention, overly theatrical coverage detracts from the more serious reporting of poverty (Lugo-Ocando 2014). Poverty and the inhuman living conditions in the camp seem to play second fiddle to Sienna Miller's 'escape'. This appears a typical example of how a PWSIE issue – poverty – is often relegated to a more marginal role within a news item.

Another ITV story focused on the other extreme of the wealth continuum versus those suffering in the Lebanon. Since the so-called 'Shareholder Spring' in 2012 (see Thomas 2016), a number of news stories focused on the high pay awards to a range of corporate and sporting figures. While this is not surprising, it is notable that the moral/ethical element of high pay was often marginalized in favour of a fascination about the personal opportunities for acquisition enabled by such wealth. Take for example ITV's report on 1 September 2014 shown in Figure 8.3, which explained that football club Manchester United had just signed the Colombian striker, Falcao.

The report features anchor Mark Austin and sports correspondent Ian Payne, and like many other stories about wealth, is typically episodic and focuses on the large sums involved and what spending opportunities such wealth provides. Payne's lexical choice of 'wages' implicitly encourages viewers to compare the sum to their own 'wages' and is somehow incongruous, since 'wages' suggests a more blue-collar level of reward. Despite the general tone of incredulity expressed by both journalists, neither questions the system allowing such large sums. Payne's perceived 'big question' indeed is not how such salaries are justified against the prevailing socio-economic backdrop where inequality was growing, but instead concerns how such amounts might be spent. Of course, this might have been a light-hearted and rhetorical way to conclude the item, but even so, it was the only 'big question' that was posed. Others including 'how can such salaries be justified?' were absent. Viewers are invited to consider how they might spend £346,000 per week, even though many of those watching would likely be more concerned about covering their essential monthly costs. In simple terms,

Figure 8.3 ITV's report that Manchester United have signed Falcao on 1 September 2014.

the emphasis of the report does not move beyond an almost light-hearted discussion about consumerism and acquisition, similar to the way that the good fortune of lottery winners is often reported. In these cases, too, there is a regular emphasis on 'the first thing' that the winner will buy with their new found wealth.

However, the emphasis on consumerism predated the financial crisis beginning in 2008. There was another pertinent example in 2007 when both channels reported the trial and subsequent imprisonment of Conrad Black, the ennobled former newspaper owner who was accused of defrauding his shareholders. Both channels featured interviews with journalist Andrew Neil, described as someone that knew Black well. In the ITV report of Black being found guilty on 13 July 2007 (Figure 8.4), anchor James Mates continued the preoccupation with the spending power of wealth by asking Neil whether Black's parties were 'as extravagant as made out in court'. Neil answered accordingly that this seemed to be the case. When on 10 December 2007, the BBC reported the sentencing of Conrad Black to 6 and a half years' imprisonment (also Figure 8.4) it too called upon the testimony of Andrew Neil, who responded with a similar assessment. Both reports typify the dominant episodic framings evident within wealth coverage across years and channels, with the narratives strongly focusing on lifestyle details and referring to examples such as the '$6,000 toilet seat', the '$2,000 handbag', 'toys', 'private jets' and 'parties' attended by royalty.

Perhaps even more significantly however, was Andrew Neil's consistent focus on 'the rules' within both his contributions, several months apart, on different channels. He suggests that Conrad Black was not being punished for his lifestyle, but for how his wealth had been acquired. The inference is that although such illegal behaviour is unacceptable, the way capitalism incentivizes such behaviour is legitimate, so long as the 'rules' are observed. Neil presupposes that the 'rules' themselves are legitimate, and the point is not challenged within either interview. The idea that it might be the 'rules' themselves that might be insufficiently robust to prevent the potentially unethical and unpopular acquisition of wealth – as was alleged about numerous bankers during the

Figure 8.4 Andrew Neil's comments about Conrad Black on ITV in 13 July 2007 and BBC on 10 December 2007.

crisis – is not mentioned. Ironically, however, 'rules' might be entirely the wrong word in this case, since it seems clear that the system that allows record levels of wealth and poverty to coexist is actually characterized by systemic deregulation.

8.5 Neoliberalism: The fewer 'rules' the better

In 2014, towards the end of the crisis when the news more widely revealed narratives of mismanagement, greed, excess and criminality, both BBC and ITV seemed intent on regularly defending a neoliberal approach. Figure 8.5 shows various prominent interjections on both channels that provide a robust defence of free markets. The first example comes from the BBC on 30 July 2014 and a report about how bank bonuses might be repaid by those found to have acted unethically. Within the report, Anthony Browne from the British Bankers Association suggests that when compared with bankers in other financial centres, London bankers are the most regulated and lowest paid. He articulates this as a tangible threat to jobs and taxation revenue. Of course, his views are understandable given his role with an association supporting the British banking sector, but the point is that though this contributor was given the chance to build a defence, those with contrasting opinions were not.

In the next example, from ITV on 16 January 2014, employer Leanne Hewitt claims that an increase in the minimum wage – often seen as a Keynesian intervention that disturbs free market economics – will ultimately mean that some of her employees would lose their jobs. The inference is that being able to offer the lowest price in a competitive market takes precedence over a fractional increase in the minimum wage. In the final example, a BBC story about rent capping on 1 May 2014 was punctuated by a soundbite from Andrew Wernick, described simply as a 'Landlord'. His impassioned defence of the free market suggests that this is the 'nanny state' exerting its influence and that suppressing 'free enterprise' is a folly. Of course, these are not journalists talking, but these interjections have been selected as part of an edited package, and as such can be thought of as the work of journalists and editors.

On other occasions, it is the journalist that actually constructs a similar argument. For example, in a story on BBC on 3 February 2014 describing how Lloyds Bank had improved its performance, anchor Huw Edwards begins by explaining that Lloyds Banking Group was selling £5 billion worth of shares, but that the share price had fallen after the announcement that £1.8 billion was being allocated to settle claims arising from the mis-selling of payment protection insurance (PPI). Thereafter, Robert Peston's report suggested that the PPI refunds actually represented a 'massive silver lining', in that the money being given back to consumers would contribute significantly to the country's growing economy. By any measure, this seems to be a very positive spin on what many would consider a financial scandal, fuelled by an insufficiently rigorous regime of financial regulation.

But perhaps this is not the most explicit example of a journalist defending a neoliberal economic system where regulations are perceived as restrictive. As per Anthony Browne's argument (Figure 8.5), a key defence is that unfettered wealth creates jobs for others and generates significant tax revenue. In 2007 – before income inequality became an even more serious issue – a BBC report introduced by anchor Fiona Bruce on 20 June 2007 focused on the suggestion that 'billion-pound private

Figure 8.5 Various defending of free markets.

Figure 8.6 The 'cost' of increasing the taxation system to Britain on the BBC on 20 June 2007.

equity deals' were being criticized for the low rate of tax they are subject to. Concluding the report (Figure 8.6), Robert Peston interviews 'investments superstar' Guy Hands who warns that if the UK taxation regime changed, then these business leaders – and presumably the businesses that they run and jobs that they provide – would move overseas. Perhaps most compelling of all is Peston's final comment. He repeats this alert by once again warning about the 'cost' to Britain; however, he dodges the ethical and moral dimensions of the issue that he himself earlier in the report had defined as equity bosses actually paying 'lower rates of tax than their cleaners'. Notwithstanding that the taxes being referred to are different – income tax for the cleaners and capital gains for the equity bosses – the inequality of their respective situations is clear.

This stout defence, however, is not confined to the BBC. On 15 January 2014, ITV Business editor Laura Kuenssberg concluded her interview with anchor Mark Austin with a similar warning as that voiced by Peston, in that 'we have to be careful how far we go …' when it comes to regulating the banking sector with any restricting of bonus payments. In both these examples, viewers are left with the final (and therefore perhaps, also the most memorable) message that the financial sector should be protected and not further regulated. This message, of course, is supportive of those who have earned millions in bonuses, and in turn this further drives inequality. Such qualitative examples can be added to the fact that in this large sample, there was less PWSIE news after the financial crisis than before and that such issues were less prominent. In 2007, as we have heard, Robert Peston suggested that income inequality was 'the great debate'; if indeed it was – and the compelling evidence suggests that it should have been – then the unavoidable conclusion is that it was not being debated on TV news.

8.6 But why is inequality not being discussed?

On a superficial level at least, the UK's TV news landscape – as represented here by BBC and ITV – apparently provides the right conditions for reporting serious news and topics associated with social justice. Such issues are generally covered within longer news conventions providing opportunities for more detailed reporting. However, there was generally less coverage of poverty and inequality, and PWSIE issues were featured less prominently. Moreover, both ITV and BBC seemed reluctant to interrogate the financial system seemingly enabling increasing income inequality. Even more damning, the defence of neoliberal economics and the promotion of systematic deregulation are so explicit that it hardly requires the sharp incisive potential of CDA at all. The evidence here supports Grisold and Theine's (2017: 4278) analysis of the coverage of inequality in that there seems a lack of 'diversity of information on economic inequality' and 'a neglect of the positive implications of redistributional policies to diminish inequality'.

One explanation for the lack of news about income inequality is that it is simply not newsworthy enough, that it may have lacked some key news values – those characteristics in a news story such as negativity, unexpectedness and so on that editors anticipate the audience will be drawn to – and that as a story by itself, income inequality may be too complex to understand (McCall 2013). Kitzinger (1999), for example, proposes that media portray 'risk' irresponsibly, preferring sensational impacts over cumulative outcomes, with events taking precedence over backgrounds. Indeed, the complex, gradual nature of income inequality may be less newsworthy than other stories because it is a 'slow burn' issue. According to the 'burglar alarm' model (Zaller 2003), for example, extraordinary events such as catastrophes, trials and misdemeanours are needed to promote stories onto news agendas. As such, income inequality might be considered similar to climate change; both might actually be getting worse but at the same time are both background issues that rarely make the news. News channels are unlikely to simply report that 'the environment is still being damaged' or 'there is still great inequality'; it might take a research project or a statement by someone famous to generate sufficient news value for it to feature within a news programme containing on average between 9.7 and 12.5 stories per bulletins (see Table 8.1).

This, however, does not explain why income inequality would be less newsworthy after the financial crisis, especially since the likes of Wilkinson and Pickett (2010), Piketty (2014), Dorling (2014) and others had made the issue much more prominent than before, reaching wider audiences with information about its potential dangers. The answer, perhaps, goes beyond on-the-hoof editorial decisions made in busy newsrooms, and concerns the wider grip of, and deep reliance on, capitalism.

Empirical evidence indicates quite clearly that across mainstream media platforms, the maintenance of capitalism through economic growth is presented as unequivocally positive (Lewis and Thomas 2015; Thomas 2018). Logically, increased output of goods and services (growth) is driven by continuing demand. Irrespective of any environmental concerns (Lewis and Thomas 2015), relentless consumption is therefore fuelled by advertising. Capitalism therefore can be considered to hold modern democracies in a vice-like grip, and based on the quantitative and qualitative evidence here, TV news does not offer any critiques or alternatives. Put more succinctly, it is hard to contest the conclusion offered by Kay and Salter (2014) that at a point when free market economics should be justifiably held to account by public service media, they fail to do so, and instead, it continues to promote what appears to be a flawed model serving the few and not the many.

The idea that the pro-business media organizations generally shy away from discussing income inequality is supported by some simple analysis comparing the *Telegraph* (a UK broadsheet allied to the political right and whose owners have extensive business interests) to the *Guardian* (which has a liberal-minded ethos and an ownership model that does not benefit 'a proprietor or shareholders' ('The Scott Trust: Values and History', 2015)).

Generated with the help of the Nexis database, Figure 8.7 shows how often the phrase 'income inequality' was used in all print editions (including Sunday editions) of these newspapers between 2007 and 2018. Even without the notable spike in 2016, *The Guardian* consistently features the phrase far more than the *Telegraph*. Indeed, for the *Telegraph*, the 'great debate' only merited 157 mentions in 11 years. In short, where there is a need to generate value for owners and shareholders, capitalism and commercialism are the dominant codes, and income inequality is marginalized. This particular comparison is pertinent to the discussion when the TV news data herein is not considered holistically, and the channels are looked at more as separate entities.

Of course, there are some similarities between the BBC and ITV. Not least, there is some travel back and forth involving key journalist staff; indeed since this research was

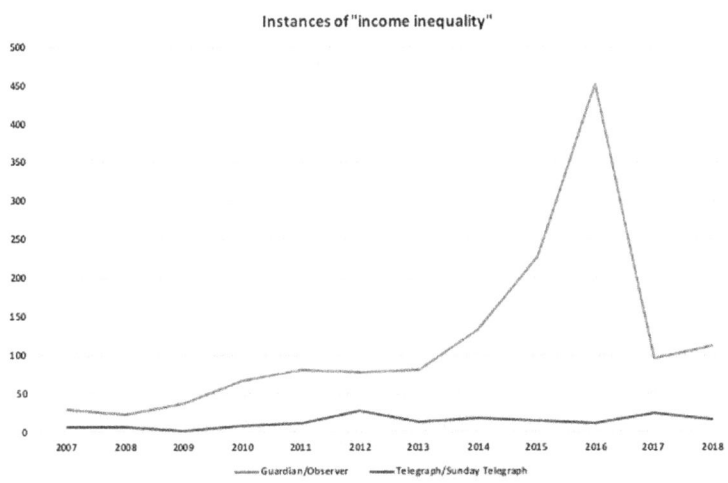

Figure 8.7 'Income inequality' in the *Telegraph* and the *Guardian*.

conducted, both Robert Peston and Laura Kuenssberg moved from one channel to the other. In 2015, Peston became political editor of ITV News, and Keunssberg took over the same role at the BBC. But there are some fundamental differences in terms of what might be expected from each. For example, with its primary position as the nation's public service broadcaster, one might reasonably expect that the BBC would put the interests of its wider viewership first, especially since it is funded by a licence fee. ITV, on the other hand, has lighter public service obligations, and relies on capitalism – manifested as advertising – to pay for its broadcast content.

For different reasons, both channels might be fundamentally unsuited to the reporting of income inequality, and the reasons involve mechanisms embracing themes of power, politics, governance, public service, funding and tradition. ITV's general support of a neoliberal system might be more simply explained in that since it wishes to attract advertisers it is unlikely to undermine the economic system enabling such potential investors to thrive. However, the BBC's apparent unwillingness to challenge capitalism seems more difficult to explain. There are historical suggestions that the BBC's business reporting traditionally avoids questioning the financial status quo, instead preferring a more superficial focus (see, inter alia, Svennevig 2007; Lewis 2013b; Jones 2014). Given its public-serving objective, the BBC might even be considered to be in breach of such noble objectives, especially in face of 'the incessant prodding of commercial interests, combined with the Thatcherite love of the market' (McChesney 2000: 249).

More widely, there are suggestions that business journalism might be beset with bias and vested interests (Shaw 2015). More specifically, some notable empirical studies (inter alia Wahl-Jorgensen et al. 2013; Cushion, Lewis and Callaghan 2017; Lewis and Cushion 2019) support a general thesis that politically the BBC has moved to the right. While still employed by the BBC, for example, Robert Peston conceded that 'the broadcaster actually veers towards a right-wing, pro-establishment view for fear of criticism' (Sommers 2014).

The persuasive argument is that BBC output reflects the preferences of those who run it and produce its content. According to Freedman (2019: 209), 'Senior editorial appointments also reflect an underlying commitment to an aggressive defence of the status quo'; many key correspondents, he suggests, are 'establishment insiders'. Both Jones (2014) and Freedman (2019) provide detailed and compelling examinations of BBC hierarchy from Chairmen to editors, producers and senior journalists, and both conclude therein a widespread and indisputable support for conservative ideology and free market ideals. Robert Peston, who was a key onscreen figure in both 2007 and 2014 research samples, describes the BBC as preoccupied with not breaking accepted rules and conventions when training its journalists (Higgins 2015). Freedman (2019) also points to key figures oscillating between the BBC and organizations that would naturally support free markets, the potential collusion between the BBC and the government when deciding the licence fee, and finally, an assertion that the corporation's key positions are held by members of the most elite strata of British society.

The suggestion is that 'while the BBC claims scrupulously to adhere to its obligation to respect due impartiality', its journalism 'deliberately bows down to a prevailing neoliberal consensus' (Freedman 2019: 211). Such a notion has considerable support (see Kay and Slater 2014; Kelsey et al. 2016) and is difficult to resist.

8.7 Where now?

This all leads to some inevitable questions. First, will the 'big debate' on TV news ever address the serious elements of wealth, poverty and inequality? Second, if we cannot rely on our public service broadcasting system to report income inequality – a critical issue relating to our collective well-being and allegedly 'the big debate' – then who *can* we rely on?

And yet, there is still hope. Irrespective of the evidence here, both ITV and the BBC are capable of meeting its obligations to responsibly report such issues. Emerging from this wider research were examples of ITV demonstrating that they were more than capable of holding a major bank to account with critical and probing journalism. ITV journalists relentlessly reported the problems experienced by Barclays PLC even though the very bulletins containing the censorious reporting were punctuated by advertisement breaks actually featuring commercials for the very same organization (see Thomas 2019). Similarly, even though it was the only story to address income inequality in terms of its causes, consequences and cures within over 9,000 news stories and 350 hours of news, on 28 January 2014, the BBC featured a story about how governor of the Bank of England Mark Carney gave a speech that was highly critical of city greed and rising inequality. In concluding a wide-ranging report suggesting that progressive taxation might solve the problem, Business editor Kamal Ahmed concluded with the words 'if capitalism is to flourish, it is time for reform'. One suspects that before income inequality can become a less serious problem, such reform is required to extend beyond the prevailing economic system of neoliberalism and must reach the practices of the UK's broadcasting system.

Notes

1 This was a DVD archive at Cardiff School of Journalism, Media and Cultural Studies containing a library of DVD recordings that had been made by the technical team at this department. The archive comprised of DVD recordings of each day's key news programmes throughout the year. A quantity of 2007 bulletins were missing from the archive, but I believe a total of 171 still represents a large percentage of what was broadcast.
2 Of the Krippendorf Alpha scores calculated for the intercoder phase of study, variables exceeded 0.77, meaning that all were 'substantial' with many rated as 'almost perfect' (Landis and Koch 1977: 165).

9

The democracy we live in

Can there be democracy without equality?

Wolfgang Teubert

> Rise like Lions after slumber
> In unvanquishable number –
> Shake your chains to earth like dew
> Which in sleep had fallen on you –
> Ye are many – they are few.
>
> Percy Bysshe Shelley, The Masque of Anarchy, composed shortly after the Peterloo massacre

9.1 The aim of this paper

'We live in a democracy – this means "rule by the people". It is therefore important that people should have a say in what happens and what is decided.' This is the first sentence of a brochure issued by the Scottish Parliament, titled: 'How can people get involved in politics?' (Scottish Parliament n.d.). This is what people can do, we are told: vote, campaign, sign petitions, join a party, join a pressure group. What they cannot do is decide. Is this 'rule by the people'?

My aim in this chapter is to show that what we take to be democracy in the Western world is spurious if this notion is to mean that citizens participate actively in decisions concerning the common weal of a nation. The interests of the few still govern politics, and by bestowing this pruned version of 'democracy' upon the multitude, by telling them they are in charge, the few keep them from rebelling, while growing inequality has tolled the death knell of any real governance by the people. It is true that every four or five years we are called to vote for people to fill our national parliaments, and similarly for local, regional and even supranational assemblies. In these elections we can freely choose between the candidates put forward by more or less relevant political parties, and the result, we are told, is a parliament whose members represent the interests of us, the people. We are to believe these convocations will put the will of the people into practice.

In most countries, though, these representatives or deputies, once elected, are not bound by their voters in the decisions they make; the people who voted for them cannot call them back for not keeping their promises. At times, it seems as if these members of parliament often show more loyalty to their party agenda, their sponsors and to the eminent people inviting them to their dining tables. When it comes to unpopular measures, often favouring those at the top, they prefer to wash their hands of them by devolving them to quangos, quasi-autonomous non-governmental organizations without parliamentary oversight, for instance, dealing with education (Ofsted), serious fraud (SFO) or the national finances (Bank of England), or by outsourcing them to private contractors.

If we ask why we, the people, have to leave decision-making to others, we are frequently told that normal people are just too uninformed, too emotional, lacking the necessary experience and the intellectual qualities it takes to deal with highly complex issues. Therefore, it is only in their own interest to elect as representatives people who have an elevated background. They are much better situated to decide what is good for the country, and thus also good for the people, just as parents know what is best for their children. Another problem, we are told, with an unmitigated rule by majority, such as direct democracy, is that the rights of minorities can easily be trampled over. However, as I will show, these concerns are less about the rights of the gypsies, or black and other ethnic minorities, but the privileges of the tiny elite that is, in effect, running the country, whether due to their wealth, the inherited entitlements of certain families or the exalted position someone may hold. While this class is not uniform in its interests, it often forms a strong, solidary network, allowing them to marginalize the interests of the majority, constituted by what used to be the working class.

Taking Britain as an example, it is indeed hardly surprising that this minority, the propertied classes in particular, have fought surprisingly effectively against majority rule up to today. Before the Great War they took it for granted to control both houses of Parliament. Even as this elite conceded, step by step, reform bill by reform bill, extensions of the franchise for the Commons to almost all citizens of age, many members of the House of Lords remained proud to serve the nation without the bother of being democratically elected, because there we would find assembled not those good-for-nothing politicians, but knowledgeable, experienced and proven leaders, who place responsibility above fawning to 'hoi polloi'. For democracy is not everything, as Lord Lawson of Blaby (Nigel Lawson) said on 12 March 2007: '[W]e need to recognise that just as democracy is not the only important characteristic of an acceptable constitution – the rule of law and respect for individual freedom, for example, are at least as important – so democratic legitimacy is not the only form of legitimacy.' Whose individual freedom may he have in mind, I wonder?

In the general aftermath of the French Revolution and under the inspiration of the writings of Karl Marx and Friedrich Engels, revolutions threatened governments everywhere in Europe, and new ways had to be found to deflect them. What was needed was an exercise in public relations, in propaganda. If people could be persuaded that the political system was already democratic, because they had been listened to and all their reasonable demands had already been met, then nothing needed to be changed.

When and how did it happen that the Parliament ceased calling democracy rule by the mob and thus an irredeemable evil, and began calling it the only way to run a country? Relying on Hansard, the official record of all that has been said in Parliament, in either House or in its committees, I will focus on the discussions leading to the reform acts of 1832, 1867, 1884, 1918 and 1928 and pick out those occurrences of the word *democracy* that show how the way in which the word was paraphrased changed over time.

For those occupying the seats in either House, it was understood that this democracy only meant the right to vote, not the right to decide. And the people concurred, by and large. All they wanted was to be listened to. Once parliament had nodded through what government had proposed, the electorate rarely withheld their consent, being satisfied to live in a democracy.

9.2 This is not an exercise in linguistics proper

Discourse is not a mirror of discourse-external reality. In a world without discourse, there are no such things as 'democracy', 'equality' or 'class'. Our social reality consists of what is said about it. Talking in many voices, this discourse is self-referential; it discusses, comments on, criticizes and contradicts what has been said in previous contributions. One message, however, stands out. We live in a democracy. Parliament decides on matters of public importance. There is a party supporting what government wants, and there is an opposition usually taking a contrary view. Matters are decided by majority vote. This is, people are told, democracy at work.

This is not a scientific paper. I cannot prove my claim that the political systems of Western countries calling themselves democracies do not actually empower their citizens to run public affairs collectively, because I cannot show reality as it exists outside discourse. I argue from a constructivist position that it is not so much their personal experiences but the media discourse to which they are exposed that creates for most people the social reality that largely determines their attitudes, opinions and behaviour. No amount of methodical linguistic analysis could show what is 'really' the case, in a discourse-external reality. All we, linguists or lay persons, can do is engage in an open, unregulated dialogue, offering and comparing arguments for our respective views, discuss where we disagree, without expecting to come to a shared conclusion. This is all the true remit of the humanities, with discourse analysis being a part of it, namely what I call the art, or the craft, of interpretation. The beauty and also the weak point of interpretation is that it is largely free from methodological constraints and that there is no such thing as a true or final interpretation. Interpretations have to be interesting and controversial, and they succeed if they give rise to more interpretations. In the end, the members of such an interpretive community, as Stanley Fish (1980) envisioned it, will have raised their levels of reflection but will not have solved the issue. Discourse must remain plurivocal or it will be as dead as a dodo. What I claim in this paper is just one way to look at the way social reality is mediated.

9.3 Democracy: Does it do what it says on the tin?

Before I have a closer look at democracy, as discussed by members of the British parliament, I will look at what some other participants in public discourse have said about it. In the German academic tradition, I will start with the ancient Greeks, namely Aristotle. In his *Politics*, he discusses his experiences with Athenian democracy and defines the notion as rule by all free citizens, including those not holding any substantial amount of property (while excluding slaves and metics (μέτοικοι), the ancient equivalent of migrant workers). Aristotelian democracy is thus largely synonymous with what Karl Marx and Friedrich Engels, in their Communist Manifesto of 1848, called the dictatorship of the proletariat. In Book III, Part 8 of his *Politics*, Aristotle says: '[O]ligarchy is when men of property have the government in their hands; democracy the opposite, when the indigent, and not the men of property, are the rulers' (Aristotle 1999, Book III, Part 11). He also links inequality to injustice: 'The democrats say that justice is that to which the majority agree, oligarchs that to which the wealthier class; in their opinion the decision should be given according to the amount of property' (Aristotle 1999, Book VI, Part 3). In 1973, the German Jewish Marxist historian (and politician) Arthur Rosenberg pondered Aristotle's view on democracy, just before he was forced to emigrate to America:

> [Aristotle] does not believe that it is possible to form in a state a majority abstracting from the class contrast where there is an abyss between the poor and the wealthy. It all hinges on the question who are the 'masters' in the state, the wealthy or the poor. This is what separates democracy from oligarchy.
>
> Rosenberg 1973

Rosenberg omits to mention that Athens was not a democracy according to our modern understanding of the term, as only free citizens, actually a minority of the population, were allowed to have their say, excluding also, in the spirit of the time, women. That democracy presupposes universal franchise, however, is an argument that only gradually became mainstream in the twentieth century. But revered as Aristotle was, himself member of the elite, no one among the Athenian ruling class had any interest in putting his radical concept of democracy to the test. Then as today, rule by majority came to be seen by those in power as a grave danger for the political systems in place.

Perhaps a defining difference between the British and the continental view is the issue of sovereignty. In his *Contrat social* (1768) Jean-Jacques Rousseau had pointed out that the 'volonté générale' can only express itself in a direct democracy, implying that the sovereignty of the people cannot be delegated to representatives:

> My argument, then, is that sovereignty, being nothing other than the exercise of the general will, can never be alienated, and that the sovereign, which is simply a collective being, cannot be represented by anyone but itself – power may be delegated, but the will cannot be.
>
> Rousseau 1968

This is still, I believe, the official credo of many continental constitutions. In Britain, however, sovereignty is allocated not to the people but to the parliament. The Parliament tells us on its website:

> Parliamentary sovereignty is a principle of the UK constitution. It makes Parliament the supreme legal authority in the UK, which can create or end any law. … Parliamentary sovereignty is the most important part of the UK constitution.
>
> UK Parliament 2019

It is interesting that this introductory sentence mentions neither citizens nor democracy. But with the possible exception of Switzerland, direct democracy, unconstrained majority rule, is, apart from the occasional plebiscite, not the way Western countries are governed. They are representative democracies. All nationals, and sometimes also residents, above a defined age, are called to the ballot boxes, normally every four, five or more years. They are given the choice between candidates (usually put forward by political parties), candidates who have been selected in sometimes more, sometimes less transparent ways. Paul Cartledge, a Cambridge historian, has his doubts as to the democratic nature of this system:

> I have since found myself invited to reflect, in a wide variety of contexts and modes, on democracy ancient and modern. Or rather, on ancient as distinct from and indeed as opposed to modern. I have tried to broadcast and inculcate this historically grounded message: that direct democracy, as invented by the ancient Greeks of Athens, and indirect representative/parliamentary democracy, as invented cumulatively in England, the USA, and France between about 1650 and 1830, are two quite different, often opposed modes of political self-governance. They merely happen to share a name, which is itself a coincidence of considerable historical interest and impact, but also potentially grossly misleading.
>
> Cartledge 2018

Grassroots democracy is up to this day identified with majority rule, and majority rule with the tyranny of the majority and the oppression of minority groups. That the rights of minorities and the freedoms of individuals, especially the privileges of those at the top, are at risk in a direct democracy has been the main argument for introducing representative democracy. To protect the privileges of those at the top, the son of the last Austrian emperor, Otto Habsburg, suggests what he calls an operative democracy:

> The supreme, and most difficult, problem in politics is the protection of the legitimate rights of minorities from the whims of rulers and majorities. Only a constitution which safeguards these rights, even if they belong to a despised or unpopular group, can provide the foundation of a legitimate state. On this foundation an operative democracy can be built.
>
> Von Habsburg 1961: 3

Otto Habsburg's statement reflects the attitudes of those counting themselves among the ruling class. They still fear any form of grassroots democracy, that is the rule of the mob, as they see it. The Oxonian philosopher Chris Grayling is quite outspoken:

> Representative democracy has two fundamental features: First, those elected to serve in Parliament are representatives, not delegates; they are sent to think, examine, debate and decide on behalf of their constituents, and they have plenipotentiary powers to do so. Representative democracy is structured to ensure that decisions on complex and consequential matters are not arrived at in uninformed, hasty, emotional and populist ways, such as you expect from a referendum on a simple yes-no question. A representative democracy is precisely not a 'direct democracy' because the latter is too likely to behave as an ochlocracy.
>
> Grayling 2016

Were it up to Grayling, only those should be invited to serve as members of parliament whose education at the best schools would have taught them the meaning of the word ochlocracy ('mob rule'). But is he right to declare they 'decide on behalf of their constituents'? Are there no other interests they take into account? And Grayling does not ask why our media leave lots of people uninformed. It is not their fault that the state education they receive does not prepare them better for democratic participation. It is, by the way, the same argument that excluded the black majority from having a voice in South Africa. It suits the propertied classes if those less lucky are kept in the dark, first by substandard schools and then by the mainstream tabloids.

The remedy to rule by majority is, as people like Habsburg and Grayling see it, liberal democracy. In this form of government it seems it is mainly old families, billionaires, entrepreneurs and the managers they employ to further their interests, whose rights have to be protected. According to Wikipedia (2019), a 'liberal democracy' is based on the rule of law, a market economy, private property, human and civil rights. This is the Lockean tradition of human rights, which we also find advocated in the American *Declaration of Independence*, invoking life, liberty and the pursuit of happiness as 'unalienable rights'. While different arguments have been made as to why Thomas Jefferson replaced *property* by the *pursuit of happiness* in the draft, the *Declaration* can be read as a sanitized version of John Locke's dictum that states exist to protect the property of those who have it: 'So the great and chief purpose of men's uniting into commonwealths and putting themselves under government is the preservation of their property' (Locke 1982: 124). Property, though, defines a minority; the majority of the people may have some belongings but are excluded from being what is called *propertied* – 'owning property and land, especially in large amounts' (New Oxford English Dictionary 1998). Horses and servants may generate property, but they cannot create it for themselves: 'Thus when my horse bites off some grass, my servant cuts turf, or I dig up ore, in any place where I have a right to these in common with others, the grass or turf or ore becomes my property, without anyone's giving it to me or consenting to my having it' (Locke 1982: 28).

In a representative democracy, it is not the people (the citizens) but the representatives they have voted into parliament in whose hands all important decisions rest. As they cannot be recalled by the voters (except when they have been convicted of a crime), they are not bound by the will of their constituents. Under pressure by party whips, by the authority of the government or by powerful lobbies, members of parliament can hardly be expected to respect the interests of their voters.

That inequality is the death of democracy features prominently in Michael Toolan's new book *The Language of Inequality in the News*: 'A highly unequal society ... is inevitably also an undemocratic society' (Toolan 2018: 8). But as far as inequality is still discussed in today's media, it is carefully decoupled from the notion of democracy. So in a rare article on inequality in the *Daily Mail* on 14 August 2019 titled 'Too much inequality "puts public services at risk"', we read: 'Scientists discovered that in a very unequal society, people with higher incomes were less inclined to contribute their proportional share towards public goods and services. This, in turn, led also people on the lowest incomes to contribute less.' There is no word, though, about the implications of inequality for the working of democracy. Such narratives abstracting from any link between economic matters and democracy let people in the belief it is not the political system, but the uncontrollable 'markets' that are to blame if they live in abject conditions. This kind of mainstream media discourse supports a system where the elites, the financial elites in particular, call the shots.

As deregulation has liberated the markets from the constraints of the political will of the people and also their representatives, Angela Merkel has redefined the relationship between democracy and those who move the markets, in a revealing statement, made on 2 September 2011:

> We live in a democracy and that is a parliamentary democracy, and that is why budgetary law is a core right of Parliament and, in this respect, we will find ways in which parliamentary participation is designed in such a way that it is nevertheless in conformity with the market.
>
> Merkel 2011

The task of politicians is, in the view of Angela Merkel, to redesign the role of parliamentary democracy in such a way that it is bound to decide in favour of the interests of the tiny minority of those who move the markets. But this is nothing new. What is called liberal democracy has become a form of government designed for a neoliberal economy, an oligarchy, as Aristotle called it. Indeed, it amounts to the freedom from regulatory oversight of the economy and of those running it, an exemption from democratically imposed regulations which citizens or delegates acting in their interest would, in all probability, impose on them. The consequences are telling. As revealed by *Common Dreams*, a US alternative news outlet, on 14 June 2019, the wealth of the top 1 per cent of the US population grew by a stunning 21 trillion dollars between 1989 and 2018, while the bottom half lost 900 billion dollars over the same period (Bruenig 2019). The gurus of the so-called free market economy, none more so than Friedrich Hayek, were writing the hymn sheets from which not only neoliberal economists but also politicians sing today: 'A limited democracy might indeed be the best protector of individual liberty and be better than any other form of limited government, but an unlimited democracy is probably worse than any other form of unlimited government, because its government loses the power even to do what it thinks right if any group on which its majority depends thinks otherwise' (Hayek 1978).

The hub for spreading such post-democratic ideas is the Mont Pèlerin Society, founded already in 1947, and for many years run by Friedrich Hayek. Among its former and present members we find Milton Friedman, Ludwig von Mises, Michael Polanyi and Karl Popper. It inseminates the Davos World Economic Forum. The quotation at the top of Lars Cornelissen's 2017 contribution to the *History of European Ideas*, with the title '"How can the people be restricted?": the Mont Pèlerin Society and the problem of democracy 1947-1998' is taken from the emeritus professor of the London School for Economics, Kenneth Minogue and tells us a lot about the mentality of those who consider themselves the leaders of the Western world:

> [W]e should really be concerned with the question: How can the people be restricted? For it is their laziness and yearning for effortless and priceless security, their passion for the delusory free lunch, which is inevitably at the heart of the problem.
>
> Cornelissen 2017: 507

According to the ideology of the Mont Pèlerin Society, the danger democracy poses for the wealth of nations are first to asphyxiate the markets by regulating them and secondly to attack the rule of law by voiding the privileges the ruling class had acquired over time, in the words of Lars Cornelisen:

> [C]onsiderations by MPS members of the dangers concomitant with democracy tended to follow two lines of argumentation, the first of which considered democracy dangerous because it tends to disrupt or even destroy the market order, whereas the second hinged upon the view that democracy may undermine the separation of powers, thus imperilling individual liberty.
>
> Cornelissen 2017: 516

The markets must be obeyed. They may move in unpredictable ways, but the people moving them are not wage earners, not people paying back their mortgages over decades, but the Uncle Scrooges, now calling themselves investors, which gives them a positive image. While the people are made to believe they live in a real democracy, those who dwell at the top of the pyramid have made sure that our political system works on an unwritten constitution granting oligarchs the freedom to enrich themselves at the expense of the people.

9.4 The emergence of a class consciousness and its consequences

Of course, political classes cannot be but arbitrary constructs. But this does not mean we should cease talking about classes. When those at the top call themselves a minority and the rest of the population the multitude, they divide society into classes. In their stratification, Western societies are formed like a pyramid, with few at the top and the bulk at the bottom. From my admittedly arbitrary perspective, I would roughly define an upper class of the 1 per cent of the richest people/families in the country. Below them is an upper middle class of the 5 per cent of propertied ancient families, of other rich people including most CEOs of companies listed in the FTSE, of other people in eminent positions wielding particular influence (bishops, senior judges, very senior civil servants, members of the House of Lords, very successful entrepreneurs, media tycoons, not to forget university vice chancellors). Below them is the middle class comprising perhaps 10 per cent of the population: for instance, upper management people, head teachers, partners in big law firms, some eminent university professors, many members of the House of Commons, consultants, successful entrepreneurs, top people in the arts and in entertainment and some of the more durable celebrities. Then there is a large lower middle class, composed of highly skilled workers, clerical workers, teachers, nurses, the police and so on. The old working class seems to be disappearing, with some moving up into the middle class and a growing number turning into what is now called the precariat, that is the quickly growing number of people living in dire circumstances, in jobs not paying a living wage and often struggling to pay their rent, increasingly relying on a deteriorating welfare system.

The small segment of the population that have been and are still ruling the country, belonging to a large extent to the old guard networks, do not have to worry, it seems, about losing the privilege to be first choice when it comes to securing the best positions. As the *Elitist Britain* Report 2019 – issued jointly by the Sutton Trust and the Social Mobility Commission – shows, the privilege of attending Oxford or Cambridge (less than 1 per cent of the population) considerably improves one's professional chances in later life. Senior judges: 71 per cent; cabinet: 57 per cent; permanent secretaries: 56 per cent; diplomats: 51 per cent; newspaper columnists: 44 per cent; FTSE 350 chairs: 27 per cent. Of the members of the House of Lords, 79 per cent either went to a fee-paying or a grammar school. Of the Commons, 37 per cent of the 2010 Parliament went to 'independent' (fee-paying) schools (the Sutton Trust 2019).

How do we have to understand that this tiny minority is still calling the shots after more or less a century of democratic voting rights? Why have the lower middle and the working class not even made a serious effort to turn the tables? Why do they, against all the evidence, still believe in the fairness of the system? Why were Karl Marx and Friedrich Engels wrong in their belief in the inevitability of a revolution? The answer is, I think, that the people were led to believe that a revolution was no longer needed – the goal, democracy, had already been achieved. Therefore, when in the course of the nineteenth century the members of the British parliament, who either belonged to the ruling class or owed their seats to them, came to understand this, all they had to do was to change the narrative from 'democracy is a terrible evil' to 'you are already living in a democracy'.

9.5 Talking about democracy: Negotiating meaning in the British Parliament

Due to space constraints, I will have to restrict myself to just a few quotations from Hansard for the reform bill discussions. The first reform bill I am looking at was discussed in parliament and finally passed as the Great Reform Act in 1832, at still a time when the events in France, especially the French Revolution, had a strong impact on the situation in Britain. There was a growing and increasingly unruly population in major towns and cities, hardly represented in parliament, while there were dozens of 'rotten boroughs', largely deserted places in the countryside, where sending someone to Westminster was at the whim of the local squire. To avoid major unrest (like repetitions of what happened in 1819 in the 'Peterloo' incident), some concessions had to be made to the restive people. Due to a number of artful restrictions, the total British electorate comprised only half a million well-to-do citizens. Democracy was seen as a threat, as the dispossessed were believed to aspire to curbing the privileges of the ruling class. Here are three voices from the discussions, which took place between February and June 1832 (in those days, the speeches were transcribed into reported speech), the first by Sir George Murray:

> The great danger of this bill was the power it would give to democracy. It would give to that House the whole of the power of the Legislature. That he conceived to be the fact; and what had ever been the result of unrestrained or predominant democracy. Throughout the page of history, one common consequence was found to be the end of democracy – destruction. ... What had overthrown Athens, Rome, and, in modern Italy, Florence? Why, democracy.

A theme that repeatedly comes up in this discussion is the freedom from parliamentary oversight enjoyed by those at the top. Here is a quotation by Sir Robert Peel, who stresses that a monarchic system is best suited to keep democracy under close control:

> His attachment to monarchy was a rational attachment, founded on the conviction that where it controlled the democratic principle, it controlled it for the benefit of the governed – that secured as it was from encroachment and abuse, by a system of reciprocal control – a limited monarchy gave a stability to Government, a defence equally against popular violence and military despotism, and a protection to regulated freedom which no democratic form of Government could permanently afford.[1]

My third quotation, by Mr Offley, on the other hand, implies that the bill was the lesser of two evils as it might prevent French conditions:

> The Bill was a sweeping measure in one sense, but he was under no apprehension that it would increase the consequence of demagogues or agitators. The same measure which gave the people just rights would sweep into the same insignificance the demagogue and the boroughmongers. Frequent allusions had been made to the French Revolution, but there was one circumstance to which they did not advert, and that was, that in this country the exclusion of the people from their just rights had been long rankling in their breasts, as the privileges of the nobility had in the breasts of the French previous to the Revolution; and to the protracted refusal of any amelioration in the condition of the people was to be attributed, in a great measure, that convulsion, which was attended with such frightful consequences.

Offley sees giving the people the right to vote would quell any rebellious spirit. This was still an argument when in the deliberations of the 1867 reform bill it was mooted to extend the franchise to the growing urban professional population. When this act was passed, it led to a doubling of the electorate in England and Wales to about two million citizens, giving the vote to all those who had, in the meantime, acquired property. However, it was agreed by the members of both houses of Parliament that those without property must be kept out of any political representation. Jo Eric Khushal Murkens argues that the 'political motivation behind the Reform Acts of 1832 and 1867 was anti-democratic and served to restore and stabilise the authority of the ruling class'; he insists that 'the Second Reform Act was motivated by many things, but democracy and fair representation of the people were not among them', and he concludes that '[i]n short, Disraeli and Gladstone had not embraced democracy; they had conspirationally tamed it' (Murkens 2014: 353, 560, 562). What drove the reform spirit was also the birth of the nation state, as discussed in Anderson (1983) and Hobsbawm (1992), which demanded not just nationwide or comparable institutions, such as schools, the judiciary, the penal system, but also, and more importantly, the creation of a nationwide identity. Regional distinctions were evened out, and a collective narrative evolved encompassing seemingly all people, based on a set of distinctly English or British values ostensibly shared by all decent folk, regardless of class.

In both houses, the debates were much more plurivocal than the common denominators which are the focus of many historical studies lead us believe. Of course, on the whole, statements such as the one by Mr. Hicks-Beach are symptomatic and frequent: '[H]e did not think that the country was anxious that the rich should be ruled over by the poor, and that the intelligence and education of the nation should be subjected to the dominion of an inferior order of civilization.' But Mr. Lowe accepts there is an unresolved issue between the principle of wealth and that of democracy, and this is why he is opposed to the reform: 'You must look these matters in the face, for it is useless to suppose that, founding your institutions on democracy, you can go on legislating with a deference to established privileges and the rights of property on democracy.'

Democracy can only prevail in a society, says also Sir E. Bulwer-Lytton, that has produced, early on, 'a certain equality of manners and education', which, he insists, is not the case of England, for which 'a democracy would be a ruinous experiment'. As 'that universal and generous system of education' does not exist, 'it would be madness to make the working class the sovereign constituency of a Legislative Assembly'. Apparently most of the members of parliament accepted it as inevitable that the lower classes were, in many respects, too ignorant to be trusted with decision-making. But there was an exception, in the person of Lord Houghton:

> Among the lower classes, no doubt, there may exist many foolish opinions and mistaken sentiments; but let education be extended among the people, and there need be no fear of the admission within the pale of the Constitution of those large classes and those new interests.

The streamlining of Britain as a nation state needed more reforms, and thus we see in 1884 the Representation of the People Act, widening the electorate from just over two million to more than five million voters. What had come as quite a welcome surprise to the old guard in both houses of Parliament was that none of their fears concerning a possible uprising of the people had come true. Organizational reforms in both major parties – the Tories and the Whigs – ensured that only candidates endorsed by the leaders were put up for election. There were few radicals among the elected members of parliament. While living conditions of the working class had hardly improved since Friedrich Engels had written his *The Condition of the English Working Class* ([1845] 2009) and would not have changed when George Orwell published, in 1937, *The Road to Wigan Pier* ([1937] 2001), the enlargement of the franchise seemed sufficient to frustrate Marx' and Engels' expectation of a popular uprising.

Thus, at the time of the discussion of the 1884 reform bill, the word *democracy* had, to a large extent, shed not only its negative connotation but also its meaning. Everyone agreed that the United Kingdom was becoming a democracy, if they liked it or not, for instance, Mr. Bryce (later 1st Viscount Bryce), talking in 1886 about possible home rule for Ireland:

> But what are we? We are a democracy. Sir / a modern democracy. ... A democracy loves equality, and it could not bear to think, as it would be apt to think, that in ruling by stern laws it was oppressing the masses of the people. A democracy loves freedom. ... I say that we are a democracy, and that we must, therefore, govern on democratic principles. I may be asked 'Is it possible, then, for a democracy to govern? Are you not admitting they cannot?' I answer that it is possible for a democracy to govern, but only on democratic principles.

For Bryce, freedom was not any more the privilege of the few, but the right of the many, a hitherto unheard of statement. For Mr. Chaplin, however, the notion of democracy had not changed. In his response to Mr. Bryce, he asserts that democracy was still rule by mob, and thus intolerable:

> The hon. Member for Aberdeen said that 'a democracy loves freedom'. Of course it does. But what kind of freedom does he mean? Freedom to go about one's business, the duties of one's daily life – freedom to fulfil one's legal obligations without injury or molestation, or does he mean freedom to rob, murder, mutilate, and commit every sort of outrage with absolute impunity?

There were two more reform bills, one in 1918, which brought the right to vote to middle-class women, and finally the one in 1928, extending the franchise to all women, subject to the same conditions as male voters. Towards the end of the First World War, many soldiers on both sides, fighting in the war, as they often saw it, not for themselves but for their overlords, developed a rather strong revolutionary spirit. As by that time the ruling class had acquired quite a liking for a toothless democracy, understood as the right to vote but nothing more, it looked only logical to expand the franchise to the servicemen, and subsequently also to those involved in the war effort at home, whether male or female. The Conservative theorist, Leopold Stennet

Amery, whose view was shared by many other members of parliament, explained it in these words: 'Our system is one of democracy, but democracy by consent and not by delegation, of government of the people, for the people, with, but not by, the people' (Amery 1947: 20f.). The elected representatives were not bound by the interests who had voted for them; their challenge was rather to explain decisions made so that they would find consent.

Interestingly, the discussions of the People Bill, finally passed as the Representation of the People Act in early 1918, were much livelier in the House of Lords than in the Commons. This act expanded the franchise to all men aged twenty-one and over and, under certain restrictions, to all women aged thirty and over. Occasionally, we still find the old attitudes, for instance, in the contribution by Lord Burnham:

> There is no tyranny so great as the tyranny of the mob, and it is not giving democracy a fair chance if you refuse it the modern equipment which is necessary for its proper expression and conduct. ... Democracy, my Lords, is often unjust and often cruel, but its worst vice is its tendency on all occasions, if it can, to suppress minority opinion; and you cannot guard against that danger by any system of representation that I know or that I have heard any noble Lord suggest unless you follow the sure rule which gives minorities their proper weight in the affairs of State.

The 'sure rule' mentioned here refers to the 'first past the post' electoral system, a tool, then as today, to exclude parties not supported by mainstream media, from getting their candidates elected to the House. However, there were also more progressive lords, for example Lord Parmoor (who started out as a Conservative but later sided with Labour), who advocated proportional representation as a means to open up parliament to all classes:

> I have no fear of democracy. I welcome it, but with this proviso – that the democracy must be, a true and not a false one. It must be a democracy that is really representative. The term 'democracy' has too often been used of a particular class or a particular interest. ... We want the co-operation of all classes of this country. ... That is the argument for proportional representation.

Once again, the argument resurges that certain people are just not fit to govern, this time applied to women. As Lord Sydenham explains, it is their leaning towards socialist ideas that incapacitates them:

> Are women really fit to govern a great Empire such as ours? One immediate effect would be to add very largely to the forces of Socialism which will ruin any industrial or commercial State which submits to their operation.

By the time the last reform bill was discussed (29 March 1928), passed as the Representation of the People (Equal Franchise) Act, giving the vote to all women aged twenty-one and above, the new political system had become so entrenched in the mentality that no one disagreed when Sir Joynson-Hicks uttered his pride in Britain leading the world in matters of democracy:

> Up to the year 1832, the system of Parliamentary representation had remained practically unchanged for four centuries, but, the Act of that year, and the Acts of 1867, 1884 and 1918 effected various reforms, with which I shall deal in a few minutes; and now I have the privilege to move what I hope will probably be the final reform, which will have the effect of giving to the people of our country greater and freer Parliamentary representation than in any other democratic country in the world.

Among the very few who questioned whether parliamentary democracy as practised in Westminster really meant the implementation of the will of the people was Mr. Morris:

> [T]his Bill has very serious defects from a democratic standpoint. ... The election expenses in every constituency will be, unless there is an amendment in the law to meet the situation, increased by one-fourth of the present amount. I take a division where the expenses legally permissible at present may be £1,200, and, unless there is a new provision in the law, that limit will be extended to £1,500. ... If you are going to extend the *franchise* by increasing the election expenses by £300 on a bill of £1,200 – at least that – you are reduced to the position where the electorate must choose either a rich man or the nominee of the party caucus. ... That is the end of the House of Commons itself. The moment [members] come here as hirelings from whatever party, whether as hirelings of the brewers on the one side, of the trade unions on the other, or of the Lloyd George Fund on the other – that moment the House of Commons ceases to be an independent representation of the electorate.

After centuries of staunch opposition by the ruling class to the idea of rule by the people, the national discourse in the first half of the twentieth century had successfully established Britain as the cradle of democracy, a democracy, however, in which sovereignty did not rest with the people but with parliament.

9.6 The instrument of the ruling class: Hegemonic discourse

Karl Marx was wrong. Had he not stated that the conditions of one's material existence determined one's self-awareness ('Das Sein bestimmt das Bewusstsein')? The feeling of powerlessness of working-class members, the unfairness in their treatment, the absence of social mobility, the poverty in which many of them are forced to live, even the wrath they feel against their oppressors: it was there, and some of it may still be there, but it was not and is not strong enough to induce them to revolt, to overthrow the system. For something else has a stronger impact on the way they experience themselves and the world around them. This is the national public discourse they consume, from cradle to grave. It is the teachings of their parents, the lessons they learn at school, the word from the pulpit, the stories they read in the newspapers and magazines, the speeches of statesmen, scholars and other eminent representatives of the realm, the pronouncements of the crown and, not to forget, the world of soap operas and other forms of entertainment, as well: this is what gives the people their sense of identity and of belonging, and what shapes their views.

While there was a time when there was still a working-class discourse, with its own media, with union and party membership, with a commonality of spelt-out interests, any form of political class consciousness has now, when only few people still work in industrial production, largely vanished. The miners' strike of 1984–5 may well have been the last (unsuccessful) uprising against the ruling class. The working class today is characterized more as a culture than by a solidarity of interest directed against their oppressors. People rather want to move up class-wise, and they want to be accepted by those above them as respectable people. Hardly anyone still yearns for a change of the political system. While the gap between the rich and the poor is wider than ever, Marx's 'spectre of communism' is haunting no one. How did that happen?

It was Antonio Gramsci (the Italian philosopher who died of illness after seven years of a twenty-year prison sentence handed down by a fascist court) who first identified, in his prison notebooks, why those outside the ruling class were unable to develop a cultural identity empowering them to overthrow the existing hierarchy. Class, for him, is economically defined, by wealth, income, or the necessity to sell one's labour. But the fury at being exposed to the tyranny of one's overlords, the solidarity with other people subjected to these living conditions, the battle cries for overthrowing this tiny minority that put themselves at the top of the hierarchy they themselves have created, this class struggle can be silenced by those in charge of the public discourse and thus controlling the way reality can be talked about. The reality they construct in this discourse constitutes what Gramsci calls the hegemony exercised over the people. 'The concept of hegemony', says Thomas Bates, 'is really a very simple one. It means political leadership based on the consent of the led, a consent which is secured by the diffusion and popularization of the world view of the leading class' (Bates 1975: 352).

The voices of labour movements all over Europe, their organizations, their rallying cries, the narratives of this counter discourse, have proved impotent in the face of this omnipresent hegemonic discourse, finally put to rest by the demise of the Soviet system. The hegemonic discourse controlled by those at the top, on the other hand, has been carefully engineered to engage the hearts and minds of the public. This discourse is powerful enough to override all the contrary experience of most people. Perhaps because it is sufficiently variegated to allow some dissent, some plurality, something for everyone to identify with, because it plays to the yearnings of 'normal folk', it has succeeded in sustaining a moral platform and giving legitimacy to the political, social and economic system.

The historian T. J. Jackson Lears explains the effects hegemonic discourse has on the members of the American working class:

> In the twentieth century, working-class attitudes seem to approximate even more closely Gramsci's notion of divided consciousness. Most sociological

> studies of working-class Americans in the post-World War II era suggest that their participation in a national consensus has been limited and ambiguous. Summarizing survey data in 1970, Michael Mann concluded, 'It is not value-consensus which keeps the working class compliant, but rather a lack of consensus in the crucial area where concrete experiences and vague populism might be translated into radical politics.' Schools and mass media, implicitly denying class or group conflict, have presented a picture of competitive strivers within a benevolent nation-state. Rather than engage in indoctrination, 'the liberal democratic state' has perpetuated 'values that do not aid the working class to interpret the reality it actually experiences'. In other words, values rooted in the workers' everyday experience lack legitimacy. As Gramsci understood, the hegemonic culture depends not on the brainwashing of 'the masses' but on the tendency of public discourse to make some forms of experience readily available to consciousness while ignoring or suppressing others.
>
> Lears 1985: 577

There were two years in recent history when the hegemonic discourse of the ruling class was at risk, in parts of continental Europe, by a revolutionary counter discourse: 1848 and 1918. In both cases, success was limited. After 1848, a revolutionary movement paved the way towards a remarkably strong working-class culture, only to become gradually absorbed into hegemonic discourse. The specific working-class values, such as equality, solidarity and collectivism, for some time remained locally effective inside tight communities, for example, garden cities, but proved too weak to serve as a model for the whole nation. After the Great War, outside of the Soviet Union, no governments legitimized by workers' councils and promising a more direct form of democracy survived for longer than a few weeks, thanks to the internationalism of the ruling classes as opposed to the lack of working-class cross-border solidarity. In the long run, labour movements grudgingly accepted the model of a representative democracy, including the values promoted by the hegemonic discourse such as family, moderation, diligence, reliability and self-improvement.

In Britain, with its more or less uninterrupted continuity, a prevalent value that was adopted by the working class long before the First World War was respectability. As much as it was an insurance against gliding below into the lower orders, it also acted as a bulwark against any desire to change the social order or the political system. As Caroline Oldcorn writes in her PhD thesis *Middle Class Values and Working Class Culture in Nineteenth Century Sheffield* (1976): 'The values which respectability took and refined for its own end were essentially those which worked best in the service of capitalism, in the pursuit of profit and the maintenance of the social order' (Oldcorn 1976: 1).

Respectability is also the title of Lynsey Hanley's 2016 book, supplemented by *The Experience of Class*. Respectability, she writes, 'is still there as a signal component of what it means to be working class' (Hanley 2016: 26). For Hanley, this value engenders self-respect and aspiration and thus is the precondition for moving up the social ladder. The contrast between her book and Eribon's *Retour à Reims* (2009) could hardly be more striking. Both have moved up from working class to middle class, have become journalists and university lecturers. But while Eribon finds himself helplessly caught up in the conflict between his Marxist values and the affordances of the capitalist system, Hanley is grateful for the opportunity to move up on the social ladder.

Over the last 200 years, the key role of formulating the norms of the society, or the segment of society to which one belongs, has fallen to the traditional media, owned and controlled by the ruling class. The power of newspapers, radio, film and television, not least in its entertainment programmes, lies in the narratives they offer for ready consumption. This is, by the way, also the case for the majority of content consumed on social media.

Hegemonic discourse will accommodate a changing environment and new challenges. One value sticks out in these days: hard-working. Its purpose in times of austerity and cuts to the welfare budget to drive a wedge between people depicted as undeserving recipients of benefits and hard-working working-class and middle-class members. People are told hard work is all it takes to become rich, by quoting, for instance, Jeff Bezos, the richest man on earth, when he claims '[c]hoosing to work hard is key when it comes to being successful' (Huddlestone 2019). It is this discourse, exemplified by the *Telegraph* for the more conservative-minded, the *Times* for the managers, the *Guardian* as the official press organ for disgruntled social workers, teachers and academics, the *Daily Mail* for the lower middle class, the *Mirror* for aspiring working-class families, the *Sun* for the lower orders, that creates the acceptance of a system designed and continuously redesigned to further the interests of those at the top.

Hegemonic discourse preserves the existing power structure without physical coercion. While Marx, who defined 'class' in terms of a person's 'objective' position in the economy, had hoped once people realized how they were exploited, they would revolt in order to establish an alternative system, it was the ubiquity of hegemonic discourse that enabled the ruling class to exert dominion over the rest of the population. Gramsci thus talks of 'the "spontaneous" consent given by the great masses of the population to the general direction imposed on social life by the dominant fundamental group; this consent is "historically" caused by the prestige (and consequent confidence) which the dominant group enjoys because of its position and function in the world of production' (Gramsci 1971: 12). In order to create such consent, certain seemingly class-independent mantras are created to unite the population behind them; in the words of Eric Hobsbawm, 'Slogans such as the defence of the Republic, the defence of democracy, or the defence of civil rights and freedoms, bind rulers and ruled together for the primary benefit of the rulers' (Hobsbawm 1977: 205).

Louis Althusser (for whom the ruling class is the 'industrialist bourgeoisie') complemented Gramsci's concept of hegemony with that of the 'ideological State Apparatuses' (one of which is the media), insisting that 'no class can hold state power over a long period without at the same time exercising its hegemony over and in the Ideological State Apparatuses' (Althusser 2014: 245; emphasis in the original). For Althusser:

> the dictatorship of the bourgeoisie in the forms of a parliamentary or presidential democratic apparatus, the judicial system, the school, the family, the Church

and even the trade unions within the framework accorded to them by the legal system, are such apparatuses, and they provide the appropriate ideology to each segment of the class society: the role of the exploited (with a highly 'developed', 'professional', 'moral', 'civic', 'national' and 'apolitical' 'consciousness/conscience'), the role of the agent of exploitation, (knowing how to order workers around and talk to them), the role of the agent of repression (knowing how to issue orders and exact obedience 'without discussion'), … or professional ideologue (knowing how to treat consciousness/conscience with the appropriate respect, that is, the appropriate contempt, threats and demagogy).

Althusser 2014: 104

As Althusser sees it, the role of parliament is merely decorative, masking the dictatorship of the bourgeoisie: '[T] there is no parliamentary road to socialism. Revolutions are made by the masses, not by parliamentary deputies, even if the communists and their allies should fleetingly, by some miracle, attain a majority in the parliament' (Althusser 2014: 107). Yet these masses are nowhere to be seen.

For Stuart Hall, hegemony needs to be 'actively constructed and positively maintained'. Crises can occur. Mastery 'results from winning a substantial degree of popular consent'. He also denies the existence of a unified ruling class. 'The "leading elements" … may be only one fraction of the dominant economic class – e.g. finance rather than industrial capital; national rather than international capital' (Hall 1986: 15). But Hall admits there is active collaboration between the various factions or apparatuses making up the ruling class:

> The state is no longer conceived as simply an administrative and coercive apparatus – it is also 'educative and formative'; it is the point from which hegemony over society as a whole is ultimately exercised (though it is not the only place where hegemony is constructed). It is the point of condensation not because all forms of coercive domination necessarily radiate outwards from its apparatuses but because, in its contradictory structure, it *condenses* a variety of different relations and practices into a definite 'system of rule'.
>
> Hall 1986: 18 (emphasis in the original)

Stuart Hall's state is the conglomerate of what makes up the ruling class. The message its hegemonic discourse conveys, however, is increasingly channelled by private corporate entities, working as filters. The replacement of the Tory government in 1997 by New Labour was facilitated, to a not inconsiderable extent, by an accord between Rupert Murdoch and Tony Blair.

For Marx and Engels, and lastly also for Gramsci, class was an empirical reality of the capitalist world, regardless of whether people were aware of belonging to a certain class or not. It is perhaps symptomatic of the persuasive power of hegemonic discourse that even neo-Marxist academics now advocate a kind of liberal, pluralist democracy that is a far cry from the rule by majority Marx and Engels had in mind. Ernesto Laclau's and Chantal Mouffe's starting point in their seminal book *Hegemony and Socialist Strategy* ([1985] 2001) is that 'class' is not real but a discourse construct, in this sense no different from 'democracy' or 'hegemony'. This could explain why for them 'class' is consigned to the background in their conceptualization of democracy: the role they assign to democracy is to strike a balance between the interests of all the minorities making up society, in many ways reminding us of the arguments used over the nineteenth century against rule by majority, so that, in the end, it is not the majority constituted by the working class but, again, the ruling class pulling the strings. Laclau's and Mouffe's vision of a 'radical democracy' is a pluralism that would, it seems to me, incapacitate any power of class solidarity necessary to overcome the hegemony imposed by those at the top. Smith sums up their position:

> Radical democratic pluralism attacks all forms of domination and holds disciplinary normalization in suspicion; it takes aim at anti-democratic economic institutions, state apparatuses, social structures and cultural practices alike while it works with the democratic elements that are scattered throughout the social; it welcomes democratic forms of diversity, activism, innovation and dissent; and above all, it seeks to deepen and to broaden the advance of freedom and equality.
>
> Smith 1998: 34

In her interview with Nico Carpentier and Bart Cammaerts, Chantal Mouffe describes the objective of the book she and Ernesto Laclau authored: 'Its main aim was to reformulate the socialist project, in a way that could take the idea that the social struggles were not purely class-based into account' (Carpentier and Cammaerts 2006: 970). Class, democracy, hegemony, ethnicities or gender identities may not exist in the discourse-external world. Laclau's and Mouffe's anti-essentialism, which they set against Marx's (and also Gramsci's) empiricism, waters down the class argument when it comes to the fight for an equal and just society. Having a plurality of voices struggling to make themselves heard by organizing their own hegemonic discourses, under the umbrella of state hegemony, certainly undermines the potential of a unified working-class-based counter hegemony. It gets rid of the dreaded rule by majority by breaking up its members into minorities. It is the way to slay the spectre of democracy.

Hegemonic discourse has been largely successful in weaving a Panglossian shroud in which people envelop and understand their experience. Is it all due to the media? Chantal Mouffe does not think so:

> The media do play an important role in this reproduction, but the whole field of culture is the field where hegemony is created and reproduced. That for instance also includes the cinema, and literature. When it comes to the media, it is an important field, but my impression is that the Left has an attitude, a kind of defeatism, towards the media, saying: 'ah, but we cannot do anything, as long as the media are controlled by capitalism.'
>
> Carpentier and Cammaerts 2006: 969

Laclau and Mouffe may only have been the neo-Marxist forerunners to foreground (minority) culture at the expense of class. But does culture exist outside hegemonic discourse? As David Machin and John Richardson see it:

> For too many [academics], the study of social class, or 'social stratification' ... has been long out of date. Yet, meanwhile, it is clear we live in ... societies where who you are, who you can become, are to a significant extent shaped by your socio-economic – or class – position in society. ... [T]he emphasis on culture is important, of course, but what we must not lose sight of is that, at root, this is about economic exploitation and the unequal access to resources and power.
>
> Machin and Richardson 2008: 281–3

The mainstream media in the capitalist world, and for me this includes film as well as literature and TV entertainment programmes, is certainly more diverse than they have been in the countries of the socialist bloc. Different newspapers compete with each other for readers, and to sport a diversity of opinions can raise readership. But in the end it is again the media interpreting their own messages.

Retired people like me, with plenty of time on their hands, can form their own views by comparing the small and large differences in which a piece of news is presented. Not many people, though, have the privilege to listen to three hours of the *Today* programme on BBC Radio Four or to compare what is said on child poverty in the *Daily Mail* or in the *Guardian*. If normal people are described as too ignorant to be trusted with important decisions, we should not blame a self-induced immaturity, but the exploitative conditions in which they are forced to live.

9.7 Some last words

It is Gramsci's concept of hegemony that turns out to be more powerful than what were, for Marx, the 'objective', empirically observed living conditions of the working-class members. Hegemonic discourse keeps them from fighting for equality in the economic and the political sphere of a democracy that would lend true power to the majority this class constitutes. On 14 August 2019, one could read in the *Guardian* that 4.1 million children in the UK, 30 per cent of all children, are living 'below the breadline', that is in more or less constant hunger (Wall 2019). It was a relatively short, singular notice. Is that why it did not cause an uproar? In a country as rich as the United Kingdom, one-third of children do not have enough to eat. Is it the successful decoupling of democracy from the economy that keeps people from realizing they are living in an oligarchy?

Plebiscites are rare in most countries of the Western world. It seems people are only asked to polls when the ruling class is torn in the middle and hegemonic discourse is divided. The Brexit referendum is, I believe, such a case. But as the struggle behind the curtain goes on with their discourse veiled in secrecy, it is suddenly the hegemonic discourse that discusses itself. Where people perhaps induced to vote as they did because of what they heard and read? Should perhaps the parliament be asked to interpret what people 'really' wanted? Or should it be prorogued, temporarily closed down, until those who have the upper hand carry out their plan in disregard of the people and of parliament? The Brexit issue shows how little the voice of the people counts. Whichever way the Brexit issue will be resolved, the discourse of the winning party will tell us the will of the people has been carried out.

Note

1   *Afford* here means 'deliver'.

Afterword

Danny Dorling

As Eva Gómez-Jiménez and Michael Toolan explain in the introduction to this book, high economic inequality has, in the past, been associated with high inflation, as was the case in Germany in the 1930s, and/or with much faster than average growing debt, as has been the case in the United States until very recently. Income inequalities, and the extent to which they are high, can be measured in many ways, but the Gini coefficient is the most widely used one and hence I will use that below. It makes little difference as to which measure is used.

As I write, in late 2019, the OECD reports that the most unequal of its larger member states include both Chile and Mexico, but inequalities have fallen greatly in those two countries in recent years as the grip of the United States on their ideology slowly recedes. However, they have not fallen fast enough in Chile where the president (Sebastián Piñera) is a billionaire and widespread protests against inequality broke out in October of that year. The next most unequal is Turkey. Its income inequality Gini coefficient is 0.40 and it is ruled by President Erdoğan. Following Turkey is the United States with a Gini of 0.39, ruled by President Trump who occasionally threatens Turkey. Next most unequal of all the dozen large OECD states is the UK, where the latest Gini reported in 2019 was 0.36 at the time when Prime Minister Johnson was in power. All three states are now more unequal than Israel, where Netanyahu is Prime Minister and the Gini stands at 0.34, and Russia, with a Gini of 0.33, where the president has been Putin for some time. Inequality and despots tend to go together; but which comes first – the inequality, the man with the policies promoting inequality or the background of inequality that strongly encourages many voters to turn (in their frustration) to a reactionary strongman – is hard to determine.

By contrast, the most equitable of OECD countries are listed below with the Slovak Republic and Chile at the extreme points (the former being twice as equitable as the latter). I have not added the names of presidents and prime ministers to the list below because who they are is relatively unimportant in more equitable countries and they are often not household names because of that. It is well worth researchers remembering that not everywhere in the rich world is like Chile, Turkey, the United States, the United Kingdom, Israel or Russia. In fact, they are the outliers. If you are reading this book you probably live in one of the two states that ironically has 'United' at the start of its name. It is much more common to live somewhere more equitable. Furthermore, the majority of poorer countries in the world are currently experiencing a fall in income inequalities within them (if not between them). Poor countries tend to be more unequal; but they also tend to be seeing historical inequalities falling more often than not in recent years. People rarely know this, or celebrate it, because if they did then the pressure to continue the trend would wane and inequalities would quickly be increased again through the actions of the rich and greedy. It is possible to gain greater equality. It is possible to preserve greater equality. But to do so you need to know what happens when you do not do that and how the greedy take back control. This book shows how the UK and its media have been an object lesson in the greedy – for now at least – taking back control.

High inequality is associated with a greater rate of crime, especially the most violent crimes of murder and rape. Furthermore, almost all indicators of social progress stall when economic inequalities rise, health improvements end, educational outcomes among children begin to falter and more people find themselves homeless or very precariously or expensively housed. Given all this you might have assumed that inequality would be a gift to the press as it would enable journalists both to talk about things they talk about most often, but in more depth, and to construct a wider narrative between the stories of woe that the media so often concentrate on. However, as Eva Gómez-Jiménez and Michael Toolan in the introduction of this book explain by brilliantly summarizing Michael Sandel: 'we have passed from having a market economy, to being a market economy' (Sandel 2012) and that has altered the nature of the game that is being played and what the media then does.

When you live in a market economy you live in a world where the normal human relationships of reciprocity have been eroded away. The term 'market economy' is utterly misleading. It is neither about a market nor about an economy. A market is a place where people come together to trade. A market has a boundary around it and rules within it (which do not apply outside of the market). You might, in the past, have travelled to the market town. When you arrived you would then go to the market. At that market you might sell what you were carrying with you and then buy what you wanted. When you left the market, you left that space of exchange that was often with strangers and went back to the normal world of social interactions based on mutual respect, feudal order, clerical oversight or whatever, but you were no longer in the market.

Table A.1 The Most Equitable OECD Countries in the World as Reported in 2019 (OECD 2019)

Most Equal OECD States	Gini Coefficient Reported 2019
Sweden	0.282
Belgium	0.266
Finland	0.266
Norway	0.262
Denmark	0.261
Iceland	0.255
Czech Republic	0.253
Slovenia	0.244
Slovak Republic	0.241

The market was a place you had to go to, often the place where it was decreed by law that the market should be. There was nothing especially moral about such markets. For centuries they included slave markets. But there was a reason why they were bounded and controlled. People knew that interactions within the market tended to devalue people and life. This was one reason why markets were bounded, so that they could be controlled. It was not simply that the market was a geographically convenient place to meet. It was that the market had to be controlled, and that control included the levying of taxes.

The 'being a market economy' is not about economics but about becoming a particular type of society where everything is for sale, all the time, everywhere. Hopes, dreams and aspirations can be bought and sold. A university degree in a market economy is something you are sold with the promise that it will fulfil a dream. It is sold on false pretences. You are told, often subliminally through images of happy smiling students on university webpages, that securing it will make you happy, and, later, successful and rich.

When that does not occur and you complain, they send you to the counselling service and so the university can look as if it is caring (and defend itself against a future lawsuit), but the message you are really given is 'more fool you', you are just one individual example of market failure, but your dashed dreams are part of the creative destruction of the market economy ideology – the fire of brutal competition out of which the winner (who rightfully takes all) always emerges like a phoenix.

Being a market economy means being unequal and driving up inequalities. There are always a few spectacular winners; there must be when inequality is very high. A few people have to secure a great proportion of all the resources available at a place and time to properly become a market economy (rather than being a society with available but well controlled and limited markets).

The market economy society runs to a particular mantra. He who wins most deserved to win most. Those who lost out did not try hard enough or were unlucky. And who wishes to be unlucky? If men so often do so much better than women, well that is just what the market decreed. Nothing is out of bounds because that would be interference with the market. The market is a god, a god that is omnipresent and rewards most highly the true believers. So, believe in the market or perish.

The vast majority of people who win most when the market is god are men. But it is women who are often presented as winners. In the introduction to this book several celebrity women, Beyoncé and the Kardashians (Khloé, Kim and Kourtney) are singled out. We only know them and their stories because of media outlets holding them up high. A couple of generations ago Beyoncé would have been a singer, today she is a phenomenon and tomorrow she will be just a shadow of her celebrity memory. Kourtney was born in 1979, Kim in 1980, Beyoncé was born in 1981 and Khloé in 1984. They all became famous in their twenties when they were most saleable. They are all products. The newspaper and cable TV channels they appear on are products. The journalist is a product that can be bought and sold, hired and fired. Everything has a price. Every product has its time, and always there is a new product, a new trend, an emerging market – all the time, day and night – this has occurred to every society that has become a market. Eventually the money lenders set up stall in what used to be temples.

We are easily attracted to faiths. Being a market economy is a kind of faith. It has its own peculiar sets of rewards and punishments. As Jane Mulderrig explains in Chapter 6 of this book, being in the market economy means that a rise in childhood obesity is presented as an increase in the failings of those who have not tried hard enough (the working class). The mantra is repeated again and again that if (if only) they had tried harder they would not be working class. It is the fecklessness of these failures (people) that has caused them to be such bad parents that their children grow so fat. As the few winners rises up and up with their perfect smiles and beautiful bodies, beneath them is a sea of consumers and their fat children. That is what you are encouraged to think and say when you become a market.

When you live in a society that has become a market then none of the rise in childhood obesity is the responsibility of the food and drink industry. To curtail that industry would be heretically to intervene in the market. The market faithful stay thin, the market faithful write the news stories, the market faithful sit on the sofas on the breakfast TV programmes, having quietly vomited up their croissant in the toilet minutes earlier to ensure they fit well into the different size eight dress or fitted suit and appropriate tie each morning. The faithful write the script and hire and fire those who get to write the news. Those who are presented as being most faithful of all, like those at the top of the hierarchy of some organized religions, the most powerful of all, may not in fact be particularly 'faithful', at least in private, knowing that it is a con, an exploiting of others' credulousness. However, these people are painted the most successful just because they own entire newspapers, TV companies, huge new corporations or even entire industries, and they spend their profits promoting the faith and funding far-right think tanks to spread it even further.

And the market faithful know how to party.[1] Work hard and play hard is part of the faith. Those who call for greater equality are, above all else, no fun. The adherents of the UK being a market economy are true believers, as Richard Thomas shows in Chapter 8 of this book. By 2014 – five years after the seminal and aptly named text *The Spirit Level* was published explaining so clearly just how damaging inequality is – both the BBC and the ITV were defending the UK as a free market (otherwise called the neoliberal approach), whereas they rarely mentioned inequality. The UK is the most economically unequal state in Europe. It is the bridgehead from the United States for spreading the market economy faith. A safe place for those who resolutely believe that they have become rich because the market (god) meant them to become rich, and seeing things another way would be heresy. And through their actions they have influenced and purchased everything else, including entire political parties.

As Nuria Lorenzo-Dus and Sadiq Altamimi Almaged make clear in the first chapter of this book analysis of one million words of Britain's political leaders at their annual party conferences over the course of the last century reveals that both of Britain's two major political parties presented the poor as a group to be acted on, to be 'helped', encouraged to try harder or occasionally given a leg up. At no point did any Labour leader suggest that those suffering poverty should act to change their own circumstances. They never, in effect, said – if you are poor, if you identify with the poor because you are poor, then vote for me. The reason they do not say this is because in a very unequal society that might put off the average and modest majority who might not want to be associated with the poor. Between 2001 and 2014 both Conservative and Labour Party leaders, essentially interchangeable at that time in their approach to the economy, 'moved towards a more aggressive stance towards PSE [Poverty and Social Exclusion], increasing their use of combat metaphors'. It will be interesting to see how the speeches since 2015 are deemed to have changed when they are analysed. It may not be by as much as you may think; but they will have changed because from 2015 onwards the Labour Party began to move towards becoming a socialist party again, and the Conservative Party began to move to the far-right (it was allied in the European parliament with *Alternative für Deutschland* in 2014).

There was a time when we were much more equal. From 1913 all the way through to 1939, income and wealth inequalities in the UK were falling. Joe Spencer-Bennett in Chapter 2 of this book explains how, during the Second World War, the Ministry of Information (Orwell's Ministry of Truth) thought it had found a way of using language to control the masses, and to an extent it had. However, that control had been most overtly exercised at home. When the men came back from war in mainland Europe and voted in 1945, what they did shocked the establishment. They were supposed to have voted Winston Churchill in as leader out of gratitude. Instead they awarded Labour a landslide victory. Labour, which had been running the country at home, as the home minsters of the national government, was prepared. By, contrast the Conservatives had been running the war abroad while Labour politicians were learning how the machinery of government worked during the Second World War. Labour quickly nationalized most of what could quickly be nationalized, and despite only being in office for one term of government, managed to secure the continued reduction of income inequalities and change the behaviour of subsequent Conservative administrations that ruled from 1950 through to 1963. By then, the UK was almost unrecognizable as compared to its pre-war stuffiness and deference. When Lady Chatterley's lover was finally deemed not to be obscene in 1960s, the jury laughed at the prosecuting barrister's concern for what their wives and servants might think of the book. The prosecution was unable to make a substantial case against the novel and, at one point, prosecution counsel Mervyn Griffith-Jones shocked the jury by asking: 'Is it a book you would wish your wife or servants to read?' The jury had no servants, not all of them had wives, inequality had fallen. Only states with very high income inequality can have people being forced to be servants.

Economic *equality* continued to rise across the UK throughout the 1960s. Its high point was reached in 1976. By then, of all large European countries, only Sweden was more equitable than the UK. The UK was a market economy. It had markets and they were well bound and well regulated, and they did not extend into all walks of life. In the UK in 1976 the market had almost no place in health, a tiny (if damaging) role to play in education and was entirely absent from a third of all housing. So how was this lost? Isabelle van der Bom and Laura Paterson in Chapter 3 of this book explain how the beginnings of the surge in becoming a market economy, rather than having a market economy, began. They analysed the content of the *Times* Newspaper from the Second World War through to 2009 and showed (Table 3.1) that the welfare state had been most accepted and least commented upon in the *Times* in the 1960s and 1970s. The attack began in the 1970s but only gathered much pace in the 1980s. The critical word 'dependency' was not used in any *Times* article to refer to the welfare state until

1987, and then very frequently thereafter. Rupert Murdoch had purchased the *Times* in 1981. Rupert plays a slow game.

In Chapter 4 of this book Michael Toolan compares how the *Times* talked about child poverty when Britain was most equitable, in the 1970s, with how it later did in the early 2000s. He found that in the 1970s an analysis of articles on children and poverty was especially telling. Once the search words and almost identical ones (*child* and *poor*) were discarded, the most frequently returned words associated with stories on children and poverty in the 1970s were 'allowances', 'families', 'benefit', 'supplementary' and 'income'. In the 2000s the most frequent words were 'says', 'parents', 'families', 'people' and 'schools' (Tables 4.1 and 4.2). Thus *allowance, benefit and supplementary income* had been replaced by *says, parents, people and schools*. Michael's full analysis is far more detailed and subtle than this, but he concludes that by the start of the current century, the *Times* had changed its tune from talking about rights and allowances to claiming, for those impoverished parents who cannot afford a decent home and school for their children, 'it is unfortunate but simply in the nature of harsh reality that their children must accept inferior housing and schooling. There is no reasonable and affordable alternative.'

So how did the neoliberal headbangers win? As Ilse Ras explains (in Chapter 5), by 2004, if not earlier, most journalists in Britain had learnt, no matter what story they were covering, that it was their job to allow corporations to get away with whatever it was they had to do to succeed. She was looking at two types of stories and how these had been covered between January 2004 and December 2014 by the *Daily Mail*, the *Daily Telegraph*, the *Guardian*, the *Mirror*, the *Sun*, the *Times*, the *Financial Times*, *Mail on Sunday*, the *Sunday Times* and the *Sunday Telegraph*. This learning may have been subconscious, but it was certainly effective. As she says in her chapter, the 'newspaper coverage only covers what is already pretty clear, and fails to dig into the structural factors that continue to allow these corporations to "get away" with exploiting people and market vulnerabilities, thereby allowing the already economically powerful to continue enriching themselves to the detriment and at the expense of those less economically powerful and less well-informed'.

What will it take to escape from being the market? In Chapter 9, and in concluding this book, Wolfgang Teubert argues that we are unlikely to escape the rule of the headbangers anytime soon. He shows that very similar arguments are used in Britain today to justify very wide social divisions as were used in South Africa under apartheid. These arguments imply that it is fine for the majority to have badly funded education and to be kept subdued, and the arguments have been used just as they were used under apartheid in South Africa. In 1964, on trial for sabotage and at risk of the death penalty, Nelson Mandela delivered his four-hour speech ending famously describing a democratic and free society as 'an ideal for which I am prepared to die'. In that speech Mandela decided to quote some school spending statistics (now he is dead it is time Nelson was made the Saint of Statisticians):

> According to figures quoted by the South African Institute of Race Relations in its 1963 journal, approximately forty per cent of African children in the age group between seven and fourteen do not attend school. For those who do attend school,

the standards are vastly different from those afforded to white children. In 1960-61 the per capita Government spending [someone coughs] on African students at State-aided schools was estimated at R12.46. In the same years, the per capita spending on white children in the Cape Province (which are the only figures available to me) was R144.57.[2]

The most privileged of white children in South Africa had almost twelve times as much spent on their education as black children each did in the 1960s. In Britain today the fees at Eton are £42,501 a year which along with 'extras' and the registration fee (but no music lessons) rises to about £45,000 a year, and far more if school trips arranged during the holidays are included. The amount has been rising in recent years. By contrast, state school funding in English schools was reduced by the government by 8 per cent in real terms between 2010 and 2018 to £5,870 per child per year or £16 per child per day; as compared £123 per child per day at Eton or roughly eight times more. Britain in 2018 was not quite as bad as South Africa in the 1960s when it came to school funding inequalities. However, as Teubert says in the penultimate chapter of this book: 'It suits the propertied classes if those less lucky are kept in the dark, first by substandard schools and then by the mainstream tabloids.'

A little later Teubert continues:

The working class today is characterized more as a culture than by a solidarity of interest directed against their oppressors. People rather want to move up class-wise, and they want to be accepted by those above them as respectable people. Hardly anyone still yearns for a change of the political system. While the gap between the rich and the poor is wider than ever, Marx's 'spectre of communism' is haunting no one. How did that happen?

And concludes:

It is this discourse, exemplified by the *Telegraph* for the more conservative-minded, the *Times* for the managers, the *Guardian* as the official press organ for disgruntled social workers, teachers, and academics, the *Daily Mail* for the lower middle class, the *Mirror* for aspiring working class families, the *Sun* for the lower orders, that creates the acceptance of a system designed and continuously redesigned to further the interests of those at the top.

So, having read the above arguments about *The Discursive Construction of Economic Inequality* what do I conclude? Or could I say 'what should we conclude', if I were trying to take you and your opinion, imaginary reader, with me? I think we can see how it was done and how we were fooled, more and more clearly the more time that passes. But that does not mean we know what will happen next, or what to do.

What will most English *Telegraph* readers think when their home – the property in which most of their savings are sunk – continues to fall in value? What happens

Figure A.1 'Here's to the brave new world!' By Illingworth, Leslie Gilbert, published in the *Daily Mail*, 2 December 1942. Reproduced with permission from Solo Syndication.

Source: Associated Newspapers Ltd/ British Cartoon Archive, University of Kent, www.cartoons.ac.uk See also: http://toynbeehall.brix.fatbeehive.com/data/files/william_beveridge_spreads.pdf

as the global economy continues to slow and the managers find it harder and harder to return the profit that their shareholders demand? And how does the jolt of Brexit make that any less of a 'uncomfortable but still behaving frog in increasingly hot water' experience? How does the disgruntled social worker, teacher and academic react when they can rent a room and work – can be a servant – but can never start a family. At what point do the lower middle classes who buy the *Daily Mail* realize they have been taken for a ride. Or – more likely – at what point does the *Daily Mail* begin to change its tune in order to keep its market? It did in 1942.

And what does the no-longer-quite-so-young journalist really think – the one in one hundred that is successful, and gets to play the left-wing patsy on late-night TV, on Sky TV or the BBC, when they discuss 'what the papers say'? At what point will she no longer sit there, taking the fee, without mentioning that both the host of the programme opposite her and the right-wing commenter sitting next to her 'for balance' are both rolling in it and would never dream of using state education for their children, state health care for their parents or state housing for themselves. At what point does she say: 'You lie well, but it is beginning to wear thin?' because eventually, and always, whenever economic inequality rises it eventually falls. It just does so differently each time.

Notes

1. For example, David Koch, who died in 2019 and who was one of the richest men in the world, spent a huge amount of money on the far-right financing market economy libertarians. He owned a mansion in Southampton, New York, 'palatial homes on Park Avenue in Manhattan, in Aspen, Colo., and in Palm Beach, Fla. He kept a yacht in the Mediterranean for summer getaways and rented it out for $500,000 a week. His friends and acquaintances included Bill and Melinda Gates, Prince Charles and Winston Churchill's grandson Winston Spencer Churchill.' https://www.nytimes.com/2019/08/23/us/david-koch-dead.html
2. https://www.nelsonmandela.org/news/entry/i-am-prepared-to-die

References

Ackroyd, S. and J. Karlsson (2014), 'Critical Realism, Research Techniques and Research Design', in P. Edwards, J. O'Mahoney and S. Vincent (eds), *Studying Organizations Using Critical Realism: A Practical Guide*, 21–45, Oxford: Oxford University Press.
Addison, P. and J. A. Crang (eds) (2011), *Listening to Britain*, London: Vintage.
Almaged, A. S. (forthcoming), 'Corpus-Assisted Discourse Study Approach: A Methodological Procedure', *Midad Journal*.
Althusser, L. (2014), *On the Reproduction of Capitalism: Ideology and Ideological State Apparatuses*, London: Verso.
Amery, L. S. (1947), *Thoughts on the Constitution*, London: Geoffrey Cumberlege, Oxford University Press.
Anderson, B. (1983), *Imagined Communities*, London: Verso.
Anthony, L. (2019), AntConc (Version 3.5.8) [Computer Software], Tokyo: Waseda University. Available online: https://www.laurenceanthony.net/software (accessed 3 September 2019).
Apple, R. W. (1983), 'The Welfare State Was a Boon to Mrs. Thatcher', *New York Times*, 12 June. Available online: https://www.nytimes.com/1983/06/12/weekinreview/the-welfare-state-was-a-boon-to-mrs-thatcher.html (accessed 29 June 2019).
Appleby, J., L. Merry and R. Reed (2017), 'Root Causes: Quality and Inequality in Dental Health', *Nuffield Trust*, 2 November. Available online: https://www.nuffieldtrust.org.uk/research/root-causes-quality-and-inequality-in-dental-health (accessed 12 August 2019).
Aristotle (1999), *Politics*, trans. B. Jowett, Kitchener: Batoche Books.
Armstrong, M. (2018), 'Counting the Cost of Tooth Extractions', *British Dental Association*, 4 December. Available online: https://bda.org/news-centre/blog/counting-the-cost-of-tooth-extractions (accessed 12 August 2019).
Asthana, A. and R. Mason (2017), 'David Cameron Calls Tory Austerity Critics Selfish, Not Compassionate', *The Guardian*, 4 July. Available online: https://www.theguardian.com/politics/2017/jul/04/david-cameron-calls-tory-austerity-critics-selfish-not-compassionate (accessed 11 February 2019).
Atkinson, A. (2014), *Inequality: What Can Be Done?* Cambridge: Harvard University Press.
Atkinson, S. Roberts and M. Savage (eds) (2012), *Class Inequality in Austerity Britain: Power, Difference and Suffering*, London: Palgrave.
'Austerity' (2019), *Oxford English Dictionary*. Available online: https://www.oed.com/view/Entry/13269?redirectedFrom=austerity#eid (accessed 3 September 2019).
Babic, M., E. Heemskerk and J. Fichtner (2018), 'Who Is More Powerful – States or Corporations?', *The Conversation*, 10 July. Available online: http://theconversation.com/who-is-more-powerful-states-or-corporations-99616 (accessed 16 August 2019).
Baker, P. (2006), *Using Corpora in Discourse Analysis*, London: Continuum.
Baker, P. (forthcoming), 'Making the Needy Look Greedy: Using Corpus Methods to Examine *The Sun*'s Discourse Around Benefits', in J. Rahilly and V. Vander (eds),

Crossing Boundaries: Interdisciplinarity in Language Studies, Amsterdam: John Benjamins.

Baker, P. and E. Levon (2015), 'Picking the Right Cherries? A Comparison of Corpus-Based and Qualitative Analyses of News Articles about Masculinity', *Discourse & Communication*, 9 (2): 221–36.

Baker, P. and T. McEnery (2015a), 'Who Benefits When Discourse Gets Democratised? Analysing a Twitter Corpus Around the British Benefits Street Debate', in P. Baker and T. McEnery (eds), *Corpora and Discourse Studies*, 244–65, London: Palgrave.

Baker, P. and T. McEnery (eds) (2015b), *Corpora and Discourse Studies: Integrating Discourse and Corpora*, Basingstoke: Palgrave.

Baker, P., C. Gabrielatos, M. Khosravinik, M. Krzyzanowski, T. McEnery and R. Wodak (2008), 'A Useful Methodological Synergy? Combining Critical Discourse Analysis and Corpus Linguistics to Examine Discourses of Refugees and Asylum Seekers in the UK Press', *Discourse & Society*, 19 (3): 273–306.

Balzacq, T. (2005), 'The Three Faces of Securitization: Political Agency, Audience and Context', *European Journal of International Relations*, 11 (2): 171–201.

Barnett, S. and I. Gaber (2001), *Westminster Tales: The 21st Century Crisis in Political Journalism*, London: Continuum.

Bartley, L. (2018), 'Putting Transitivity to the Test: A Review of the Sydney and the Cardiff Models', *Functional Linguistics*, 5 (4).

Bates, T. R. (1975), 'Gramsci and the Theory of Hegemony', *Journal of the History of Ideas*, 36: 351–66.

Bayley, P. and G. Williams (eds) (2012), *European Identity. What the Media Says*, Oxford: Oxford University Press.

Bednarek, M. (2008), 'Semantic Preference and Semantic Prosody Re-examined', *Corpus Linguistics and Linguistic Theory*, 4–2: 119–39.

Beetsma, R. M. W. J. and F. Van Der Ploeg (1996), 'Does Inequality Cause Inflation?: The Political Economy of Inflation, Taxation and Government Debt', *Public Choice*, 87 (1–2): 143–62.

Beharrell, P. and Glasgow University Media Group (1976), *Bad News. Vol. 1*, London: Routledge and Kegan Paul.

Beharrell, P. and Glasgow University Media Group (1980), *Bad News. Vol. 2. More Bad News*, London: Routledge and Kegan Paul.

Bennett, J. (2013a), 'Moralising Class: A Discourse Analysis of the Mainstream Political Response to Occupy and the August 2011 British Riots', *Discourse & Society*, 24 (1): 27–45.

Bennett, J. (2013b), 'Chav-Spotting in Britain: The Representation of Social Class as Private Choice', *Social Semiotics*, 23 (1): 146–62.

Bennett, J. (2014), 'Avoiding Emotivism: A Sociolinguistic Approach to Moral Talk', *Language & Communication*, 39: 73–82.

Bennet, J. (2018), *Moral Talk: Stance and Evaluation in Political Discourse*, London: Routledge.

Berg, A. G. and J. D. Ostry (2011), 'Inequality and Unsustainable Growth: Two Sides of the Same Coin?', 8 April, International Monetary Fund. Available online: https://www.imf.org/external/pubs/ft/sdn/2011/sdn1108.pdf (accessed 4 September 2019).

Bernstein, B. (1971), *Class, Codes and Control. Volume 1*, London: Routledge & Kegan Paul.

Billig, M. (1992), *Talking of the Royal Family*, London: Routledge.

Blanden, J. (2009), 'How Much Can We Learn from International Comparisons of Intergenerational Mobility?,' CEE Discussion Papers 0111, Centre for the Economics of Education, LSE. Available online: http://cee.lse.ac.uk/ceedps/ceedp111.pdf (accessed 4 September 2019).
Bourdieu, P. (1984), *Distinction*, trans. R. Nice, Cambridge: Harvard University Press.
Bourdieu, P. (1991), *Language and Symbolic Power*, trans. G. Raymond and M. Adamson, Cambridge: Harvard University Press.
Briggs, A. and P. Burke (2009), *A Social History of the Media*, 3rd edn, Cambridge: Polity.
British Phonographic Industry (2019), 'BPI Calls on Government to Tackle Growing Inequality in Access to Music in State Schools', 8 March. Available online: https://www.bpi.co.uk/news-analysis/bpi-calls-on-government-to-tackle-growing-inequality-in-access-to-music-in-state-schools/ (accessed 3 September 2019).
British Political Speech (2019), *British Political Speech Archive*. Available online: http://www.britishpoliticalspeech.org (accessed 3 September 2019).
British University Film and Video Council (2018), *Box of Broadcast*. Available online: https://learningonscreen.ac.uk/ondemand (accessed 3 September 2019).
Bruenig, M. (2019), *Top 1% Up $21 Trillion. Bottom 50% Down $900 Billion*, People's Policy Project, 14 June. Available online: https://www.peoplespolicyproject.org/2019/06/14/top-1-up-21-trillion-bottom-50-down-900-billion (accessed 2 August 2019).
Brunsdon, C. and D. Morley (1978), *Everyday Television: Nationwide*, London: BFI.
Burgess, A. (1980), *1985*, London: Arrow.
Burns, J. K., A. Tomita and A. S. Kapadia (2014), 'Income Inequality and Schizophrenia: Increased Schizophrenia Incidence in Countries with High Levels of Income Inequality', *International Journal of Social Psychiatry*, 60 (2): 185–96.
Butterick, K. (2015), *Complacency and Collusion: A Critical Introduction to Business and Financial Journalism*, London: Pluto.
Caldas-Coulthard, C. (1993), 'From Discourse Analysis to Critical Discourse Analysis: The Differential Re-Presentation of Women and Men Speaking in Written News', in G. Fox, M. Hoey and J. M. Sinclair (eds), *Techniques of Description: Spoken and Written Discourse*, London: Routledge.
Caldas-Coulthard, C. R. and R. Moon (2010), '"Curvy, Hunky, Kinky": Using Corpora as Tools for Critical Analysis', *Discourse & Society*, 21 (2): 99–133.
Calder, A. (1969), *The People's War*, London: Pimlico.
Calder, A. (1985), 'Mass Observation 1937-1949', in M. Bulmer (ed), *Essays on the History of British Sociological Research*, 121–36, Cambridge: Cambridge University Press.
Cameron, D. (1995), *Verbal Hygiene*, London: Routledge.
Carpentier, N. and B. Cammaerts (2006), 'Hegemony, Democracy, Agonism and Journalism: an Interview with Chantal Mouffe', *Journalism Studies*, (7): 964–75.
Cartledge, P. (2018), 'A Brief History of Democracy: Does It Still Convey the "Will of the People"?', *The Independent*, 26 May.
Charles, S. D. (1939), 'Letter About Mass Observation Broadcast', *The National Archives*, 11 October, INF 1/261.
Charteris-Black, L. (2013), *Analysing Political Speeches: Rhetoric, Discourse and Metaphor*, Basingstoke: Palgrave Macmillan.
Chief Medical Officer (2003), *Annual Report of the Chief Medical Officer 2002*, London.
Child Poverty Action Group (2019), *Child Poverty Facts and Figures*. Available online: https://cpag.org.uk/child-poverty/child-poverty-facts-and-figures (accessed 5 August 2019).
Chilton, P. (2004), *Analysing Political Discourse: Theory and Practice*, London: Routledge.

Chouliaraki, L. and N. Fairclough (1999), *Discourse in Late Modernity*, Edinburgh: Edinburgh University Press.
Clark, A. (2012), *Political Parties in the UK*, London: Palgrave.
Clarke-Billings, L. (2015), 'Sunday Times Rich List: Number of Billionaires in Britain Doubles in Five Years', *Independent*, 26 April. Available online: https://www.independent.co.uk/news/uk/home-news/sunday-times-rich-list-number-of-billionaires-in-britain-doubles-in-five-years-10205138.html (accessed 3 September 2019).
Cohn, A., E. Fehr and L. Goette (2015), 'Fair Wages and Effort Provision: Combining Evidence from a Choice Experiment and a Field Experiment', *Management Science*, 61 (8): 1777–94.
Cohn, A., E. Fehr, B. Herrmann and F. Schneider (2011), 'Social Comparison in the Workplace: Evidence from a Field Experiment', IZA Discussion Paper No. 5550. Available online: https://ssrn.com/abstract=1778894 (accessed 4 September 2019).
Colvile, R. (2014), 'Yes, CEOs Are Ludicrously Overpaid. And Yes, It's Getting Worse', *Telegraph*, 13 October. Available online: http://www.telegraph.co.uk/comment/columnists/robert-colvile/11158607/Yes-CEOs-areludicrously-overpaid.-And-yes-its-getting-worse.html (accessed 3 September 2019).
Corak, M. (2016), 'Inequality from Generation to Generation: The United States in Comparison', IZA Discussion Paper No. 9929. Available online: http://ftp.iza.org/dp9929.pdf (accessed 4 September 2019).
Cornelissen, L. (2017), '"How Can the People Be Restricted?" the Mont Pèlerin Society and the Problem of Democracy, 1947–1998', *History of European Ideas*, 43 (5): 507–24.
Corner, J. (2003), *Media and the Re-styling of Politics: Consumerism. Celebrity and Cynicism*, London: Sage.
Cribb, J., P. Johnson and R. Joyce (2012), *Jubilees Compared: Incomes, Spending and Work in The Late 1970s and Early 2010s*, Institute of Fiscal Studies Briefing Note 128, Swindon UK: Economic and Social Research Council.
Crossman, R. (1939), 'Memorandum on the Report of Mass Observation Upon the Red Posters', *The National Archives*, 26 October, INF 1/261.
Crowley, T. (2003), *Standard English and the Politics of Language*, 2nd edn, Basingstoke: Palgrave Macmillan.
Cushion, S. and R. Thomas (2013), 'The Mediatization of Politics: Interpreting the Value of Live Versus Edited Journalistic Interventions in U.K. Television News Bulletins', *The International Journal of Press/Politics*, 18 (3): 360–80.
Cushion, S., J. Lewis, and R. Callaghan (2017), 'Data Journalism, Impartiality and Statistical Claims', *Journalism Practice*, 11: 1198–215.
Dados, N. and R. Connell (2018), 'Neoliberalism in World Perspective: Southern Origins and Southern Dynamics', in D. Cahill, M. Cooper, M. Konings and D. Primrose (eds), *The Sage Handbook of Neoliberalism*, 28–39, London: Sage.
Daly, M., M. Wilson and S. Vasdev (2001), 'Income Inequality and Homicide Rates in Canada and the United States', *Canadian Journal of Criminology*, 43 (2): 219–36.
Darbyshire, N. (2000), 'Children Who Are Sent to "The Circus". One of the *Daily Telegraph*'s Christmas Charities is Trying to Stop Young Nepalese Girls Being Enslaved as Prostitutes', *The Daily Telegraph*, 27 December: 24.
Dean, M. (2010), *Governmentality: Power and Rule in Modern Society*, London: Sage.
De Melo Resende, V. (2016), 'Discursive Representation and Violation of Homeless People's Rights: Symbolic Violence in Brazilian Online Journalism', *Discourse & Communication*, 10 (6): 596–613.
Demmen, J., Jeffries, L. and Walker, B. (2018), 'Charting the Semantics of Labour Relations in House of Commons Debates Spanning Two Hundred Years: A Study of

Parliamentary Language Using Corpus Linguistic Methods and Automated Semantic Tagging', in M. Kranert and G. Horan (eds), *Doing Politics: Discursivity, Performativity and Mediation in Political Discourse*, 81–104, Amsterdam: John Benjamins.

De Vogli, R., R. Mistry, R. Gnesotto and G. A. Cornia (2005), 'Has the Relation Between Income Inequality and Life Expectancy Disappeared? Evidence from Italy and Top Industrialised Countries', *Journal Epidemiol Community Health*, 59: 158–62.

De Vreese, C. (2003), *Framing Europe: Television News and European Integration*, Amsterdam: Aksant Academic Publishers.

De Vries, R., S. Gosling and J. Potter (2011), 'Income Inequality and Personality: Are Less Equal U.S. States Less Agreeable?', *Social Science and Medicine*, 72: 1978–85.

Dibley, B. and M. Kelly (2015), 'Morale and Mass Observation: Governing the Affective Atmosphere on the Home-Front', *Museum & Society*, 13 (1): 22–41.

Dimsdale, N. and A. Hotson (2014), *British Financial Crises Since 1825*, Oxford: Oxford University Press.

DOH (1992), *The Health of the Nation: A Strategy for Health in England*, London.

DOH (2008a), *Healthy Weight, Healthy Lives: Consumer Insight Summary*, London.

DOH (2008b), *Healthy Weight, Healthy Lives: A Cross-Government Strategy for England*, London.

DOH (2009), *Change4Life Marketing Strategy: In Support of Healthy Weight, Healthy Lives*, London.

Dorling, D. (2014), *Inequality and the 1%*, London and New York: Verso.

Dorling, D. (2016a), *A Better Politics: How Government Can Make Us Happier*, London: London Publishing Partnership.

Dorling, D. (2016b), 'Danny Dorling on Brexit, Empire, Inequality…and Eurovision', *British Politics and Policy at LSE*, 14 May. Available online: http://blogs.lse.ac.uk/politicsandpolicy/should-we-stay-or-should-we-go/ (accessed 4 September 2019).

Dorling, D., J. Rigby, B. Wheeler, D. Ballas, B. Thomas, E. Fahmy, D. Gordon and R. Lupton (2007), *Poverty, Wealth and Place in Britain, 1968 to 2005*, York: Joseph Rowntree Foundation.

Doyle, G. (2007), 'Financial News Journalism: A Post-Enron Analysis of Approaches Towards Economic and Financial News Production in the UK', *Journalism*, 7 (4): 433–52.

Dunning, T. (1993), 'Accurate Methods for the Statistics of Surprise and Coincidence', *Computational Linguistics*, 19 (1): 61–74.

Durant, A. (2006), 'Raymond Williams's *Keywords*: Investigating Meanings "Offered, Felt for, Tested, Confirmed, Asserted, Qualified, Changed"', *Critical Quarterly*, 48 (4): 1–26.

Durante, F., S. T. Fiske, N. Kervyn, A. J. C. Cuddy, A. Akande, B. E. Adetoun, M. F. Adewuyi, M. M. Tserere, A. A. Ramiah, K. A. Mastor, F. K. Barlow, G. Bonn, R. W. Tafarodi, J. Bosak, E. Cairns, C. Doherty, D. Capozza, A. Chandran, X. Chryssochoou, T. Iatridis, J. M. Contreras, R. Costa-Lopes, R. González, J. I. Lewi, G. Tushabe, J. Leyens, R. Mayorga, N. N. Rouhana, V. S. Castro, R. Perez, R. Rodríguez-Bailón, M. Moya, E. M. Marente, M. P. Gálvez, C. G. Sibley, F. Asbrock and C. C. Storari (2013), 'Nations's Income Inequality Predicts Ambivalence in Stereotype Content: How Societies Mind the Gap', *British Journal of Social Psychology*, 52: 726–46.

Edwards, D. and J. Potter (1992), *Discursive Psychology Inquiries in Social Construction*, London: Sage.

Ekström, M. (2001) 'Politicians Interviewed on Television News', *Discourse & Society*, 12 (5): 563–84.

Elgar, F. J. and N. Aitken (2010), 'Income Inequality, Trust and Homicide in 33 Countries', *European Journal of Public Health*, 21 (2): 241–6.

Elgar, F. J., K. E. Pickett, W. Pickett, W. Craig, M. Molcho, K. Hurrelmann and M. Lenzi (2013), 'School Bullying, Homicide and Income Inequality: A Cross-National Pooled Time Series Analysis', *International Journal of Public Health*, 58: 237–45.

Engels, F. ([1845] 2009), *The Condition of the Working Class in England*, London: Penguin.

Eribon, D. (2009), *Retour à Reims*, Paris: Fayard.

Evans, M. (2016), *A Critical Stylistic Analysis of the Textual Meanings of 'Feminism', 'Feminist(s)' and 'Feminist' in UK National Newspapers, 2000-2009*, PhD diss., University of Huddersfield. Available online: http://eprints.hud.ac.uk/id/eprint/30184/ (accessed 3 September 2019).

Evans, M. and B. Walker, B. (2020), 'The Beginning of "The Age of Austerity": A Critical Stylistic Analysis of David Cameron's 2009 Spring Conference Speech', *CADAAD Journal*, 11 (2): 169–86.

E3G (2018), 'UK Has Sixth-Highest Rate of Excess Winter Deaths in Europe'. Available online: https://www.e3g.org/news/media-room/uk-has-sixth-highest-rate-of-excess-winter-deaths-in-europe (accessed 3 September 2019).

Fahy, D., M. O'Brien and V. Poti (2010), 'From Boom to Bust: A Post-Celtic Tiger Analysis of the Norms, Values and Roles of Irish Financial Journalists', *Irish Communications, Review* 12: 5–20.

Fairclough, I. (2016), 'Evaluating Policy as Argument: The Public Debate over the First UK Austerity Budget', *Critical Discourse Studies*, 13 (1): 57–77.

Fairclough, N. (1992), *Discourse and Social Change*, Cambridge: Policy.

Fairclough, N. (1995), *Critical Discourse Analysis: The Critical Study of Language*, London: Longman.

Fairclough, N. (2000), *New Labour, New Language?*, London: Routledge.

Fairclough, N. (2002), 'Language in New Capitalism', *Discourse & Society*, 13 (2): 163–6.

Fairclough, N. (2003), *Analysing Discourse: Textual Analysis for Social Research*, London: Routledge.

Fairclough, N. (2005), 'Critical Discourse Analysis in Trans-disciplinary Research on Social Change: Transition, Re-scaling, Poverty and Social Inclusion', *Lodz Papers in Pragmatics*, 1: 37–58.

Fairclough, N. (2012), 'Language in New Capitalism', *Discourse & Society*, 13 (2): 163–6.

Fairclough, N. (2015), *Language and Power*, 3rd edn, London: Routledge.

Fairclough, N. and I. Fairclough (2012), 'Analysis and Evaluation of Argumentation in Critical Discourse Analysis: Deliberation and the Dialectic of Enlightenment', *Argumentation et Analyse du Discours*, 9: 1565–896.

Fairclough, N. and R. Wodak (1997), 'Critical Discourse Analysis', in T. van Dijk (ed), *Discourse as Social Interaction*, Vol. 2, 258–84, London: Sage.

Farnsworth, K. and Z. Irving (2017), 'Crisis, Austerity, Competitiveness and Growth: New Pathologies of the Welfare State', in D. Horsfall and J. Hudson (eds), *Social Policy in an Era of Competition: From Global to Local Perspectives*, 187–99, Bristol: Policy Press.

Farrelly, M. and E. Seoane (2012), 'Democratization', in T. Nevalainen and E. Cross Traugott (eds), *The Oxford Handbook of the History of English*, 392–401, Oxford: Oxford University Press.

Faucher-King, F. (2005), *Changing Parties: An Anthropology of British Political Party Conferences*, New York: Palgrave.

Finlayson, A., J. Martin and K. Philips (2016), *Rhetoric, Politics and Society*, New York: Palgrave.

Fish, S. (1980), *Is There a Text in This Class?*, Cambridge: Harvard University Press.

Foley, W. (1997), *Anthropological Linguistics*, Oxford: Blackwell.

Fooks, G., A. Gilmore, J. Collin, C. Holden and K. Lee (2012), 'The Limits of Corporate Social Responsibility: Techniques of Neutralization, Stakeholder Management and Political CSR', *Journal of Business Ethics*, 1 (12): 283–99.
Foresight (2007), *Tackling Obesities: Future Choices*, Government Office for Science. Available online: https://assets.publishing.service.gov.uk/government/uploads/system/uploads/attachment_data/file/287937/07-1184x-tackling-obesities-future-choices-report.pdf (accessed 3 September 2019).
Forsey, A. (2017), 'Hungry Holidays: A Report on Hunger Amongst Children During School Holidays', Report, All-Party Parliamentary Group on Hunger. Available at: http://www.frankfield.co.uk/upload/docs/Hungry%20Holidays.pdf (accessed 4 September 2019).
Foucault, M. (2007), *Security, Territory, Population: Lectures at the College de France 1977-1978*, Basingstoke: Palgrave Macmillan.
Fowler, R. (1991), *Language in the News*, London: Routledge.
Fowler, R. (1995), *The Language of George Orwell*, Basingstoke: Macmillan.
Fowler, R. (1996), 'On Critical Linguistics', in T. A. van Dijk (ed), *Handbook of Discourse Analysis. Vol. 4: Discourse Analysis in Society*, 61–82, Orlando: Academic Press.
Fowler, R., B. Hodge, G. Kress and T. Trew (1979), *Language and Control*, London: Routledge and Kegan Paul.
Frank, R. H., A. S. Levine and O. Dijk (2014), 'Expenditure Cascades', *Review of Behavioral Economics*, 1 (1–2): 55–73.
Fraud Act 2006 (c. 35), London: The Stationery Office.
Freedman, D. (2019), '"Public Service" and the Journalism Crisis: Is the BBC the Answer?', *Television & New Media*, 20 (3): 203–18.
Fuchs, C. (2016), 'Neoliberalism in Britain: From Thatcherism to Cameronism', *Triple*, 14 (1): 163–88.
Gabrielatos, C. (2007), 'Selecting Query Terms to Build a Specialised Corpus from a Restricted-Access Database', *ICAME Journal*, 31: 5–43.
Gabrielatos, C. (2018), 'Keyness Analysis: Nature, Metrics and Techniques', in C. Taylor and A. Marchi (eds), *Corpus Approaches to Discourse: A Critical Review*, 225–58, London: Routledge.
Gabrielatos, C. and P. Baker (2008), 'Fleeing, Sneaking, Flooding: A Corpus Analysis of Discursive Constructions of Refugees and Asylum Seekers in the UK Press 1996-2005', *Journal of English Linguistics*, 36 (1): 5–38.
Gabrielatos, C., T. McEnery, P. J. Giddle and P. Baker (2012), 'The Peaks and Troughs of Corpus-Based Contextual Analysis', *International Journal of Corpus Linguistics*, 17 (2): 1569–9811.
Gale (n.d.), *The Times Digital Archive*. Available online: https://www.gale.com/intl/c/the-times-digital-archive (accessed 1 June 2019).
Garcia da Silva, D. (2008), 'A Pobreza no Context Brasileiro da Exclusão Econômica e Social a Rupture Familiar', *Discurso & Sociedad*, 2 (2): 265–96.
Gardiner, J. (2004), *Wartime: Britain 1939-1945*, London: Headline.
Gazeley, I. (2003), *Poverty in Britain, 1900–1965*, New York: Palgrave Macmillan.
Georgakopoulou, A. and D. Goutsos (1997), *Discourse Analysis: An Introduction*, Edinburgh: Edinburgh University Press.
Gephart, R. (2004), 'Qualitative Research and the Academy of Management Journal', *Academy of Management Journal*, 47 (4): 454–62.
Gibbs, R. (2017), *Metaphor Wars: Conceptual Metaphors in Human Life*, Cambridge: Cambridge University Press.

Glennerster, H. (2002) 'United States Poverty Studies and Poverty Measurement: The Past Twenty-Five Years', *Social Service Review* (March): 83–107.

Glennerster, H., J. Hills, D. Piachaud and J. Webb (2004), *One Hundred Years of Poverty and Policy*, York: Joseph Rowntree Foundation.

Goatly, A. (2007), *Washing the Brain – Metaphor and Hidden Ideology*, Amsterdam: John Benjamins Publishing Company.

Gómez-Jiménez, E. (2018), '"An Insufferable Burden on Businesses?" On Changing Attitudes to Maternity Leave and Economic-Related Issues in the *Times* and *Daily Mail*', *Discourse, Context & Media*, (26): 100–107.

Graham, P. (2012), 'Hypercapitalism: Language, New Media and Social Perceptions of Value', *Discourse & Society*, 13 (2): 227–49.

Graham, C. and B. K. O'Rourke (2019), 'Cooking a Corporation Tax Controversy: Apple, Ireland and the EU', *Critical Discourse Studies*, 16 (3): 298–311.

Gramsci, A. (1971), *Selections from the Prison Notebooks*, New York: Smith.

Grayling, A. C. (2016), 'Parliament, the Nation, and Brexit'. Available online: http://acgrayling.com/parliament-the-nation-and-brexit (accessed 2 August 2019).

Gregoriou, C. and I. A. Ras (2018), '"Call for Purge on the People Traffickers": An Investigation into UK News Media's Portrayal of Transnational Human Trafficking, 2000-2016', in C. Gregoriou (ed), *Representations of Transnational Human Trafficking: Present-Day News Media, True Crime, and Fiction*, 25–60, London: Palgrave.

Gregory, I. and L. L. Paterson (2020), 'English Language and Spatial Humanities: Representations of Poverty in Historical Newspapers', in S. Adolphs and D. Knight (eds), *The Routledge Handbook of English Language and Digital Humanities*, London: Routledge.

Gregory, I. N., P. Atkinson, A. Hardie, A. Joulain-Jay, D. Kershaw, C. Porter, P. Rayson and C. J. Rupp (2016), 'From Digital Resources to Historical Scholarship with the British Library 19th Century Newspaper Collection', *Journal of Siberian Federal University: Humanities and Social Sciences*, 9 (4): 994–1006.

Grisold, A. and H. Silke (2019), 'Denying, Downplaying, Debating: Defensive Discourses of Inequality in the Debate on Piketty', *Critical Discourse Studies*, 16 (3): 264–81.

Grisold, A. and H. Theine (2017), 'How Come We Know? The Media Coverage of Economic Inequality', *International Journal of Communication*, 11: 4265–84.

Guerini, M., D. Giampiccolo, G. Moretti, R. Sprugnoli and C. Strapparava (2013), 'The New Release of CORPS: A Corpus of Political Speeches Annotated with Audience Reactions', in I. Poggi, F. D'Errico, L. Vincze and A. Vinciarelli (eds), *Multimodal Communication in Political Speech: Shaping Minds and Social Action*, 86–98, Berlin: Springer.

Guy's and St Thomas' Charity (2018), *Bite Size: Breaking Down the Challenge of Inner-City Childhood Obesity*. Available online: https://www.gsttcharity.org.uk/what-we-do/bitesize (accessed 3 September 2019).

Habsburg, O. (1961), 'The Primacy of the Judiciary', Box 5, conference 12, Turin 1961, folder 1/1, 3-4.

Hall, S. (1986), 'Gramsci's Relevance for the Study of Race and Ethnicity', *Journal of Communication Inquiry*, (10): 5–27.

Hall, S., C. Critcher, T. Jefferson, J. Clarke and B. Roberts (1978), 'The Social Production of News', in S. Hall et al., *Policing the Crisis: Mugging, the State, and Law and Order*, 53–60, London: Macmillan.

Halliday, M. A. K. (1985), *A Short Introduction to Functional Grammar*, London: Edward Arnold.

Halliday, M. A. K. and J. R. Martin (1993), *Writing Science: Literacy and Discursive Power*, Pittsburgh: University of Pittsburgh Press.
Halliday, M. A. K. and C. M. I. M. Matthiessen (2014), *Halliday's Introduction to Functional Grammar* (4th edn), London: Routledge.
Hampe, B. and J. Grady (2005), *From Perception to Meaning: Image Schemas in Cognitive Linguistics*, Berlin: Mouton de Gruyter.
Hanley, L. (2016), *Respectable: The Experience of Class*, London: Allan Lane.
Hansard (1940), War-Time Social Survey, 1st August 1940, Volume 363. Available online: https://hansard.parliament.uk (accessed 21 February 2019).
Hansard (2019). Available online: https://hansard.parliament.uk (accessed 2 August 2019).
Hansen, A. and D. Machin (2013), *Media and Communication Research Methods: An Introduction*, Basingstoke: Palgrave.
Hardie, A. (2012), 'CQPweb - Combining Power, Flexibility and Usability in a Corpus Analysis Tool', *International Journal of Corpus Linguistics*, 17 (3): 380–409.
Hardie, A. (2014), 'Log Ratio: An Informal Introduction' [Blog post], Lancaster: ESRC Centre for Corpus Approaches to Social Science (CASS). Available online: http://cass.lancs.ac.uk/log-ratio-an-informal-introduction (accessed 11 February 2019).
Hare, K. (2014), *How Small Newsrooms Can Go Big When News Comes to Town*. Available online: https://www.poynter.org/reporting-editing/2014/how-small-newsrooms-can-go-big-when-news-comes-to-town/ (accessed 3 September 2019).
Harkins, S. and J. Lugo-Ocando (2016), 'How Malthusian Ideology Crept into the Newsroom: British Tabloids and the Coverage of the "Underclass"', *Critical Discourse Studies*, 13 (1): 78–93.
Harrisson, T. (1939a), 'Note on Conversation with Richard Crossman', 30 August, *Mass Observation* 43 2/E.
Harrisson, T. (1939b), 'Note on Ministry of Information Meeting', 6 October, *Mass Observation* 43 2/E.
Harrisson, T. (1939c), 'Note on Visit to the Ministry of Information', 12 October, *Mass Observation* 43 2/B.
Harrisson, T. (1939d), 'Note on Senate House Postcards', 19 October, *Mass Observation* 43 2/E.
Harrisson, T. and C. Madge (1937), *Mass-Observation*, London: Frederick Muller.
Hart, C. (2010), *Critical Discourse Analysis and Cognitive Science: New Perspectives on Immigration Discourse*, 196–208, London: Palgrave.
Hart, C. (2014), *Discourse, Grammar and Ideology*, London: Bloomsbury.
Harvey, L., K. Allen and H. Mendick (2015), 'Extraordinary Acts and Ordinary Pleasures: Rhetorics of Inequality in Young People's Talk About Celebrity', *Discourse & Society*, 26 (4): 428–44.
Hatherley, O. (2016), *The Ministry of Nostalgia*, London: Verso.
Hayek, F. (1978), 'Letter to *The Times*', 11 July.
Heath, A., D. Fisher, G. Rosenblatt, D. Sanders and M. Sobolewska (2013), *The Political Integration of Ethnic Minorities in Britain*, Oxford: Oxford University Press.
Heimann, J. (1998), *The Most Offending Soul Alive: Tom Harrisson and His Remarkable Life*, Honolulu: University of Hawai'i Press.
Hewitt, R. (1994), 'The Beggar's Blanket: Public Scepticism and the Representation of Poverty', in U. H. Meinhof and K. Richardson (eds), *Text, Discourse and Context: Representations of Poverty in Britain*, 122–46, London and New York: Longman.
Higgins, C. (2015), *This New Noise: The Extraordinary Birth and Troubled Life of the BBC*, London: Guardian Faber.

Highmore, B. (2002), *Everyday Life and Cultural Theory*, London: Routledge.
Hills, J. and K. Stewart (eds) (2005), *A More Equal Society? New Labour, Poverty, Inequality and Exclusion*, Bristol: Policy Press.
Hinton, J. (2013), *The Mass Observers: A History, 1937-1949*, Oxford: Oxford University Press.
Hobsbawm, E. J. (1977), 'Gramsci and Political Theory', *Marxism Today*. Available online: http://banmarchive.org.uk/collections/mt/pdf/07_77_205.pdf (accessed 2 August 2019).
Hobsbawm, E. J. (1992), *Nations and Nationalism Since 1780*, Cambridge: Cambridge University Press.
Hobsbawm, E. J. (1994), *The Age of Extremes: 1914-1991*, London: Abacus.
Hoggart, R. (1957), *The Uses of Literacy*, Harmondsworth: Penguin.
House of Commons Health Committee (2004), *Obesity: Third Report of Session 2003-04*, London: TSO.
Hsieh, C. C. and M. D. Pugh (1993), 'Poverty, Income Inequality, and Violent Crime: A Meta-Analysis of Recent Aggregate Data Studies', *Criminal Justice Review*, 18 (2): 182–202.
Huddlestone, T. (2019), 'Jeff Bezos: Making This 1 Choice Is the Key to Success', CNBC, 21 February. Available online: https://www.cnbc.com/2019/02/20/amazon-ceo-jeff-bezos-this-choice-is-the-key-to-success.html (accessed 2 August 2019).
Hulbert, J. (2015), 'UK Financial Journalists Quizzed by MPs', in S. Schifferes and R. Roberts (eds), *The Media and Financial Crises*, 279–90, London and New York: Routledge.
Hunston, S. (2002), *Corpora in Applied Linguistics*, Cambridge: Cambridge University Press.
Iacoviello, M. (2008), 'Household Debt and Income Inequality, 1963-2003', *Journal of Money, Credit and Banking*, 40 (5): 929–65.
Idrovo, A., M. Ruiz-Rodriguez and A. Manzano-Patino (2010), 'Beyond the Income Inequality Hypothesis and Human: A Worldwide Exploration', *Rev Saude Publica*, 44 (4): 695–702.
'In Quotes: Margaret Thatcher' (2013), *BBC News Politics*, 8 April. Available online: https://www.bbc.com/news/uk-politics-22068157 (accessed 11 February 2019).
Inman, P. and R. Booth (2019), 'Poverty Increases Among Children and Pensioners Across UK', *Guardian*, 28 March. Available online: https://www.theguardian.com/society/2019/mar/28/poverty-increases-among-children-and-pensioners-across-uk (accessed 4 September 2019).
International Labour Office and Walk Free Foundation (2017), *Global Estimates of Modern Slavery: Forced Labour and Forced Marriage*. Available online: https://www.ilo.org/wcmsp5/groups/public/@dgreports/@dcomm/documents/publication/wcms_575479.pdf (accessed 20 January 2019).
Jeffery, T. (1978), *Mass Observation – A Short History*. CCCS Stencilled Occasional Papers, Birmingham: University of Birmingham.
Jeffries, L. (2003), 'Not a Drop to Drink: Emerging Meanings in Local Newspaper Reporting of the 1995 Water Crisis in Yorkshire', *Text - Interdisciplinary Journal for the Study of Discourse*, 23 (4): 513–38.
Jeffries, L. (2010), *Critical Stylistics*, London: Palgrave.
Jeffries, L. (2011), 'Radicalisation and Democracy: A Linguistic Analysis of Rhetorical Change', in V. Bryson and P. Faber (eds), *Redefining Social Justice: New Labour, Rhetoric and Reality*, 37–56, Manchester: Manchester University Press.

Jeffries, L. (2014), 'Critical Stylistics', in M. Burke (ed), *The Routledge Handbook of Stylistics*, 408–21, London: Routledge.
Jeffries, L. and M. Evans (2015), 'The Rise of Choice as an Absolute "Good": A Study of British Manifestos (1900-2010)', *SRW Working Papers*, 5: 1–24.
Jeffries, L. and B. Walker (2018), *Keywords in the Press: The New Labour Years*, London: Bloomsbury.
Jeffries, L. and B. Walker (2019), 'Austerity in the Commons: A Corpus Critical Analysis of Austerity and Its Surrounding Grammatical Context in Hansard (1803– 2015)', in K. Power, T. Ali and E. Lebdušková (eds), *Discourse Analysis and Austerity: Critical Studies from Economics and Linguistics*, 53–79, London: Routledge.
Jensen, T. (2014), 'Welfare Commonsense, Poverty Porn and Doxosophy', *Sociological Research Online*, 19 (3): 1–7.
Jewkes, Y. (2011), *Media and Crime*, 2nd edn, London: Sage.
Jones, O. (2014), *The Establishment: And How They Get Away with It*, London: Allen Lane.
Johnson, K., J. Sonnett, M. Dolan, R. Reppen and L. Johnson (2010), 'Interjournalistic Discourse About African Americans in Television News Coverage of Hurricane Katrina', *Discourse and Communication*, 4 (3): 243–61.
Joseph Rowntree Foundation (2015), *JRF Response to HBAI Figures*. Available online: https://www.jrf.org.uk/press/jrf-response-hbai-figures (accessed 4 September 2019).
Joseph Rowntree Foundation (2018), *UK Poverty 2018*. Available online: https://www.jrf.org.uk/report/uk-poverty-2018?gclid=EAIaIQobChMIzuPxws_c4QIVwuF3Ch3uaA9-EAAYASAAEgLl2fD_BwE (accessed 4 September 2019).
Joseph Rowntree Foundation (2019), *UK Poverty: Causes, Costs and Solutions*, London. Available online: https://www.jrf.org.uk/file/49551/download?token=fRbyhlDk&filetype=full-report (accessed 3 September 2019).
Joyce, R. (2014), *Child Poverty in Britain: Recent Trends and Future Prospects*, London: Institute of Fiscal Studies. Available online: https://www.ifs.org.uk/uploads/publications/wps/WP201507.pdf (accessed 3 September 2019).
Joye, S. (2010), 'News Discourses on Distant Suffering: A Critical Discourse Analysis of the 2003 SARS Outbreak', *Discourse & Society*, 21 (5): 586–601.
Kalogeropoulos, A., E. Albæk, H. de Vreese, and A. Van Dalen (2015), 'The Predictors of Economic Sophistication: Media, Interpersonal Communication and Negative Economic Experiences', *European Journal of Communication*, 30 (4): 385–403.
Kasser, T. and R. M. Ryan (1993), 'A Dark Side of the American Dream: Correlates of Financial Success as a Central Life Aspiration', *Journal of Personality and Social Psychology*, 65 (2): 410–22.
Kawachi, I., B. Kennedy, K. Lochner and D. Prothrow-Smith (1997), 'Social Capital, Income Inequality, and Mortality', *American Journal of Public Health*, 87 (9): 1491–8.
Kay, J. and L. Salter (2014), 'Framing the Cuts: An Analysis of the BBC's Discursive Framing of the ConDem Cuts Agenda', *Journalism*, 15 (6): 754–72.
Keane, W. (2003), 'Semiotics and the Social Analysis of Material Things', *Language & Communication*, 23 (3–4): 409–25.
Kelley, K. and K. P. Preacher (2012), 'On Effect Size', *Psychological Methods*, 17 (2): 137–52.
Kelsey, D., F. Mueller, A. Whittle and M. Khosravinik (2016), 'Financial Crisis and Austerity: Interdisciplinary Concerns in Critical Discourse Studies', *Critical Discourse Studies*, 13 (1): 1–19.
Kennedy, J. (2018), *Authentocrats*, London: Repeater.

Kilgarriff, A., V. Baisa, J. Bušta, M. Jakubíček, V. Kovář, J. Michelfeit, P. Rychlý and V. Suchomel (2014), 'The Sketch Engine: Ten Years On', *Lexicography*, 1: 7-36. Available online: https://www.sketchengine.eu/ (accessed 3 September 2019).

Kitzinger, J. (1999), 'Researching Risk and the Media', *Health, Risk and Society*, 1 (1): 55-69.

Klein, N. (2000), *No Logo*, London: Harper Collins.

Koller, V. and P. Davidson (2008), 'Social Exclusion as Conceptual and Grammatical Metaphor: A Cross-Genre Study of British Policy-Making', *Discourse & Society*, 19 (3): 307-31.

Kondo, N., G. Sembajwe, I. Kawachi, R. M. Van Dam, S. V. Subramanian and Z. Yamagata (2009), 'Income Inequality, Mortality, and Self-rated Health: Meta-Analysis of Multilevel Studies', *BMJ*, 339: b4471.

Krahn, H., T. F. Hartnagel and J. W. Gartrell (1986), 'Income Inequality and Homicide Rates: Cross-National Data and Criminological Theories', *Criminology*, 24 (2): 269-94.

Kress, G. (1985), *Linguistic Processes in Sociocultural Practice*, 2nd edn, Oxford: Oxford University Press.

Kress, G. (1994), 'Text and Grammar as Explanation', in U. H. Meinhof and K. Richardson (eds), *Text, Discourse and Context: Representations of Poverty in Britain*, 24-46, London and New York: Longman.

Kress, G. and R. Hodge (1979), *Language as Ideology*, London: Routledge.

Kress, G. and T. van Leeuwen (1996), *Reading Images: The Grammar of Visual Design*, London: Routledge.

Kress, G. and T. van Leeuwen (2001), *Multimodal Discourse: The Modes and Media of Contemporary Discourse*, London: Hodder Arnold.

Kress, G. and T. V. Leeuwen (2002), '"Colour" as a Semiotic Mode: Notes for a Grammar of Colour', *Visual Communication*, 1 (3): 343-68.

Kumhof, M. and R. Rancière (2010), *Inequality, Leverage and Crises*, November, International Monetary Fund. Available online: https://www.imf.org/external/pubs/ft/wp/2010/wp10268.pdf (accessed 4 September 2019).

Labov, W. (1972), *Sociolinguistic Patterns*, Philadelphia: University of Pennsylvania Press.

Lacerda, D. (2015), 'Rio de Janeiro and the Divided State: Analysing the Political Discourse on Favelas', *Discourse & Society*, 26 (1): 74-94.

Laclau, E. and C. Mouffe ([1985] 2001), *Hegemony and Socialist Strategy*, 2nd edn, London: Verso.

Lakoff, G. and M. Johnson (1980), *Metaphors We Live By*, Chicago: University of Chicago Press.

Lambert, T. (2013), 'A Brief History of Poverty in Britain', *A World History Encyclopedia*. Available online: www.localhistories.org/povhist.html (accessed 3 September 2019).

Lancee, B. and H. G. Van der Werfhorst (2012), 'Income Inequality and Participation: A Comparison of 24 European Countries', *Social Science Research*, 41: 1166-78.

Landis, J. and G. Koch (1977), 'The Measurement of Observer Agreement for Categorical Data', *Biometrics*, 33 (1): 159-74.

Langer, A. I. (2007), 'A Historical Exploration of the Personalisation of Politics in the Print Media: The British Prime Ministers (1945 - 1999)', *Parliamentary Affairs*, 60 (3): 371-87.

Lansley, S. (2012), 'Inequality, the Crash and the Ongoing Crisis', *The Political Quarterly*, 83 (4): 754-61.

Lawson (2007), *House of Lords: Reform*. Available online: https://www.theyworkforyou.com/lords/?id=2007-03-12b.441.98&p=13427 (Accessed 2 August 2019).

Lears, T. J. (1985), 'The Concept of Cultural Hegemony', *American Social Review*, (30): 567–93.
Lederman, D., P. Fajnzylber and N. Loayza (2002), 'Inequality and Violent Crime', *Journal of Law and Economics*, 45 (1): Part 1.
Levitas, R. (2005), *The Inclusive Society?*, 2nd edn, London: Sage.
Lewis, J. (2013a), 'Evolution Not Revolution: News in the Digital Age', *Journalism, Media and Culture*. Available online: http://www.jomec.co.uk/blog/evolution-not-revolution-news-in-the-digital-age (accessed 3 September 2019).
Lewis, J. (2013b), *Beyond Consumer Capitalism: Media and the Limits to Imagination*, Cambridge: Polity.
Lewis, J. and S. Cushion (2019), 'Think Tanks, Television News and Impartiality', *Journalism Studies*, 20 (4): 480–99.
Lewis, J. and R. Thomas (2015), 'More of the Same: News, Economic Growth and the Recycling of Conventional Wisdom', in G. Murdock and J. Gripsrud (eds), *Money Talks: Media, Markets, Crisis*, 83–99, Polity: Bristol.
Lewis, N. (2017), *Keep Calm and Carry On: The Truth Behind the Poster*, London: Imperial War Museum.
'Liberal Democracy' (2019), *Wikipedia, The Free Encyclopedia*. Available online: https://en.wikipedia.org/w/index.php?title=Liberal_democracy&oldid=909535630 (accessed 18 August 2019).
Locke, J. (1982), *Second Treatise of Government*, Arlington Heights: Harlan Davidson.
Longmate, N. (1973), *How We Lived Then: A History of Everyday Life During the Second World War*, London: Arrow.
Lorenzo-Dus, N. and S. Marsh (2012), 'Bridging the Gap: Interdisciplinary Insights into the Securitization of Poverty', *Discourse & Society*, 23: 274–96.
Louw, B. (1993), 'Irony in the Text or Insincerity in the Writer? The Diagnostic Potential of Semantic Prosodies', in M. Baker, G. Francis, and E. Tognini-Bonelli (eds), *Text and Technology: In Honour of John Sinclair*, 157–75, Amsterdam: John Benjamins.
Lugo-Ocando. J. (2014), *Blaming the Victim: How Global Journalism Fails Those in Poverty*, London: Pluto Press.
Lundström, R. (2013), 'Framing Fraud: Discourse on Benefit Cheating in Sweden and the UK', *European Journal of Communication*, 28 (6): 630–45.
Lyengar, S. (1990), 'Framing Responsibility for Political Issues: The Case of Poverty', *Political Behavior*, 12 (1): 19–40.
Machin, S. (2015), *Real Wages and Living Standards: The Latest UK Evidence. British Politics and Policy at LSE*, 26 May. Available online: http://blogs.lse.ac.uk/politicsandpolicy/real-wages-and-living-standards/ (accessed 3 September 2019).
Machin, D. and J. E. Richardson (2008), 'Renewing an Academic Interest in Structural Inequalities', *Critical Discourse Studies*, 5 (4): 281–7.
Mair, C. (2006), *Twentieth-Century English*, Cambridge: Cambridge University Press.
Malinowski, B. (1938), 'A Nation-Wide Intelligence Service', in *Mass-Observation, First Year's Work 1937-38*, 81–121, London: Lindsay Drummond.
'Margaret Thatcher: A Life in Words' (2013), *The Daily Telegraph*, 8 April. Available online: https://www.telegraph.co.uk/news/politics/margaret-thatcher/9979399/Margaret-Thatcher-A-life-in-words.html (accessed 11 February 2019).
Marmot, M. G. (2010), *Fair Society, Healthy Lives: The Marmot Review*, London: The Marmot Review.
Marquand, D. (2013), *Mammon's Kingdom: An Essay on Britain Now*, London: Allen Lane.

Martin, J. and P. White (2008), *The Language of Evaluation: Appraisal in English*, London: Palgrave.
Marx, K. and F. Engels (2015), *The Communist Manifesto*, Scotts Valley: Create Space Independent Publishing Platform.
Mass-Observation (1937), *May 12th Mass-Observation Day Surveys*, London: Faber & Faber.
Mass-Observation (1938a), *First Year's Work 1937-38*, London: Lindsay Drummond.
Mass-Observation (1938b), *Labour Crusade Meeting*, 24 September, Worktown Collection 7B, Labour Party.
Mass-Observation (1939, 2), *Government Posters in War-Time*, 18 October.
Mass-Observation (1939, 3), *The Public Information Leaflets*, 18 October.
Mass-Observation (1939, 5), *Six Railway Posters*, 27 October.
Mass-Observation (1940), *War Begins at Home*, London: Chatto & Windus.
Mass-Observation (1940, 84), *'Fifth Column' Pilot Test*, 29 April.
Mass-Observation (1940, 112), *Reaction to Eden's Speech*, 17 May.
Mass-Observation (1940, 193), *A New Attitude to the Problem of Civilian Morale*, 12 June.
Mass-Observation (1940, 197), *Propaganda Ideas*, 13 June.
Mass-Observation (1940, 219), *Ministry of Information Speaker in Hyde Park*, 21 June.
Mass-Observation (1940, 250), *The Yardstick Memo*, 5 July.
Mass-Observation (1940, 298), *The Rout Rumour Rally*, 26 July.
Mass-Observation (1940, 305), *Unintelligible Words*, 27 July.
Mass-Observation (1940, 363), *The Word 'Crusade'*, 20 August.
Mass-Observation (1940, 448), *Personification Processes (YOU)*, 10 October.
Mass-Observation (1941, 681), *Gas Mask Leaflet*, 1 May.
Mass-Observation (1941, 795), *Songwriters*, 22 July.
Mass-Observation (1947, 2462), *The Language of Leadership*, 20 March.
Mautner, G. (1995), '"Only Connect." Critical Discourse Analysis and Corpus Linguistics', *UCREL Technical Papers* 6. Available online: http://ucrel.lancaster.ac.uk/papers/techpaper/vol6.pdf (accessed 3 September 2019).
Mautner, G. (2010), *Language and the Market Society: Critical Reflections on Discourse and Dominance*, New York: Routledge.
McCall, L. (2005), *Do They Know and Do They Care? Americans' Awareness of Rising Inequality*, Berkeley: Russell Sage Foundation Social Inequality Conference.
McCall, L. (2013), *The Undeserving Rich: American Beliefs About Inequality, Opportunity, and Redistribution*, Cambridge: Cambridge University Press.
McChesney, R. (2000), *Rich Media, Poor Democracy*, Chicago: University of Illinois Press.
McChesney, R. (2003), 'The Problem of Journalism: A Political Economic Contribution to an Explanation of the Crisis in Contemporary US Journalism', *Journalism Studies*, 4 (3): 299–329.
McEnery, T. and H. Baker (2017), 'The Poor in Seventeenth-Century England: A Corpus Based Analysis', *A Journal of English Linguistics*, 6: 51–83.
McIntyre, D. and B. Walker (2019), *Corpus Stylistics: Theory and Practice*, Edinburgh: Edinburgh University Press.
McKendrick, J., S. Sinclair, A. Irwin, H. O'Donnell, G. Scott and L. Dobbie (2008), *The Media, Poverty and Public Opinion in the UK*, York: Joseph Rowntree.
McLaine, I. (1979), *Ministry of Morale*, London: George Allen and Unwin.
Meinhof, U. H. (1994), 'From the Street to the Screen: *Breadline Britain* and the Semiotics of Poverty', in U. H. Meinhof and K. Richardson (eds), *Text, Discourse and Context: Representations of Poverty in Britain*, 67–92, London and New York: Longman.

Meinhof, U. H. and K. Richardson (1994), *Text, Discourse and Context: Representations of Poverty in Britain*, London and New York: Longman.

Mendick, H., K. Allen and L. Harvey (2015), '"We Can Get Everything We Want If We Try Hard": Young People, Celebrity, Hardwork', *British Journal of Education Studies*, 63 (2): 161–78.

Merkel, A. (2011), 'Merkel: "Marktkonforme Demokratie"', *NachDenkSeiten*, 2 September. Available online: https://www.nachdenkseiten.de/?p=10611 (accessed 2 August 2019).

Merriam Webster Thesaurus (2019), Merriam Webster. Available online: https://www.merriam-webster.com (accessed 3 September 2019).

Merrill, G. (2012), 'The Revolution Must Wait: Economic, Business and Financial Journalisms Beyond the 2008 Crisis', *Ethical Space: The International Journal of Communication Ethics*, 9 (1): 41–51.

Modern Slavery Act 2015 (c.30), London: The Stationery Office.

Monaghan, A. and J. Elgot (2017), '"Brexit Boom" Gives Britain Record 134 Billionaires, Fuelling Inequality Fears', *Guardian*, 7 May. Available online: https://www.theguardian.com/business/2017/may/07/brexit-boom-creates-record-number-of-uk-billionaires-sunday-times-rich-list (accessed 3 September 2019).

Montgomery, M. (2007), *The Discourse of Broadcast News: A Linguistic Approach*, London: Routledge.

Mooney, A. and E. Sifaki (eds), (2017) *The Language of Money and Debt*, London: Palgrave.

Moran, J. (2008), 'Mass-Observation, Market Research, and the Birth of the Focus Group, 1937-1997', *Journal of British Studies*, 47 (4): 827–51.

Morley, J. and P. Bayley (eds) (2009), *Corpus-Assisted Discourse Studies on the Iraq Conflict*, London: Routledge.

Morrisson, C. and F. Murtin (2013), 'The Kuznets Curve of Human Capital Inequality: 1870-2010', *The Journal of Economic Inequality*, 11 (3): 283–301.

Mount, F. (2012), *The New Few: Or a Very British Oligarchy*, London: Simon & Schuster.

Mugglestone, L. (2003), *Talking Proper*, Oxford: Oxford University Press.

Mulderrig, J. (2007), *Equalities and Human Rights: Key Concepts and Issues*, Edinburgh: University of Edinburgh.

Mulderrig, J. (2011), 'The Grammar of Governance', *Critical Discourse Studies*, 8 (1): 45–68.

Mulderrig, J. (2015), '"Enabling" Participatory Governance in Education: A Corpus-Based Critical Policy Analysis', in P. Smyers, D. Bridges, N. Burbules and M. Griffiths (eds), *International Handbook of Interpretation in Educational Research*, 441–70, Berlin: Springer.

Mulderrig, J. (2017), 'The Language of "Nudge" in Health Policy: Pre-empting Working Class Obesity Through "Biopedagogy"', *Critical Policy Studies*, 13 (1): 101–21.

Mulderrig, J. (2018), 'Multimodal Strategies of Emotional Governance: A Critical Analysis of "Nudge" Tactics in Health Policy', *Critical Discourse Studies*, 15 (1): 39–67.

Mulderrig, J. (forthcoming), 'Analysing Orders of Discourse of Neoliberal Rule: Health "Nudges" and the Rise of Psychological Governance', in M. Montessori, M. Farrelly and J. Mulderrig (eds), *Critical Policy Discourse Analysis*, London: Edward Elgar.

Mulderrig, J., Montessori, M., Farrelly, M. (2019). 'Introducing Critical Policy Discourse Analysis', in Montessori, M. Farrelly and J. Mulderrig (eds), *Critical Policy Discourse Analysis*, 1–22. London: Edward Elgar.

Murkens, J. E. K. (2014), 'Unintended Democracy: Parliamentary Reform in the UK', in K. L. Grotke and M. J. Prutsch (eds), *Constitutionalism, Legitimacy, and Power: Nineteenth-Century Experiences*, 351–70, Oxford: Oxford University Press.

National Assistance Act (1948). Available online: http://www.legislation.gov.uk/ukpga/Geo6/11-12/29 (accessed 4 August 2019).

National Audit Office (2001), *Tackling Obesity in England*, London.

National Evaluation of Sure Start (NESS) Team and Others (2010), *The Impact of Sure Start Local Programmes on Five-Year-Olds and Their Families*, London: Department for Education. Available online: https://assets.publishing.service.gov.uk/government/uploads/system/uploads/attachment_data/file/182026/DFE-RR067.pdf (accessed 3 September 2019).

National Health Service Act (1946). Available online: https://www.legislation.gov.uk/ukpga/Geo6/9-10/81/enacted (accessed 4 August 2019).

New Oxford English Dictionary (1998), Oxford: Clarendon Press.

News Statesman and Nation (1940), 11 May, in I. McLaine, *Ministry of Morale*, 39, London: George Allen and Unwin.

Nexis (2019). Available online: https://www.nexis.com/ (accessed 4 September 2019).

NHS (2012), 'Sweet Breakfast Cereals "Too Sugary for Kids"', 16 February. Available online: https://www.nhs.uk/news/food-and-diet/sweet-breakfast-cereals-too-sugary-for-kids/ (accessed 12 August 2019).

NRC (2013), 'Participatiesamenleving Uitgeroepen tot Woord van het Jaar 2013', *NRC*, 16 November. Available online: https://www.nrc.nl/nieuws/2013/11/16/participatiesamenleving-uitgeroepen-tot-woord-van-het-jaar-2013-a1429701 (accessed 31 May 2019).

NHS (2019), Statistics on Obesity, Physical Activity and Diet, England, 8 May. Available online: https://digital.nhs.uk/data-and-information/publications/statistical/statistics-on-obesity-physical-activity-and-diet/statistics-on-obesity-physical-activity-and-diet-england-2019/part-4-childhood-obesity (accessed 12 August 2019).

Nunn, A. (2016), 'The Production and Reproduction of Inequality in the UK in Times of Austerity', *British Politics*, 11 (4): 469–87.

O'Connor, A. (2001), *Poverty Knowledge*, Princeton: Princeton University Press.

OECD (2019), *Income Inequality (indicator)*. Available online: https://data.oecd.org/inequality/income-inequality.htm#indicator-chart (accessed 2 August 2019).

Ofcom (2018), *News Consumption in the UK-2018*. Available online: https://www.ofcom.org.uk/__data/assets/pdf_file/0024/116529/news-consumption-2018.pdf (accessed 3 September 2019).

Offer, A., R. Pechey, and S. Ulijaszek (2012), *Insecurity, Inequality, and Obesity in Affluent Societies*, Oxford: Oxford University Press.

Office for National Statistics (2015), *Child and Infant Mortality in England and Wales: 2013*. Available online: https://www.ons.gov.uk/peoplepopulationandcommunity/birthsdeathsandmarriages/deaths/bulletins/childhoodinfantandperinatalmortalityinenglandandwales/2015-03-10#socio-economic-status (accessed: 12 August 2019).

Office for National Statistics (2018), 'Wealth in Great Britain Wave 5: 2014 to 2016', Newport: Office for National Statistics. Available online: https://www.ons.gov.uk/peoplepopulationandcommunity/personalandhouseholdfinances/incomeandwealth/bulletins/wealthingreatbritainwave5/2014to2016 (accessed: 12 August 2019).

Office for National Statistics (2019a), 'Household Income Inequality, UK: Financial Year Ending 2019 (Provisional)', Newport: Office for National Statistics. Available online: https://www.ons.gov.uk/peoplepopulationandcommunity/personalandhouseholdfinances/

incomeandwealth/bulletins/householdincomeinequalityfinancial/financialyearendin g2019provisional (accessed 3 September 2019).
Office for National Statistics (2019b), 'Average Household Income, UK: Financial Year Ending 2019 (Provisional)', Newport: Office for National Statistics. Available online: https://www.ons.gov.uk/peoplepopulationandcommunity/personalandhouseholdfin ances/incomeandwealth/bulletins/householddisposableincomeandinequality/financial yearending2019provisional (accessed 3 September 2019).
Oldcorn, C. (1976), *Middle Class Values and Working Class Culture in Nineteenth Century Sheffield*, University of Sheffield. Available online: http://etheses.whiterose.ac.uk/1281 5/1/540913.pdf (accessed 2 August 2019).
Organisation for Economic Co-operation and Development (2015), *Income Inequality Data Update and Policies Impacting Income Distribution*, Paris: OECD Publishing. Available online: http://www.oecd.org/unitedkingdom/OECD-Income-Inequality-UK.pdf (accessed 3 September 2019).
Ortu, C. (2008), 'The Denial of Class Struggle by British Governments in Their Anti-union Discourse (1978-2007)', *Critical Discourse Studies*, 5 (4): 289–301.
Orwell, G. ([1940] 1968), 'War-Time Diary, 24 June 1940', in S. Orwell and I. Angus (eds) *The Collected Essays, Journalism and Letters of George Orwell, Volume II*, 353–6, London: Secker and Warburg.
Orwell, G. ([1937] 2001), *The Road to Wigan Pier*, Harmondsworth: Penguin.
Orwell, G. ([1947] 2001), 'The English People', in P. Davison (ed), *Orwell's England*, 290–333, London: Penguin.
Orwell, G. ([1946] 2004), 'Politics and the English Language', in *Why I Write*, 102–20, London: Penguin.
Orwell, G. ([1944] 2010), 'Propaganda and Demotic Speech', in J. E. Joseph (ed), *Language and Politics, Volume 1*, 22–48, London: Routledge.
Osbourne, G. (2012), 'George Osborne's Speech to the Conservative Conference: Full Text', *New Statesman*. Available online: https://www.newstatesman.com/blogs/politics/2012/10/george-osbornes-speech-conservative-conference-full-text (accessed 20 March 2019).
Oswald, A. J. (1997), 'Happiness and Economic Performance', *The Economic Journal*, 107: 1815-1831.
Oxford Thesaurus (2019), 'Lexico'. Available online: https://www.lexico.com/en/english-thesaurus (accessed 3 September 2019).
Pardo, M. L. (2013), 'The Aesthetics of Poverty and Crime in Argentinean Reality Television', in N. Lorenzo-Dus and P. G. C. Blitvich (eds), *Real Talk: Reality Television and Discourse Analysis in Action*, 115–39, Palgrave Macmillan, London.
Pardo-Abril, N. (2008), 'La Representación de lo Mensurable sobre la Pobreza en la Prensa Colombiana', *Discurso & Sociedad*, 2 (2): 394–421.
Partington, A. (2006), *The Linguistics of Laughter: A Corpus-Assisted Study of Laughter-Talk*, London: Routledge.
Partington, A. (2010), 'Modern Diachronic Corpus-Assisted Discourse Studies (MD-CADS) on UK Newspapers: An Overview of the Project', *Corpora*, 5 (2): 83–108.
Partington, A., A. Duguid and C. Taylor (2013), *Patterns and Meanings in Discourse: Theory and Practice in Corpus-Assisted Discourse Studies (CADS)*, Amsterdam: John Benjamins.
Partington, A., J. Morley and L. Haarman (eds) (2004), *Corpora and Discourse*, Bern: Peter Lang.

Paterson, L. L. and I. N. Gregory (2019), *Representations of Poverty and Place: Using Geographical Text Analysis to Understand Discourse*, Basingstoke: Palgrave Macmillan.

Paterson, L. L., L. Coffey-Glover and D. Peplow (2016), 'Negotiating Stance within Discourses of Class: Reactions to *Benefits Street*', *Discourse & Society*, 27 (2): 195–214.

Paterson, L., D. Peplow and K. Grainger (2017), 'Does Money Talk Equate to Class Talk? Audience Responses to Poverty Porn in Relation to Money and Debt', in A. Mooney and E. Sifaki (eds), *The Language of Money and Debt*, 205–31, London: Palgrave.

Pearce, M. (2005), 'Informalization in UK Party Election Broadcasts 1966-97', *Language and Literature*, 14 (1): 65–90.

Piketty, T. (2014), *Capital in the Twenty-First Century*, Cambridge: The Belknap Press of Harvard University Press.

Piquero, N. L., S. G. Tibbetts and M. B. Blankenship (2005), 'Examining the Role of Differential Association and Techniques of Neutralization in Explaining Corporate Crime', *Deviant Behavior*, 26 (2): 159–88.

Pope, R., A. Pratt and B. Hoyle (1986), *Social Welfare in Britain 1885–1985*, London: Croom Helm.

Potts, A., M. Bednarek and H. Caple (2015), 'How Can Computer-Based Methods Help Researchers to Investigate News Values in Large Datasets? A Corpus Linguistic Study of the Construction of Newsworthiness in the Reporting on Hurricane Katrina', *Discourse and Communication*, 9 (2): 149–72.

Poverty and Social Exclusion (2013), *Payday Loans Used to Pay for Food*. Available online: http://www.poverty.ac.uk/editorial/payday-loans-used-pay-food (accessed 3 September 2019).

Powell, K. (2017), 'Brexit Positions: Neoliberalism, Austerity and Immigration – The (Im)Possibilities? of Political Revolution', *Dialect Anthropology*, 41: 225–40.

Pryor, F. L. (2012), 'The Impact of Income Inequality on Values and Attitudes', *The Journal of Socio-Economics*, 41: 615–22.

Public Health England (2018), *Obesity and the Environment: Density of Fast Food Outlets*, PHE Publication Gateway Reference 2018064. Available online: https://assets.publishing.service.gov.uk/government/uploads/system/uploads/attachment_data/file/741555/Fast_Food_map.pdf (accessed 3 September 2019).

Punch, M. (1996), *Dirty Business: Exploring Corporate Misconduct*, London: Sage.

Quirk, R., S. Greenbaum, G. Leech and S. Svartvik (1985), *A Comprehensive Grammar of the English Language*, London: Longman.

Rahman, F. (2019), *The Generation of Poverty: Poverty over the Life Course for Different Generations*, London: Resolution Foundation. Available online: https://www.resolutionfoundation.org/app/uploads/2019/05/Generation-of-Poverty-Report.pdf (accessed 3 September 2019).

Raine, K. (1991), *Autobiographies*, London: Skoob Books.

Rampton, B. (2006), *Language in Late Modernity*, Cambridge: Cambridge University Press.

Ras, I. A. (2017), *A Corpus-Assisted Critical Discourse Analysis of the Reporting on Corporate Fraud by UK Newspapers 2004-2014*, PhD diss., University of Leeds.

Rayson, P. (2009), 'Wmatrix: A Web-Based Corpus Processing Environment, Computing Department, Lancaster University'. Available online: http://ucrel.lancs.ac.uk/wmatrix/ (accessed 3 September 2019).

Rayson, P. (n.d.), 'Log-Likelihood and Effect Size Calculator', University of Lancaster. Available online: http://ucrel.lancs.ac.uk/llwizard.html (accessed 1 February 2019).

Reece, D. (2009), 'Austerity or Inflation. That's the Choice for the Next Government', *The Daily Telegraph*, 22 April.

Reisigl, M. and R. Wodak (2001), *Discourse and Discrimination: Rhetorics of Racism and Anti-semitism*, London: Routledge.

Reith, J.C.W. (1949), *Into the Wind*, London: Hodder & Stoughton.

Richardson, K. (1994), 'Interpreting *Breadline Britain*', in U. H. Meinhof and K. Richardson (eds), *Text, Discourse and Context: Representations of Poverty in Britain*, 93–121, London and New York: Longman.

Rieder, M. and H. Theine (2019), '"Piketty Is a Genius, but…": An Analysis of Journalistic Delegitimation of Thomas Piketty's Economic Policy Proposals', *Critical Discourse Studies*, 16 (3): 248–63.

Roberts, C. (2017), 'The Language of "Welfare Dependency" and "Benefit Cheats: Internalising and Reproducing the Hegemonic and Discursive Rhetoric of "Benefit Scroungers"', in A. Mooney and E. Sifaki (eds), *The Language of Money and Debt*, 189–204, London: Palgrave.

Roberts, C. and M. Lawrence (2017), *Wealth in the Twenty-First Century Inequalities and Drivers*, London: Institute for Public Policy Research. Available online: https://www.ippr.org/publications/wealth-in-the-twenty-first-century (accessed 4 September 2019).

Roberts, C., G. Blakeley, L. Rankin and R. Statham (2019), *The UK in the Global Economy*, London: Institute for Public Policy Research. Available online: https://www.ippr.org/research/publications/uk-in-the-global-economy (accessed 4 September 2019).

Robinson, F., R. Else, M. Sherlock and I. Zass-Ogilvie (2009), *Poverty in the Media: Being Seen and Getting Heard*, York: Joseph Rowntree Foundation. Available online: https://www.jrf.org.uk/report/poverty-media-being-seen-and-getting-heard-0 (accessed 3 September 2019).

Rosenberg, A. (1973), 'Aristoteles über Diktatur und Demokratie', in P. Steinmetz (ed), *Schriften zu den Politika des Aristoteles*, New York: Hildesheim.

Rosoff, S. M., H. N. Pontell, and R. H. Tillman, (2010), *Profit Without Honor: White-Collar Crime and the Looting of America*, 5th edn, Boston: Prentice Hall.

Rothstein, B. and E. M. Uslaner (2005), 'ALL FOR ALL: Equality, Corruption, and Social Trust', *World Politics*, 58 (1): 41–72.

Rousseau, J. (1968), *The Social Contract*, Harmondsworth: Penguin Classics.

Rowlingson, K. (2011), 'Does Income Inequality Cause Health and Social Problems?', Joseph Rowntree Foundation. Available online: https://www.jrf.org.uk/sites/default/files/jrf/migrated/files/Rowlingson-Income-eBook.pdf (access 4 September 2019).

Rowlingson, K. (2012), *Wealth Inequality: Key Facts*, Birmingham: University of Birmingham Policy Commission on the Distribution of Wealth.

Sandel, M. J. (2012), *What Money Can't Buy: The Moral Limits of Markets*, London: Penguin.

Sarbanes-Oxley Act (2002), Public Law 107-204, 30 July 2002. Congress of the United States of America. Available online: https://www.sec.gov/about/laws/soa2002.pdf (accessed 13 August 2019).

Sayer, A. (2014), *Why We Can't Afford the Rich*, Bristol: Policy Press.

Schifferes, S. and S. Coulter (2013), 'Downloading Disaster: BBC News Online Coverage of the Global Financial Crisis', *Journalism*, 14 (2): 228–52.

Schneider, A. and H. Ingram (1993), 'Social Construction of Target Populations: Implications for Politics and Policy', *American Political Science Review*, 87 (2): 334–47.

Scott, M. (2009), *Wordsmith Tools*. Available online: https://lexically.net/downloads/version7/HTML/index.html (accessed 4 September 2019).

Scott, M. (2010), 'Problems in Investigating Keyness, or Clearing the Undergrowth and Marking Out Trails', in M. Bondi and M. Scott (eds), *Keyness in Texts*, 43–57, Amsterdam: John Benjamins.

Scott, M. (2019), *Wordsmith Tools* (Version 7.0) [Computer Software], Stroud: Lexical Analysis Software. Available online: https://www.lexically.net/wordsmith/downloads/ (accessed 3 September 2019)

Scott, M. and C. Tribble (2006), *Textual Patterns: Key Words and Corpus Analysis in Language Education*, Amsterdam: John Benjamins.

Scottish Parliament (n.d.), 'How Can People Get Involved in Politics?'. Available online: http://www.parliament.scot/EducationandCommunityPartnershipsresources/Natio nal_Getting_Involved.pdf (Accessed 16 August 2019).

Shaw, I. (2015), *Business Journalism: A Critical Political Economy Approach*, London and New York: Routledge.

Silke, H., F. Quinn and M. Rieder (2019), 'Telling the Truth About Power? Journalism Discourses and the Facilitation of Inequality', *Critical Discourse Studies*, 16 (3): 241–7.

Silverstein, M. (2003), 'Indexical Order and the Dialectics of Sociolinguistic Life', *Language and Communication*, 23: 193–229.

Simpson (1993), *Language, Ideology, and Point of View*, London: Routledge.

Sinfield, A. (2019), 'The Benefits and Inequalities of Fiscal Welfare', In M. Powell (ed), *Understanding the Mixed Economy of Welfare*, 135–58, Bristol: Policy Press.

Smith, A. M. (1998), *Laclau and Mouffe: The Radical Democratic Imaginary*, London: Routledge.

Solt, F. (2008), 'Economic Inequality and Democratic Political Engagement', *American Journal of Political Science*, 52 (1): 48–60.

Solt, F. (2010), 'Does Economic Inequality Depress Electoral Participation? Testing the Schattschneider Hypothesis', *Political Behaviour*, 32: 285–301.

Sommers, J. (2014), 'Robert Peston Claims BBC Is "Obsessed" With Covering Same Stories as Daily Mail', *Huffington Post*, 6 June. Available online: http://www.huffingto npost.co.uk/2014/06/06/robert-peston-says-bbcleftwing-bias-bollocks_n_5458619.ht ml (accessed 3 September 2019).

Stadler, W. A. and M. L. Benson (2012), 'Revisiting the Guilty Mind: The Neutralization of White-Collar Crime', *Criminal Justice Review*, 37 (4): 494–511.

Stierli, M., A. Shorrocks, J. B. Davies, R. Lluberas and A. Koutsoukis (2014), *Global Wealth Report 2014*, Zurich: Credit Suisse AG Research Institute. Available at: https://economics.uwo.ca/people/davies_docs/credit-suisse-global-wealth-report-2014.pdf (accessed 11 February 2019).

Stiglitz, J. (2009), 'Moving Beyond Market Fundamentalism to a More Balanced Economy', *Annals of Public and Cooperative Economics*, 80 (3): 345–60.

Stiglitz, J. (2012), *The Price of Inequality*, London: Penguin.

Street, B. (1994), 'The International Dimension', in U. H. Meinhof and K. Richardson (eds), *Text, Discourse and Context: Representations of Poverty in Britain*, 47–66, London and New York: Longman.

Strong, S. (in press), 'Food Banks, Actually Existing Austerity and the Localisation of Responsibility', *Geoforum*. Available online: https://www.sciencedirect.com/science/article/pii/S0016718518302835 (accessed 11 February 2019).
Stubbs, M. (1996), *Text and Corpus Analysis*, Oxford: Blackwell.
Stubbs, M. and A. Gerbig (1993), 'Human and Inhuman Geography: On the Computer-Assisted Analysis of Long Texts', in M. Hoey (ed), *Data, Description, Discourse. Papers on the English Language in Honour of John Sinclair on His Sixtieth Birthday*, 64–85, London: Harper Collins.
Summers, J. (2006), *The Poverty of News Discourse: The News Coverage of Poverty in New Zealand*, PhD diss., University of Canterbury.
Sutherland, E. H. (1949), *White Collar Crime*, New Haven: Yale University Press.
Sutherland, E. H. and D. R. Cressey (1955), *Principles of Criminology*, 5th edn, Chicago: J.B. Lippincott.
Svennevig, M. (2007), *BBC Coverage of Business in the UK. A Content Analysis of Business News Coverage*, Leeds: University of Leeds.
Sykes, G. M. and D. Matza (1957), 'Techniques of Neutralization: A Theory of Delinquency', *American Sociological Review*, 22 (6): 664–70.
Szlendak, T. and A. Karwacki (2012), 'Do the Swedes Really Aspire to Sense and the Portuguese to Status? Cultural Activity and Income Gap in the Member States of the European Union', *International Sociology*, 27 (6): 807–26.
Tambini, D. (2010), 'What Are Financial Journalists For?', in S. Schifferes and R. Roberts (eds), *The Media and Financial Crises*, 121–39, London and New York: Routledge.
Taylor, C. and A. Marchi (eds) (2018), *Corpus Approaches to Discourse: A Critical Review*, London: Routledge.
Taylor, P. and J. L. Powell (2017), 'The UK Welfare System with Special Reference to the Mental Health Care System', in C. Aspalter (ed), *Routledge International Handbook to Welfare State Systems*, 191–202, London: Routledge.
Tenorio, E. (2011), 'Critical Discourse Analysis: An Overview', *Nordic Journal of English Studies*, 10 (1): 183–210.
Tepe-Belfrage, D. and S. Wallin (2016), 'Austerity and the Hidden Costs of Recovery: Inequality and Insecurity in the UK Households', *British Politics*, 11: 389–95.
The Equality Trust (2017), *Pay Tracker: Comparing Chief Executive Officer Pay in the FTSE 100 with Average Pay and Low Pay in the UK*, London: The Equality Trust. Available online: https://www.equalitytrust.org.uk/sites/default/files/resource/attachments/Pay%20Tracker%20%20-%20web_0.pdf (accessed 4 September 2019).
The Equality Trust (2019a), *How Is Economic Inequality Defined?*, London: The Equality Trust. Available online: https://www.equalitytrust.org.uk/how-economic-inequality-defined (accessed 4 September 2019).
The Equality Trust (2019b), 'A Nation of Ferraris and Foodbanks – UK Rich Increase Wealth by £253 Billion over Five Years', London: The Equality Trust. Available online: https://www.equalitytrust.org.uk/news/nation-ferraris-and-foodbanks-uk-rich-increase-wealth-%C2%A3253-billion-over-five-years (accessed 4 September 2019).
Thesaurus (2019), Dictionary.com. Available online: https://www.thesaurus.com (accessed 3 September 2019).
'The Scott Trust: Values and History' (2015), *Guardian*, 26 July. Available online: http://www.theguardian.com/the-scott-trust/2015/jul/26/the-scott-trust (accessed 3 September 2019).
The Social Metrics Commission (2019), *Measuring Poverty*, London: Social Metrics Commission. Available online: https://socialmetricscommission.org.uk/wp-

content/uploads/2019/07/SMC_measuring-poverty-201908_full-report.pdf (accessed 3 September 2019).

The Sutton Trust (2019), *Elitist Britain Report*. Available online: https://www.suttontrust.com/wp-content/uploads/2019/06/Elitist-Britain-2019.pdf (accessed 2 August 2019).

Thomas, R. (2016), '"I Think It's Absolutely Exorbitant!": How UK Television News Reported the Shareholder Vote on Executive Remuneration at Barclays in 2012', *Critical Discourse Studies*, 13 (1): 94–117.

Thomas, R. (2018), 'The Economic Recovery on TV news', in L. Basu, S. Schifferes and S. Knowles (eds), *The Media and Austerity: Comparative Perspectives*, 63–79, Abingdon: Routledge.

Thomas, R. (2019), 'Biting the Hand: Using the Relationship between ITV and Barclays to Examine Political Economy', *Journalism Studies*, 20 (4): 585–607.

Thompson, B. (2007), 'Effect Sizes, Confidence Intervals, and Confidence Intervals for Effect Sizes', *Psychology in the Schools*, 44 (5): 423–32.

Thompson, D. F. (1980), 'Moral Responsibility of Public Officials: The Problem of Many Hands', *American Political Science Review*, 74 (4): 905–16.

'Thousands Attend Anti-austerity Rallies across UK' (2015), *BBC News*, 20 June. Available online: https://www.bbc.com/news/uk-politics-22068157 (accessed 11 February 2019).

Toft, A. (2014), 'Contesting the Deviant Other: Discursive Strategies for the Production of Homeless Subjectivities', *Discourse & Society*, 25 (6): 783–809.

Toolan, M. (2016), 'Peter Black, Christopher Stevens, Class and Inequality in the *Daily Mail*', *Discourse & Society*, 27 (6): 642–60.

Toolan, M. (2018), *The Language of Inequality in the News: A Discourse Analytic Approach*, Cambridge: Cambridge University Press.

Toolan, M. (this volumen, 2020), 'What Can Be Done about Child Poverty? What the *Times* Said Then and What It Says Now', in E. Gómez-Jiménez and M. Toolan (eds), *The Discursive Constructions of Economic Inequality: CADS Approaches to the British Public Discourse*, London: Bloomsbury.

Topham, G. (2013), 'Executive Pay Rises by 14% as Awards Linked to Shares Soar', *Guardian*, 18 November. Available online: http://www.theguardian.com/business/2013/nov/18/executive-pay-up-14-percent (accessed 3 September 2019).

Torre, R. and M. Myrskylä (2013), 'Income Inequality and Population: A Panel Data Analysis on 21 Developed Countries', *Population Studies: A Journal of Demography*, 68 (1): 1–13.

Townsend, P. and D. Gordon (2002), *World Poverty: New Policies to Defeat an Old Enemy*, Bristol: The Policy Press.

UK Office for National Statistics (2019), *Persistent Poverty in the UK and EU: 2017*. Available online: https://www.ons.gov.uk/peoplepopulationandcommunity/personalandhouseholdfinances/incomeandwealth/articles/persistentpovertyintheukandeu/2017 (accessed 3 September 2019).

UK Parliament (2019), *UK Parliament*. Available online: www.parliament.uk (accessed 2 August 2019).

Ulijaszek, S. J. and A. K. McLennan (2016), 'Framing Obesity in UK Policy from the Blair Years, 1997-2015: The Persistence of Individualistic Approaches despite Overwhelming Evidence of Societal and Economic Factors, and the Need for Collective Responsibility', *Obesity Reviews*, 17 (5): 397–411.

UN General Assembly (2000), 'Protocol to Prevent, Suppress and Punish Trafficking in Persons, Especially Women and Children, Supplementing the United Nations

Convention against Transnational Organized Crime', 15 November. Available online: https://www.ohchr.org/Documents/ProfessionalInterest/ProtocolonTrafficking.pdf (accessed 13 August 2019).

van der Bom, I., L. Paterson, D. Peplow and K. Grainger (2018), '"It's Not the Fact They Claim Benefits but They're Useless, Lazy, Drug Taking Lifestyles We Despise": Analysing Audience Responses to *Benefits Street* Using Live Tweets', *Discourse, Context & Media*, 21: 36–45.

van Dijk, T. A. (1988), *News as Discourse*, London: Lawrence Erlbaum Associates.

van Dijk, T. A. (1991), *Racism and the Press*, London: Routledge.

van Dijk, T. A. (1993), 'Principles of Critical Discourse Analysis', *Discourse & Society*, 4 (2): 249–83.

van Dijk, T. A. (1995a), 'Aims of Critical Discourse Analysis', *Japanese Discourse*, 1 (1): 17–28.

van Dijk, T. A. (1995b), 'Discourse Semantics and Ideology', *Discourse & Society*, 6 (2): 243–89.

van Dijk, T. A. (1995c), 'Discourse Analysis as Ideology Analysis', in C. Schaffner and A. I. Wenden (eds), *Language and Peace*, 17–36, Amsterdam: Harwood Academic Publishers.

van Dijk, T. A. (1998), *Ideology: A Multidisciplinary Approach*, London: Sage.

van Dijk, T. A. (2002), 'El análisis crítico del discurso y el pensamiento social', *Athenea Digital*, 1: 18–24.

van Leeuwen, T. (1996), 'The Representation of Social Actors', in C. Caldas-Coulthard and M. Coulthard (eds) *Texts and Practices: Readings in Critical Discourse Analysis*, 32–70, London: Routledge.

van Treeck, T. (2014), 'Did Inequality Cause the U.S. Financial Crisis?', *Journal of Economic Surveys*, 28 (3): 421–48.

'Turkeys Voting for Christmas' (2017), *Fear and Loathing in Great Britain*. Available online: https://fearandloathingingreatbritain.wordpress.com/tag/turkeys-voting-for-christmas/ (accessed 3 September 2019).

Wæver, O. (1995), 'Securitization and Desecuritization', In D. Ronnie (ed), *On Security*, 35–66, New York: Columbia University Press.

Wahl-Jorgensen, K., R. Sambrook, M. Berry, K. Moore, L. Bennett, J. Cable, I. Garcia-Blanco, J. Kidd, L. Dencik, and A. Hintz (2013), *BBC Breadth of Opinion Review Content Analysis*, Cardiff School of Journalism, Media and Cultural Studies. Available online: http://orca.cf.ac.uk/52553/1/content_analysis.pdf (accessed 3 September 2019).

Wall, T. (2019), 'Every Day We See Really Hungry Kids. They Shouldn't Be Living Like This', The *Guardian*, 14 August. Available online: https://www.theguardian.com/society/2019/aug/14/uk-holiday-hunger-schemes-deprived-children-summer (accessed 3 September 2019).

Waterfield, B. (2013), 'Old, Sick or Disabled Dutch People Will Be Asked to Work in Return for Care', *Telegraph*, 3 October. Available online: https://www.telegraph.co.uk/news/worldnews/europe/netherlands/10353781/Old-sick-or-disabled-Dutch-people-will-be-asked-to-work-in-return-for-care.html (accessed 31 May 2019).

Watt, P. (2008), '"Underclass" and "Ordinary People" Discourses: Representing/Re-presenting Council Tenants in a Housing Campaign', *Critical Discourse Studies*, 5 (4): 345–357.

Watt, N. (2013), 'Boris Johnson Invokes Thatcher Spirit with Greed Is Good Speech', *Guardian*, 27 November. Available online: http://www.theguardian.com/politics/2013/nov/27/boris-johnson-thatcher-greed-good (accessed 3 September 2019).

Welch, D. (2016), *Persuading the People: British Propaganda in World War II*, London: The British Library.

Welfare Reform Act (2012). Available online: http://www.legislation.gov.uk/ukpga/2012/5/contents/enacted (accessed 04 August 2019).

Westergaard, J. (2012), *Who Gets What? The Hardening of Class Inequality in the Late 20th Century*, London: Polity Press.

Whitworth, A. (2012), 'Inequality and Crime Across England: A Multilevel Modelling Approach', *Social Policy and Society*, 11 (1): 27–40.

Wiggan (2012) ,'Telling Stories of 21st Century Welfare: The UK Coalition Government and The Neo-Liberal Discourse of Worklessness and Dependency', *Critical Social Policy*, 32 (3): 383–405.

Wilkinson, R. and K. Pickett (2009), 'Income Inequality and Social Dysfunction', *Annual Review of Sociology*, 35: 493–511.

Wilkinson, R. and K. Pickett (2010), *The Spirit Level: Why Equality Is Better for Everyone*, London: Penguin.

Williams, P. (2011), *Aggression: From Fantasy to Action*, London: Karnac Books.

Williams R. ([1979] 1983), *Keywords: A Vocabulary of Culture and Society*, London: Fontana.

Williams, R. ([1969] 2005), 'Advertising: The Magic System', in *Culture and Materialism*, 170–95, London: Verso.

Wilson, M. (2008), 'Crisis? What Crisis? But It's Great TV', *British Journalism Review*, 19 (3): 57–61.

Winckler, V. (2012), 'Conclusions: Taking Stock', in G. Calder, J. Gass and K. Merrill-Glover (eds), *Changing Directions of the British Welfare State*, 213–20, Cardiff: University of Wales Press.

Wodak, R. (1996), *Disorders of Discourse*, London: Longman.

Wodak, R. (2001), 'What Is CDA About: A Summary of Its History, Important Concepts and Its Developments', in R. Wodak and M. Meyer (eds), *Methods of Critical Discourse Analysis*, 1–13, London: Sage.

Wodak, R. and M. Meyer (2009), *Methods for Critical Discourse Analysis*, London: Sage.

Woolard, K. and B. A. Schieffelin (1994), 'Language Ideology', *Annual Review of Anthropology*, 23 (1): 55–82.

World Bank Organization. (2006), *World Development Report 2006*. Available at: http://documents.worldbank.org/curated/en/435331468127174418/pdf/322040World0Development0Report02006.pdf (accessed 3 September 2019).

Zaller, J. (2003), 'A New Standard of News Quality: Burglar Alarms for the Monitorial Citizen', *Political Communication*, 20 (2): 109–30.

Index

9/11   18, 27, 30

Ackroyd and Karlsson   150
actor/agency, representation of   27–9, 31, 61, 111, 115, 119–20, 139–40
ad hoc, data-driven categorization of keywords   132–4
Addison and Crang   36
affluent, the   5, *see also* rich, the
affordability   13, 58–60, 69, 71, 77, 88, 140, 144, 147, 177
allowance, family   70, 77, 86
Althusser   177–8
Amery, Leopold Stennet   172–3
Anderson   171
Anthony   8, 97, 131
anthropology   7, 36
   linguistic   34
Apple   59
Appleby, Merry and Reed   122
Aristotle   164, 167
Armstrong   122
Asda   112, 120
'at risk' groups   10, 107–23
Atkinson   143
August 2011 British riots   6
austerity   6, 10, 49–50, 71, 121, 125, 127–41, 143, 177
authentocracy   46

Babic, Heemskerk and Fichtner   92
Baker   5, 7, 14, 16, 51, 52, 54, 97
Baker, Gabrielatos, Khosravinik, Krzyzanowski, McEnery and Wodak   19
'balancing the books'   128, 135
Baldwin, Stanley   20
Balzacq   16
Bank of English   8
Barnett and Gaber   145

Bates   175
Bayley and Williams   7
Beetsma and Van Der Ploeg   2
benefits
   child   70, 71, 74, 76, 88
   claimants   5, 15, 62, 70
   health   17
   incapacity   62
   maternity leave   77
   recipients   51, 56, 65, 177
   statutory   85
   supplementary   70
Benefits Streets (TV programme)   5, 15, 64
Bennett   6, 9, 33, 60–5, 187, *see also* Spencer-Bennett
Berg and Ostry   2
Bernstein   33, 40
Bevan Foundation   70
Beveridge Report   18, 49, 70
Beyoncé   5, 185
Billig   5
Black, Conrad   152
Black, Peter   15
Blair, Tony   17, 18, 80, 178
Blair years, the   125
Blanden   2
Bourdieu   33, 46
Box of Broadcasts   145
Brexit   135, 180–1, 190
Briggs and Burke 35
British National Corpus   8, 74, 78
   Written Informative   81
   Written Sampler   95
British Phonographic Industry   72
British Political Speech Archive   19
Brown   74
Brown, Gordon   17, 80, 129
Brunsdon and Morley   145
Bryce, Viscount   172
budget   50, 125, 128, 129–30, 135, 141, 177
   speech   137–8

Burgess, Anthony 38
Burnham, Lord 173
Burns, Tomita and Kapadia 2
Business, the 96
Butterick 143

Calder 34–6, 38, 44–5
Cameron, David 126–8, 129, 147
capitalism 6, 177–8, 180
  hypercapitalism 3
  new 3
Carpentier and Cammaerts 179
Cartledge 165
celebrities 5, 151, 169, 185
central value system 4
CEO 3, 4, 143, 169
Change4Life 10, 107, 112, 117, 119, 121
  move structure of TV adverts 118–19
Chaplin, Mr 172
Charles 37
chav 63
Childcare 1, 70
Child Poverty Act 69
Child Poverty Action Group 74, 77
children, living in poverty 8–10, 18, 69–89, 180, 186, 188, 189
children, representation of in obesity documents 115–20
Children's Centres in England 7
Chilton 15
Chouliaraki and Fairclough 4
Churchill, Winston 18, 20, 187
Clark 17, 143
Clark-Billings 143
class (or social class, or socioeconomic group) 1, 6, 9, 15, 35, 47, 62, 64–5, 99, 163, 168–9, 171, 173, 175, 177–80
  artisan 40
  dominant 178
  layabout 63
  lower 171
  lower middle 169, 177, 190
  middle 40, 70, 80, 113, 116–17, 121–2, 169, 172, 176
  political 168
  poor 110, 113
  propertied 162, 166, 189
  ruling (also leading) 11, 164, 166, 168–80, 176
  struggle 6, 175
  underclass 9, 15, 53, 62–3, 65–6, 72
  upper 33, 37, 39, 42, 44, 46, 169
  upper middle 169
  wealthy 164
  working 10, 34–5, 40–7, 162, 169, 171–2, 174–7, 179–80, 186, 189
cluster 8, 15, 54, 113
Cohn, Fehr and Goette 2
collocate 9, 52–8, 60, 62, 65, 76, 78, 80, 98, 112, 115–16
  c-collocate 10, 97–101, 103–4
collocation 11, 49, 52, 54, 76, 78, 80, 98, 116, 135
Colvile 144
comment article 72
concordance 9–10, 21, 51–4, 58–9, 62, 76, 98
concordancer (software) 8
conservatism 16
Conservative Party 8, 9, 13–32, 55, 59, 66, 126, 128, 129, 187
Cooper, Duff 36
Cooper, Jack 56
Corak 2
Cornelissen 168
Corner 31
corporation 5, 92, 94–5, 98, 102, 104, 147, 158, 186, 188
corpus-assisted discourse studies 6–8, 10, 14, 107, 112, 125
corpus linguistics 8, 11, 14, 19, 51
corpus tools 7, 8, 10, 19
Corpus of Political Speeches 19
cost
  economic 49–50, 91–3, 112, 151, 155
  housing 69, 71, 85
  human 135
co-text 9, 49, 52–4, 61, 126, 128, 131–2, 135–6, 139–40
CQPweb 9, 49–50
crash, 2008 financial 50, 53, 126
crisis, 2008 global financial 1, 6, 10, 18, 94, 121, 138, 140, 143–5, 148–9, 152–6

critical discourse analysis   2, 4–8, 11–12, 14–15, 74, 107–8, 146, 156
Crossman, Richard   35, 37, 46
Crowley   44
Cushion and Thomas   147
Cushion, Lewis and Callaghan   147, 158
cut, economic   71–2, 133, 144, 147, 166, 177

Dados and Connell   62
Daily Edition, the   96
Daily Express, the   35
Daily Mail, the   5, 15, 94, 96, 130, 167, 177, 180, 188, 190
Daily Star, the   96
Daily Star Sunday, the   96
Daily Telegraph, the   94, 96, 130, 188
Daly, Wilson and Vasdev   2
Darbyshire   92
Darling, Alistair   129
data-driven analysis   132
Dean   108
debt   2, 128, 183
deception   92
deixis   9, 30, 32, 47
De Melo Resende   14
Demmen, Jeffries and Walker   127
democracy, direct or grassroots *vs.* parliamentary or representative   11, 161–7
denial
  of class structure   6
  of harm or injury   93, 102
  of responsibility   10, 93, 104
  of the victim   93
Department for Work and Pensions   69
depression, economic   17–18
deregulation   167, *see also* regulation
De Vogli, Mistry, Gnesotto and Cornia   2
de Vries, Gosling and Potter   2
Dibley and Kelly   33
Dimsdale and Hotson   18
discourse
  'anti-union'   6
  'austerity'   6, 140
  counter   175–6
  of economic inequality   6, 125
  elite   16
  'finance'   20–1, 26

'hardship'   20–1, 27, 30–1
hegemonic   6, 174–7, 179–80
'idle poor'   15, 16, 51, 62, 63
managerial   111
mass media   50
media   163, 167
moral   65
national public   174–5
neoliberal   62, 65
news discourse   49, 50, 52
policy   10, 108, 121
political   1, 6, 31–4
'poor as victim'   15
poverty   5
PSE   19–21, 26–7, 30–2
public   6, 8, 11, 109, 111, 164, 174–5
'rich get richer'   15
scientific discourse   117, 119
'scrounger'   51
'undeserving poor'   6, 61
welfare   54
working-class   175
dispersion   8
Dorling   2, 11, 144, 156
Dorling, Rigby, Wheeler, Ballas, Thomas, Fahmy, Gordon and Lupton   17
Doyle   147
Dunning   131
Durant   127
Durante, Fiske, Kervyn, Cuddy, Akande, Adetoun, Adewuyi, Tserere, Ramiah, Mastor, Barlow, Bonn, Tafarodi, Bosak, Cairns, Doherty, Capozza, Chandran, Chryssochoou, Iatridis, Contreras, Costa-Lopes, González, Lewi, Tushabe, Leyens, Mayorga, Rouhana, Castro, Perez, Rodríguez-Bailón, Moya, Marente, Gálvez, Sibley, Asbrock and Storari   2

E3G   13
economics   3, 57, 134, 137, 185
Eden, Anthony   18, 28
editorial   10, 73, 74, 76, 77, 80, 86
education   3, 10, 13, 17, 44, 49, 53, 62, 66, 71, 80, 121, 162, 166, 171, 187–90
  early   70
  free   62, 66
  state school   80

Edwards and Potter 26
Ekström 146
Elgar and Aitken 2
Elgar, Pickett, Pickett, Craig, Molcho, Hurrelmann and Lenzi 2
elite 14, 46, 91, 158, 162, 164, 167
  corporate 91
  political 32
  schools 80
elitism, linguistic 47
Elitist Britain 169
employment 1, 5, 13, 54, 71, 85, 93
End of Child Poverty Programme 18
Enfield, Harry 143
Engels, Friedrich 162, 164, 171–2, 178
English, varieties of
  British 33, 44
  vernacular 34, 44
  working-class 44
Enough Food for Everyone campaign 19
entrepreneurship 59
equality 93, 98, 109, 122, 135, 141, 161, 163, 176, 180, 184, 186–7
The Equality Trust 1, 3
Erdoğan, Recep Tayyip 183
Eribon 176–7
Evans 141
Evans and Walker 125
Every Child Matters 71
Express, the 96

Fahy, O'Brien and Poti 147
Fairclough 3, 4, 6–8, 14, 34, 45, 50, 60, 65, 108, 113
Fairclough and Fairclough 17
Fairclough and Wodak 50
family clusters, typology of 114
Farnsworth and Irving 62
Farrelly and Seoane 34, 44
Faucher-King 17
Field, Frank 77
Financial Times, the 94, 130, 188
Finlayson, Martin and Philips 17
Firth, Raymond 36
Foley 33
Fooks, Gilmore, Collin, Holden and Lee 93
Foresight 110–11, 122
Foucault 107–8, 115

Fowler 4, 7, 26, 44–5, 50
Fowler, Hodge, Kress and Trew 7, 28
Frank, Levine 2
fraud, corporate 10, 91–2, 94–5, 98, 100–4
Fraud Act, UK 2006 92
Freedman 158
frequency 8, 19–21, 54, 62, 78, 81, 84–5, 97–8, 104, 112, 131–2, 137–8
  normalized 53
  relative 21, 97–8
Friedman, Milton 64

G8 19
Gabrielatos 95, 131
Gabrielatos and Baker 7, 97
Gale (database) 50, 73
Gammans, David 54–5
García da Silva 14
Gardiner 34–5, 38, 47
Gazeley 18
gender 1, 4–5, 99, 118, 179
general elections, UK 1, 4, 18, 44, 58, 125, 129–30, 147
geographical text analysis 5
Georgakopoulou and Goutsos 146
George VI, King 36
Gephart 149
Gibbs 58
Glennerster 17
Glennerster, Hills, Piachaud and Webb 18, 70
Goatly 26
Gómez-Jiménez 1–12, 15, 50–1, 59, 70, 77, 183–4
Gómez-Jiménez and Toolan 1–12, 183–4
government
  British/UK 6, 10, 17, 33–48, 70, 72, 77, 80, 107–24, 125, 127–9, 158, 163
  Conservative 18, 59, 60, 86, 141
  European 162
  Labour 18, 50, 55, 60, 70, 71, 84, 111
  neoliberal 110–11
governmentality 107–9, 121
Graham and O'Rouke 3
Grainger 6
Gramsci, Antonio 175, 177–80
granularity 76
Grayling, Chris 166

Great Reform Act, 1832   170
Green Party   74
Gregoriou and Ras   94–5
Gregory and Paterson   51
Gregory, Atkinson, Hardie, Joulain-Jay, Kershaw, Porter, Rayson and Rupp   51
Grisold and Silke   6
Grisold and Theine   156
Guardian, the   5, 94, 96, 130, 157, 177, 180, 188

Habsburg, Otto   165–6
Hall   178
Hall, Critcher, Jefferson, Clarke and Roberts   4
Halliday   26, 29, 112, 115, 138, 139
Halliday and Martin   26
Halliday and Matthiessen   29, 112, 115, 138
Hammond, Philip   129
Hampe and Grady   28
Hanley, Lynsey   176–7
Hansard   1, 11, 36, 126–7, 137, 163, 167
Hansen and Machin   146
Hardie   9, 49–50, 54, 131
Hare   150
Harkins and Lugo-Ocando   6
Harrisson, Tom   35–7, 41, 45
Hart   7, 29
Hayek   167–8
health   2–3, 17, 71, 113, 144, 187
health and safety   92
healthcare (or health support)   1, 17, 49, 53, 70, 190
Healthy Weight, Healthy Lives: Consumer Insight Summary   111–13, 115–17, 121–2
hegemony *vs.* coercion   11, 27, 31, 109, 175–9
Heimann   36, 45
Hewitt   5, 153
hierarchy   47, 52, 158, 175, 186
Higgins   158
Highmore   36, 44
Hinton   36, 45–6
Hobsbawm   34, 171, 177
Hoggart   45–6
Houghton, Lord   171

household   1, 3, 69
  income   70
housing   51, 69, 71, 88, 147, 187–8, 190
Howell, Ralph   85
Hsieh and Pugh   2
Huddlestone   177
Hudson, Walter   20
Hulbert   143
Hundred Years' War   35

Iacoviello   2
ideology   6, 10, 14, 16, 21, 52, 60, 66, 72, 125–7, 146, 158, 168, 183, 185
ideo-textual analysis   9, 19
Idrovo, Ruiz-Rodriguez and Manzano-Patino   144
immorality   53, 60
income   3, 13, 26, 69, 147, 167, 175
  national   2
  Supplement, Family (or family credit)   70
  support   70
  tax credit   18, 70, 76
Independent, the   74, 96, 130
Independent on Sunday, the   96
inequality (or disparity)
  economic (or class-based)   1–12, 65, 91, 144, 156, 183–4, 189–90
  health   107–24
  income   1–2, 11, 100, 110, 128, 143–50, 155–9, 183, 187
  individual *vs.* social responsibility for   110–11
  inequality, as not newsworthy   156
  pay   1
  social   6, 34–5, 49, 109–10, 117, 121–2
  wealth   1, 8, 13, 15, 70–1, 91–2, 104, 128
inflation   2, 18, 69, 129, 143, 183
Inman and Booth   69
International Labour Office   92
interventionism (or state intervention)   16–17, 59, 72, 76–7, 80, 88, 107–9, 111–12, 117, 121, 122, 128, 153
investment, state   88, 94, 121
It's That Man Again (radio programme)   35

Jefferson, Thomas 166
Jeffery 46
Jeffries 9–10, 19–21, 30, 127, 131, 136
Jeffries and Walkers 6, 10, 125–41
Jeffries and Evans 141
Jensen 5
Jewkes 94
Johnson, Boris 144, 183
Johnson, Sonnett, Dolan, Reppen and Johnson 146
Jones 158
Joseph Rowntree Foundation (or Rowntree Foundation) 3, 70, 144
journalism 4, 7, 145
Joyce 70
Joye 146
Joynson-Hicks 174

Krahn, Hartnagel and Gartrell 2
Kalogeropoulos, Albæk, de Vreese and Van Dalen 145
Kardashians 5, 185
Kasser and Ryan 2
Kawachi, Kennedy, Lochner and Prothrow-Smith 2
Kay and Salter 157
Keane 34
Kelley and Preacher 33, 131
Kellogg's 123
Kelsey, Mueller, Whittle and Khosravinik 158
Kennedy 46
keyness, semantic 78, 81–5
keyword, socio-political 126, 136
keyword, statistical 75–81, 128, 130–1
  analysis 10, 74, 78, 130–1, 140
  in context 76, 84
Kilgarriff, Baisa, Bušta, Jakubíček, Kovář, Michelfeit, Rychlý and Suchomel 8, 19
Kitzinger 156
Klein 3
Koller and Davidson 15
Kondo, Sembajwe, Kawachi, Van Dam, Subramanian and Yamagata 2
Krahn, Hartnagel and Gartrell 2
Kress 5, 7, 16
Kress and Hodge 7
Kress and van Leeuwen 112, 118
Kumhof and Rancière 2

Labour Party 8, 9, 13–32, 60, 70, 129, 187
  New Labour (or Third Way) 17, 60, 125, 178
Labov 33
Lacerda 14
Laclau, Ernesto 179–80
Lakoff and Johnson 58
Lambert 17
Lancee and Werfhorst 2
Langer 31
language
  demotic 34, 45
  mass 9, 45–7
  metalanguage 34
  of propaganda 37, 42, 46
  working-class 34, 44
Lawson, Nigel 162
Lawson, Richard 74, 86
Lears 176
Lederman, Fajnzylber and Loayza 2
van Leeuwen 112
letter to the editor 73, 77
Levitas 65
Lewis 38, 144, 147, 158
Lewis and Thomas 157
Lewis and Cushion 158
liberalism 16, 121, 153–8, *see also* neoliberalism
linguistic democratization 44
Lister, Ruth 74
Locke, Anthony 74
Locke, John 166
log-likelihood 97
log ratio 54, 131
Longmate 38
Lorenzo-Dus 5, 15–16
Lugo-Ocando 6, 151
Lundström 56
Lyengar 147

McCall 144, 145, 156
McChesney 147, 158
McEnery and Baker 16
Machin 143
Machin and Richardson 5, 180
McIntyre and Walker 132
McKendrick, Sinclair, Irwin, O'Donnell, Scott and Dobbie 144
McLaine 33, 35–6, 47

McLennan 110
MacMillan, Harold (or Lord MacMillan) 18, 34
macrostructure (or macroproposition) 9, 15, 52–3, 58, 60, 62, 65
Madge, Charles 36, 44–5
Mail on Sunday, the 94, 96, 188
Mair 33–4
Malinowski, Bronislaw 36
Mandela, Nelson 188
market economy, free *vs.* regulated 3, 11, 50, 59–60, 107, 110, 121, 153–4, 157–8, 167–8, 184–6
marketing, social 107–22
marketization 50, 60
Martin and White 26
Marx, Karl 162, 164, 169, 172, 174, 175, 177, 178
mass, the (or the masses) 33, 35–6, 38, 40, 44–7, 177–8, 187
Mass-Observation 9, 33–47
Mautner 7–8, 146
Meade, James 74
media 4, 5, 11, 14, 52, 66, 70, 129, 140, 144, 148, 151, 156–7, 166–7, 169, 175, 179–80, 184
  British/UK 8, 14, 15, 63, 65, 184
  discourse 163
  mainstream 173, 180
  mass 1, 4, 14, 50
  news 4, 125
  social 6, 112, 122, 177
  traditional 177
Meinhof 5
Meinhof and Richardson 14
Mendick, Allen and Harvey 5
Merkel, Angela 167
Merrill 147
metaphor 9, 15, 27, 30, 32, 55, 56–8, 118, 141, 187
  conceptual theory 58
MI3 54
Miliband, Ed 6, 15
millennial 3
Miller, Sienna 150–1
Ministry of Information 187
Mirror, the 94, 96, 130, 177, 188
mobility, social 2, 174
modality 7, 27–8, 53, 118–19
  boulomaic 63

Monaghan and Elgot 143
Montgomery 146
morality 9, 61, 65, 77
moral talk 60
Morley and Bayley 7
Morrisson and Murtin 2
Mouffe, Chantal 179–80
Mugglestone 44
Mulderrig 10, 107–23, 186
Mulderrig, Montessori and Farrelly 108
multimodality 10, 118
Murkens 171
Murray, Sir George 170
mutual information 54

naming 10, 21–4, 61, 136–9
National Assistance Act 1948 18, 53
National Health Service Act 1946 53, 66
National Housing Federation 69
national income, share of 2
National Insurance Act 17
naturalization 15, 50, 125
Neil, Andrew 152–3
neoliberalism 50, 59, 61–2, 65–6, 153–6, 159
neutralization 91–3, 104
New Labour 17, 60, 125, 178
New Review, the 96
New Statesman and Nation, the 35
newsworthiness 53, 156
Nexis (or Lexis Nexis) 73, 94–6, 157
NHS Trust 136
nominalization 26
normativity 107–9, 112–13, 145, 177
Northern Rock bank 143
NRC 66
Nunn 128

obesity
  in UK 110
  UK government policy on 107, 110–18, 122
Observer, the 96
Occupy Movement 6
O'Connor 13
Ofcom 144
Offer, Pechey and Ulijaszek 2
Office for National Statistics 3, 13, 110, 114

Oldcorn 176
opinion article 4, 8
optical character recognition 51
Organization for Economic Cooperation and Development 3, 13, 110, 143, 183–4
origin, country of 1, 5
Ortu 6
Orwell, George 172, 187
Osborne, George 129
Oswald 2

parasite 15, 62
Pardo 14
Pardo-Abril 14
parents, representation of in obesity documents 115–20
Parliament, Scottish 161
Parliament, UK 11, 35–6, 59, 126, 162–5, 169–74
Parmoor, Lord 173
Partington 7–8, 19
Partington, Duguid and Taylor 7–8, 19
Partington, Morley and Haarman 7
Paterson and Gregory 5, 51
Paterson, Coffey-Glover and Peplow 5, 62
Paterson, Peplow 6
Pearce 33
Peel, Sir Robert 170
People, the 96
per capita 18, 189
personalization 31–2, 34, 45
personification 37, 43, 139
philosophy 7, 125
Piketty 144, 156
Piñera, Sebastián 183
Piquero, Tibbetts and Blankenship 93
policy (or policies) 1, 10, 15, 17, 30, 49, 57, 80, 125, 128, 135, 143
 austerity 66, 128–9, 131, 138, 140
 benefit 3
 change 50
 conservative 128
 economic 129–30
 egalitarian 15
 health 17
 home 39

income 18
inequality 183
maternity leave 15, 51
neoliberal 62
NHS and educational 66
obesity 10, 107–23
party 17, 58
redistributional 156
security 27
socialist 17
welfare state 50, 53, 60
politics 6, 14–15, 125, 147, 158, 161
 British 17
poor, the 2–6, 15–16, 70–2, 77, 85–6, 88, 91, 110, 113, 125, 128, 144, 175, 186–7
Pope, Pratt and Hoyle 16
poverty 3, 5, 11, 51, 110, 144–7, 150–1, 153, 156, 159, 174, 186
 child 8–10, 69–90, 180, 188
 levels 141
 line 69, 76
 relative 3
 and social exclusion 9, 13–32, 187
poverty-porn genre 5
Powell, Enoch 46, 50, 128
press, the (or newspapers) 4–6, 49–50, 70–1, 129, 140, 157, 175, 177, 180, 185–7
 broadsheet 130, 157
 right-of-centre 50
 tabloid 6, 130, 166
 UK/British (or national) 10, 15, 80, 91–106, 125–42
privileged, the 92, 189
productivity, labour 2
propaganda 1, 33–8, 42–7
property 1–2, 26, 147, 164, 166, 171, 189
property and rights 166
proposition 31, 52–3, 74, 77
Protocol to Prevent, Suppress and Punish Trafficking in Persons, especially Women and Children, UN 95
Pryor 2
Public Health Responsibility Deal 121
Punch 104
Purves, Libby 72, 86, 88
p-value 97, 132

qualitative method (or qualitative analysis)   7–8, 10, 19, 26, 36, 51, 58, 94, 107, 112, 125, 130–1, 135, 138, 140, 149, 155, 157
quantitative method (or qualitative analysis)   7–8, 19, 45, 52, 157
query   51, 52, 53, 94–5
  node   52

race   4–5, 99
Rahman   69
Raine, Kathleen   44
Rampton   33
Ras   10, 91–106, 188
Rayson   76, 97
redistribution   15, 17, 71, 128, 156
Reece   129
regulation   61, 102–3, 107–8, 153–6, see also deregulation
Reisigl and Wodak   7
Reith, John   33, 35
Relative Query Term Relevance   95
religion   1, 2, 5
Representation of the People (Equal Franchise) Act, 1928   173
Representation of the People Act, 1884   171
Representation of the People Act, 1918   173
Resolution Foundation   69
respectability   176
review, TV programme   15, 63
rheme (*vs.* theme)   29, 31
rhetoric, political   17
rich, the   3, 6, 15, 110, 125, 128, 144, 169, 175, 177, 184
Richardson   5
Rieder and Theine   6
Roberts   5
Roberts and Lawrence   3
Roberts, Blakeley, Rankin and Statham   3
Robinson, Else, Sherlock and Zass-Ogilvie   147
Rosenberg, Arthur   164
Rosoff, Pontell and Tillman   94
Rothstein and Uslaner   2
Rousseau, Jean-Jacques   164
Rowlingson   2
Royal Family, British   5

Sandel   3, 11, 184
Sarbanes-Oxley Act 2002, US   98, 103
Saturday Magazine, the   96
Sayer   144
Schifferes and Coulter   145
Schneider and Ingram   107, 109
Scott and Tribble   8, 131
Second World War   1, 9, 33–48, 187
securitization   5, 9, 16
semantic field (or semantic domain)   52, 56–8, 65, 78, 81, 85, 98
Semtag   85–7
sexual orientation   1, 5
Shaw   158
Shelley, Percy Bysshe   161
Silke, Quinn and Rieder   4, 6
Silverstein   63
Simpson   26–8, 63
Sinfield   70
slavery, modern   10, 91–2, 94–6, 98, 100–1, 103–4
Slavery Act, Modern   2015   92, 95, 98
Smith, Owen   46, 179
Schneider and Ingram   107, 109
social deixis   47
socialism   17, 55, 60, 173, 178–80
social media   6, 112, 122, 177
Social Metrics Commission   69
social security   76
socio-constructionism   4
software tools   8, 52, 112, 131, 135, 138
  Antconc   8, 78, 97, 131–2
  Sketch Engine   8, 19, 112
  WMatrix   76, 78
Solt   2
Sommers   158
South Africa   166, 188–9
speech   6, 9, 17–32, 46, 66, 126, 127, 129, 159, 170, 175, 187
  budget   137–8
  demotic   45
  political   13–32
  working-class   42
Spencer-Bennett   9, 33–47, 187, *see also* Bennett
Stadler and Benson   93
statistical significance   54, 97, 131
statistics   7, 54, 71, 109, 122, 126, 132, 135, 147, 149, 150, 188

stereotype (also stereotyping) 2, 9, 14, 32, 34, 46, 61, 64–6, 88, 91, 93
Steven, Christopher 15
Stierli, Shorrocks, Davies, Lluberas and Koutsoukis 128
Stiglitz 2
Street 5, 14
Stubbs 7, 127
Stubbs and Gerbig 7
Summers 14
Sun, the 94, 96, 130, 177, 188
Sunday Business, the 96
Sunday Express, the 96
Sunday Mirror, the 96
Sunday Telegraph, the 94, 188
Sunday Times, the 94, 96, 188
Sure Start Team 70
Sutherland 91–2
Sutherland and Cressey 93
Svennevig 158
Sydenham, Lord 173
Sykes and Matza 91, 93, 102, 104
Szlendak and Karwacki 2

Tambini 147
Taylor and Powell 50
Tenorio 146
Tepe-Belfrage and Wallin 128
Teubert 161–81, 188–9
textual conceptual functions 20–1, 29–32, 131, 136
Thatcher, Margaret 1, 16–18, 59–62, 125, 140, 158
theme (or topic) 38, 51–3, 117, 120, 146, 158, 170
thesaurus dictionary
    Merriam-Webster 19
    Oxford 19
    Thesaurus.com 19
Thomas 11, 143–59, 166, 186
Thompson 91, 93, 102, 104, 131
threshold (or cut-off point) 54, 81, 85, 94, 97, 132
Times, the 8, 9, 10, 15, 49–68, 69–90, 94, 96, 130, 177, 188
Toft 14
token 4, 95–6, 136–7
Toolan 13, 15, 50–1, 63, 69–89, 167, 188
Topham 143

Torre and Myrskylä 144
transfer of responsibility 102
transitivity 7, 10, 32, 112, 115, 136, 138–9
Turkeys Voting for Christmas 125
tweet 4, 51, 64
Twitter 4, 15, 51
    responses 5, 15

Ulijaszek and McLennan 2, 110
underclass 9, 15, 53, 62–3, 65–6, 72
unemployed, the 13, 17, 49, 62, 85–6, 88, 150
unemployment 10, 18, 76, 85–6
Universal Credit Scheme 71

van der Bom and Paterson 9, 49–67, 187
van der Bom, Paterson, Peplow and Grainger 5, 15, 51, 61, 64
van Dijk 4, 7, 9, 27, 31, 34, 50, 52–3, 64
van Treeck 2
Vine, Sarah 63–4

Wæver 16
wage 1, 3, 30, 76, 77, 84, 92–3, 143, 147–8, 151, 168–9
    minimum 9, 17, 77, 85, 153
Wahl-Jorgensen, Sambrook, Berry, Moore, Bennett, Cable, Garcia-Blanco, Kidd, Dencik, and Hintz 158
Walk Free Foundation 92
Wall 180
Wallin 128
Waterfield 66
Watson, Tom MP 122
Watt 15, 144
wealth (or riches, *vs.* poverty) 3, 17, 110, 128, 144–8, 151–4, 159, 162, 167–8, 171, 175
Welch 38, 44
Welfare Reform Act 2012 50
welfare state (or welfare system) 1, 9, 18, 49–67, 80, 110, 127–8, 187
Whitworth 2
Whyte, Jamie 77
Wiggan 62
wildcard 51, 97
Wilkinson and Pickett 2, 110, 144, 156
Willem-Alexander (King of the Netherlands) 66

Williams   7, 17
Williams, Raymond   126–7
Wilson, Michael   144
Winckler   50
Wodak   7
Wodak and Meyer   7
Woolard and Schieffelin   34

worker   6, 17, 31, 59, 92, 164, 169, 176
 manual   4
 non-unionized   59
World Bank Organization   13

Zaller   156

www.ingramcontent.com/pod-product-compliance
Lightning Source LLC
Chambersburg PA
CBHW072149290426
44111CB00012B/2013